Building English Skills

Purple Level

Yellow Level

Blue Level

Orange Level

GREEN LEVEL

Red Level

Gold Level

Silver Level

Aqua Level

Brown Level

Plum Level

Pink Level

Kindergarten Level

Building English Skills

Green Level
Revised Edition

Joy Littell, EDITORIAL DIRECTOR

McDougal, Littell & Company
Evanston, Illinois
Sacramento, California

Prepared by the Staff of
THE WRITING IMPROVEMENT PROJECT

Joy Littell, Editorial Director, McDougal, Littell & Company

Donna Rae Blackall, Chairperson, English Department, Miner Junior High School, Arlington Heights, Illinois

J. A. Christensen, East High School, Salt Lake City, Utah

William H. Horst, Henrico County Schools, Virginia

Eric L. Kraft, Writer and Editor, Stow, Masachusetts

Debbie Rosenberger, formerly, Henrico County Schools, Virginia

Kathleen Bell Welch, Department of English, University of Miami, Coral Gables, Florida

For their cooperation in the development of the sections on grammar, usage, and mechanics, grateful acknowledgment is made to Thomas Clark Pollock, John P. Milligan, and Richard L. Loughlin.

Acknowledgments: See page 524.

ISBN: 0-88343-866-6

The twelve sections on grammar, usage, and mechanics contain, in revised form, some materials that appeared originally in *The Macmillan English Series, Grade 8,* by Thomas Clark Pollock et al., copyright © 1963, 1960, 1954 by The Macmillan Company. Used by arrangement.

Contents

Grammar, Usage, and Mechanics

SPECIAL FEATURES OF THIS TEXT

The Composition Chapters (First half of text)

Vocabulary Development. Chapter 1 emphasizes procedures for learning word meanings from context: definition, restatement, examples, comparison, and contrast. An adequate vocabulary and the ability to use words precisely are necessary for good writing and speaking.

Using the Dictionary. Chapter 2 shows students how to use the dictionary: how to locate words; how to divide, pronounce, and define them; and how to select precise synonyms.

Sentence Combining. Chapter 3 presents a basic introduction to sentence combining. Its purpose is to help students create mature sentences, and to help them become aware of the choices they have in combining ideas.

The Process of Writing. Chapter 4 analyzes the three major steps in writing: pre-writing; writing the first draft; and rewriting, or revising, which includes proofreading.

The Paragraph. Chapters 5, 6, and 7 comprise an intensive study of the paragraph. Chapter 5 introduces the form of the structured paragraph and explains the function of a topic sentence. Chapter 6 treats in detail three ways of developing paragraphs: using sensory details, using examples, and using facts or figures. Chapter 7 provides a working explanation of three kinds of paragraphs: narrative, descriptive, and explanatory. These chapters provide a wealth of first-rate models along with helpful analysis. They also provide continuing opportunities for guided student writing.

Compositions and Reports. Chapter 8 provides a clear, workable blueprint for writing a composition or report. Chapter 9 deals with first-person narrative compositions, descriptive compositions, and explanatory compositions.

Writing Letters. Chapter 10 shows in detail how to go about writing friendly and business letters. The chapter contains a wide variety of model letters.

Thinking Clearly. Chapter 11 helps students understand the process of clarifying their thinking by separating fact from opinion, checking facts, making facts clear, and reasoning logically. To write clearly, students must think clearly.

Using the Library. Chapter 12 helps students understand the classification and arrangement of books, the use of the card catalog, and the kinds of reference materials.

Interviews and Group Discussions. Chapter 13 provides guidelines for conducting interviews and helps students feel comfortable about talking before a group—first informally, then more formally. It explains the various roles of responsibility in group discussions.

Grammar, Usage, and Mechanics (Second half of text)

The second half of the text consists of fourteen numbered Sections dealing with grammar, usage, and the mechanics of writing (capitalization, punctuation, spelling, and outlining.)

The text explains each topic or concept fully, then follows with examples and, where appropriate, with the definition or generalization printed in boldface type. There are abundant exercises on each topic and pages of Additional Exercises at the end of each Section. These Additional Exercises may also be used for Review.

Chapter 1

Developing Your Vocabulary

You have a group of words that you know well, use well, and feel comfortable with. These are the words that you use from day to day. You use them when you talk with friends, and your friends use them when they talk with you. This group of words that you use so comfortably in speaking is your **speaking vocabulary.**

When you sit down to write a letter or a composition, you have more time to think about the words you will use. In fact, when you are writing, you may use some words that you would not use when you are speaking. You may not feel as sure of these words as you do of the words in your speaking vocabulary. You do understand them, however, and you use them when you think about them. These words, in addition to the words in your speaking vocabulary, make up your **writing vocabulary.**

There is another group of words that you understand when you read them. You do not know these words well enough to feel comfortable about using them in speaking or in writing. But you do understand them when you come across them in your reading. These words, added to all the words in your writing vocabulary, equal your **reading vocabulary.**

The larger your reading vocabulary is, the better you will understand what you read. The larger your writing and speaking vocabularies are, the better you will be able to make people understand you. In this chapter you will learn how to make your reading vocabulary larger. You will also learn how to use words to say exactly what you mean in writing or speaking.

Part 1 Learning Word Meanings from Context

Many words have more than one meaning. For example, the word *sink* has a different meaning in each of these sentences.

> If we don't plug that leak, this boat will *sink*.
> The *sink* is full of dishes.

In one sentence, *sink* means "to go under water." In the other, it means "a tub or basin." You can easily tell which meaning fits which sentence. You can tell from the other words in each sentence.

The meaning of a word depends on its **context,** the words that come before or after it. Often the context makes the meaning clear, as it did in the two sentences above. Sometimes it does not, as in this sentence.

> We waited to see if Donna would *sink* it.

Here the context does not tell you whether Donna is playing golf or trying to sink a boat.

Context can tell you which meaning of a word fits what you are reading. It can also help you decide the meaning of a word you do not know. As you have seen, context will not always tell you enough to let you decide. But if you learn to look for certain clues, context can be a great help.

In this chapter you will learn how to use five kinds of context clues that will help you in your reading.

Context Clue 1: Definition

Sometimes a writer knows that a word will be unfamiliar to many readers. To make the word easier to understand, the writer may include a definition of the word in a sentence. It is as if the writer were saying to the reader, "I know you won't know the meaning of this word, so I am going to tell it to you." This context clue is the easiest one to spot, and it is the easiest to understand. Look at the following examples.

> At the zoo we saw a *gnu*, which is a large African antelope.
> Helium makes the balloon *buoyant;* in other words, it floats.
> The harbor is protected by a *jetty*. A jetty is a wall built out into the water.

In the first example, the writer tells you that a gnu is a large African antelope. The key words *which is* signal the definition. In the second example, the writer tells you that to be buoyant means to float. The key words *in other words* signal this definition. In the third example, the definition of *jetty* is given in a sentence of its own. The key word in this example is *is*. Watch for the key words *which is* (or *that is*), *in other words*, and *is* when you read. These key words often signal a definition.

Exercise Definition

Number a sheet of paper from 1 to 10. Read each of the following sentences. Each sentence includes a definition for the

3

italicized word. Write the meaning of each italicized word. Be ready to tell what key words helped you spot the definition.

1. We stayed in *youth hostels,* which are cheap places to stay for young people who are traveling.
2. Metal can be polished with *pumice,* which is rock formed from the lava of a volcano.
3. Clarice is *indecisive;* that is, she can't make up her mind.
4. We had to *rappel* down the face of the cliff. In other words, we had to lower ourselves on ropes.
5. I learned to use a *pantograph.* A pantograph is a mechanical gadget used to make a copy of a drawing.
6. The legs should be *perpendicular* to the top of the table. That is, they should meet the top at right angles.
7. The *marimba,* which is a kind of xylophone, is played with mallets.
8. The crops were destroyed by *locusts.* Locusts are large grasshoppers.
9. The sculpture is made of *gesso,* which is a kind of plaster.
10. Our feet were tangled in a kind of seaweed called *kelp.*

Context Clue 2: Restatement

You will not always be lucky enough to find a definition for a word in its context. More often, you will find a restatement. A restatement tells you almost as much as a definition, but it is not as easy to spot. Look at the following examples.

The walls were *buttressed,* or propped up, with sturdy logs.
We need volunteers to make *hors d'oeuvres*—appetizers—for the parents' meeting.
He had a *wan* look, pale and weak.

In the first example, the writer restates *buttressed* as "propped up." The writer has not directly said that *buttressed* means "propped up." Instead, the writer has written the same idea twice. The keys to spotting "propped up" as a restatement of *buttressed* are the word *or* and the commas that separate "or propped up" from the rest of the sentence.

In the second example, *hors d'oeuvres* is restated as "appetizers." Dashes separate *appetizers* from the rest of the sentence. These dashes are a key to spotting "appetizers" as a restatement of *hors d'oeuvres*.

The words *pale and weak* restate the idea of "wan" in the third example. The only key to *pale and weak* as a restatement is the comma that separates these words from the rest of the sentence.

The examples show three keys to spotting restatement as a context clue. They are the word *or*, a dash or a pair of dashes, and a comma or a pair of commas. Parentheses can also indicate a restatement.

Exercise Restatement

Number a sheet of paper from 1 to 10. Read each of the following sentences. Each sentence includes a restatement of the italicized word. Write the meaning of each italicized word. Tell what key or keys helped you spot the restatement.

1. The new school seemed like a *labyrinth*—a maze—to me.
2. The meeting turned into quite a *fracas*, or uproar.
3. My favorite spot at the zoo is the *aviary*, the building where the birds are kept.
4. Colonial families cleaned house with a *besom*—a broom made of twigs tied to a handle.
5. We have to *collate* these pages—put them in the right order—before we staple them.
6. Carl led us on a *devious*, or winding, route home.
7. For short hikes you may want to use a *haversack*, a small bag that you can carry over one shoulder.
8. She has always been an *upright* person, honest and just.
9. We play *quoits*, a game like horseshoes.
10. Carbon monoxide is a *noxious* (poisonous) gas.

Context Clue 3: Examples

Examples can also give you a clue to the meanings of unfamiliar words. Study the following sentences.

> *Kelp* and other kinds of seaweed can be made into food.
>
> Some kinds of seaweed, like *kelp*, can be made into food.

Neither sentence tells you just what kelp is, but both sentences tell you that kelp is one example of seaweed. Now that you have an idea of what kelp is, look at the following sentence.

> Marine algae, such as *kelp*, can be grown in underwater farms.

In this sentence, kelp is mentioned as an example of marine algae. The sentence does not tell you what *marine algae* means. It does, however, tell you that kelp is one kind of marine algae. From that clue you should be able to figure out that *marine algae* must mean something like "seaweed."

The following key words signal an example (or examples) as a context clue. The key words are in boldface type. The sentences show how they are used to give clues to the meaning of the italicized words.

> Elaine has mastered the *half gainer* **and other** difficult dives.
>
> Tony is good at difficult dives **like** the *half gainer*.
>
> Diane can do some difficult dives—the *half gainer*, **for instance.**
>
> Phil is no good at difficult dives **such as** the *half gainer*.
>
> Martha did some difficult dives—**for example,** the *half gainer*.
>
> Kurt is good at all difficult dives, **especially** the *half gainer*.

Exercise Examples

Write definitions for the italicized words in the following sentences. Use context clues alone to write your definitions. Check your definitions in a dictionary.

1. The forest was made up of pine, fir, and other *conifers*.

2. A good camper knows how to tie a *half hitch,* a *bowline,* a *clove hitch,* and other useful knots.

3. *Perishable* foods, like milk and butter, vegetables, and meats, should be kept refrigerated.

4. I like all kinds of sausage, but especially *knockwurst.*

5. In this chapter you will read about such ancient heroes as *Ulysses* and *Hercules.*

6. *Mollusks,* especially clams, oysters, and snails, may be grown on "sea farms" in the future.

7. She's studying *glaucoma* and other diseases of the eye.

8. In this display you'll find *hedgehogs* and other animals that eat insects.

9. We're learning how to make some fancy desserts—*chocolate mousse,* for example.

10. If you're serious about mountain climbing, you'll need *crampons* and other special climbing equipment.

Context Clue 4: Comparison

When you compare things, you see how they are like each other. You usually compare things that are not much alike in order to point out one important way that they are alike.

Comparisons in writing can give you clues to the meanings of unfamiliar words. Look at the following examples to see if you can get an idea of the meaning of each italicized word.

> The hot-air balloon tugged at its *tether* like a dog tugging at its leash.

> At last the balloon took off. It was as *buoyant* in the air as a cork is in water.

In the first example, the writer compares a balloon on a tether to a dog on a leash. Both are tugging, trying to get free. The balloon is like a dog. The tether is like a leash. From the comparison you should be able to see that a tether must be something like a leash.

In the second example, the writer compares a balloon in air to a cork in water. You know that a cork floats in water, and that it may bob a bit while it floats. The writer says that a balloon is buoyant in air. The writer says that a cork is buoyant in water. The buoyant balloon is compared to the buoyant cork. From the comparison you should be able to see that something buoyant is something that floats.

Key words that help you spot comparison as a context clue include *like*, *as*, and *similar to*.

Context Clue 5: Contrast

When you contrast things, you look at them to see how they are different from each other. You often contrast things that are alike in many ways in order to point out one important way that they are different. You don't usually contrast trees and rocks or buses and pickles, because you already know that these things are quite different from each other. Instead, you contrast things that are similar to show an important way in which they are different.

A contrast between two things can give you a clue to the meaning of an unfamiliar word. Look at the following examples to see if you can get an idea of the meaning of the italicized words.

> Unlike most other rats, the *bandicoot* carries its young in a pouch.
> *Rodents*, unlike most other animals, have teeth that keep growing throughout their lives.
> Tony was *reticent*, but Phyllis spoke right up.

In the first example, the bandicoot is contrasted with "most other rats." The writer points out one way in which the bandicoot is different from most other rats. Because the writer makes this contrast, you can be reasonably sure that except for this difference the bandicoot is like most other rats. A bandicoot, then, must be a kind of rat.

In the second example, the writer contrasts rodents with "most other animals." The writer points out one way in which rodents are different from most other animals. Because the writer makes this contrast, you can be reasonably sure that rodents are like most animals in other ways. Therefore, rodents must be animals.

In the third example, Tony is contrasted with Phyllis. Tony was reticent. Phyllis spoke right up. This was something that made Tony different from Phyllis. Therefore, being reticent must be different from speaking right up. Being reticent must mean something like "not speaking right up."

Key words that signal contrast as a context clue include *unlike, but, on the contrary,* and *on the other hand.*

Exercise Comparison and Contrast

Write definitions for the italicized words in the following sentences. Use context clues alone to write your definitions. Check your definitions in a dictionary.

1. Anna, unlike most *ailurophobes,* can at least stand to be in the same room with a cat.

2. Like other *marsupials,* a kangaroo carries its young in a pouch.

3. The museum has many examples of early bicycles, such as the *ordinary* and the *high wheeler.*

4. Laura spends her time reading about *griffins, unicorns,* and other imaginary beasts.

5. Some people think Paul is *irrational,* but he has always seemed reasonable to me.

6. I was *anxious,* but everyone else seemed calm and relaxed.

7. Pull the taffy until it is as *elastic* as a rubber band.

8. When you hit the bar, it will make a *plangent* sound like a bell.

9. Most of us agreed. However, Cheryl *dissented.*

10. *Stalactites* hung from the roof of the cave like icicles.

Part 2   Gaining Precision in the Use of Words

When you have something to say to someone, you want to say it in such a way that it can be understood. You don't want people to misunderstand you. Neither do you want them to only half-understand you. You can help people understand you by using words that make your meaning clear.

If your speaking and writing vocabularies are small, you won't have many words to choose from. You will not be able to say exactly what you mean.

To help people understand exactly what you mean, you must say exactly what you mean. You must choose the best words to express your meaning.

Using Synonyms

In order to be able to say exactly what you mean, you will need to know the synonyms for many words. **Synonyms** are words that have nearly the same meanings. However, they do not have exactly the same meanings. When you use a word from a group of synonyms, you must pick the one that is closest in meaning to what you want to say.

Think about the word *run*. It has many synonyms. They include *trot*, *dash*, *flee*, *scamper*, and *sprint*. Each of these synonyms has a slightly different meaning. If you want to describe a squirrel running across a park, you might use *scamper*. However, if you want to describe the finish of the Kentucky Derby, *scamper* would be the wrong word.

If you look at passages of dialogue in stories, you will find many synonyms for the word *said*. You may find some or all of the synonyms shown here and in Exercise A.

| shouted | bellowed | exclaimed |
| whispered | declared | muttered |

Which of these synonyms would you use for someone speaking in a loud voice? Which would you use for an excited person? You can see that there are important differences among these words.

Exercises Using Synonyms

A. Following is a list of synonyms for *said* that might be used in sentences 1 through 10. Choose the word that best fits each sentence.

whispered	chanted	screamed
called	cried	growled
announced	muttered	
explained	declared	

1. "I am the best violinist in class," _____ Mark.
2. "Don't look now, but someone's watching us," _____ Nancy.
3. "There will be a quiz on Friday," _____ Mr. Hunt.
4. "Wait! You forgot your notebook, hat, and pencil," _____ Madeline.
5. "I can't make this problem work out," _____ Sam.
6. "You have to multiply, not divide," _____ Mr. Crandall.
7. "Stay in line. Stay in line. Stay in line," _____ Ms. Donovan.
8. "You always get more than I do," _____ Lucy.
9. "If I get any trouble from you, you'll get plenty of trouble from me," _____ Rafferty.
10. "A giant clam has me by the foot," _____ Louise.

B. List as many synonyms as you can for the following words. Use a dictionary for help.

pull	break	hard	dull	intelligent
funny	fast	angry	tired	

Using Antonyms

Antonyms are words that are nearly opposite each other in meaning. The words *light* and *dark* are antonyms. So are *old* and *new*. So are *wide* and *narrow*.

Notice that a word may have more than one antonym. The word *old* is an antonym for *new*, but so is *ancient*. The word *new* is an antonym for old, but so are *recent* and *modern*.

You can use antonyms to clarify your ideas by making comparisons. If you are comparing two buildings, you could say that one is tall and the other is short. You could say that one is lofty and the other is squat. You could say that one is towering and the other is stumpy. Each comparison creates a different picture. You must decide which words are the best for the picture you want to create.

Exercises Using Antonyms

A. Write an antonym for each word listed in Exercise B under Using Synonyms on page 11.

B. Use antonyms to compare each of the following:

1. two people	5. two athletes	9. two places
2. two books	6. two buildings	10. two cars
3. two pets	7. two metals	
4. two moods	8. two seasons	

Review Exercises Putting Your Vocabulary Skills Together

A. Use context clues to decide the meaning of each italicized word in the following sentences. Write a definition for each word. Then be ready to tell what clue and what keys helped you decide the meaning.

1. Like all *carnivores,* wolves prefer to eat meat.
2. The design was made of three *concentric* circles; that is, three circles with the same center.
3. The new government was extremely *fragile;* in other words, it could easily fall apart.
4. You have to *interlace* the two colors of wool—weave one over and under the other.
5. For weeks the hunters lived on nothing but *pemmican,* dried meat pressed into cakes.
6. I gathered my spade, rake, hoe, and other gardening *implements.*
7. If you're going to spend the night, you'll have to put up with the creatures that haunt this castle, including *ghouls, poltergeists,* and *bogies.*
8. Joan's ideas seemed *incontestable* to me, but Frank went ahead and argued with her anyway.
9. She used to be a *retiring* type, but now she's the life of the party.
10. The disease became *pandemic;* that is, it spread through the entire country.

B. Read each of the following sentences. Try to think of a more precise synonym for each italicized word. If you need help, use a dictionary.

1. That was a really *good* dinner.
2. There's a *cold* wind blowing from the north.
3. Elaine *said* that she could beat any of us at ping-pong.
4. I *jumped* over the fence and ran for my life.
5. The quake *moved* the buildings as if they were toys.
6. She *moved* quickly across the floor.
7. Cars *moved* along the highway at rush hour.
8. It was a *bad* place to be.
9. The elephant *walked* slowly down the ramp.
10. The boy *walked* aimlessly down the street.

Chapter 2

Using the Dictionary

How many words are there in the English language? Would you guess 100,000? 200,000? 500,000? A good guess would be more than 500,000, but no one is really sure how many words there are. Old words die out and new ones are born all the time. Some words have short lives. Some live on and on. Some are used often by nearly everyone. Some are not used much at all. No one can know the meanings of so many words. That is why everyone runs into an unfamiliar word now and then. When that happens, a person turns to a dictionary.

Just what is a dictionary? How can a dictionary help you? A dictionary is a list of words, with information about each word. It will divide the words into syllables and tell you how to pronounce them. It will tell you the meanings of the words. It will tell you what words are related in meaning. Finally, it will tell you the history of each word. This chapter will show you how to get the most out of a dictionary.

Part 1   Alphabetical Order

The words in a dictionary are listed in alphabetical order. All words that begin with *a* come first. All words that begin with *b* come next. Words that begin with *s* come before words that begin with *t*, and so on. When words begin with the same letter, they are alphabetized according to the second letter. If the second letter is the same, the words are alphabetized according to the third letter, and so on.

The words in these columns are in alphabetical order.

anteater	aardvark	grasshopper
groundhog	albatross	greyhound
hedgehog	anteater	griffin
mole	armadillo	groundhog

To find words quickly, learn to open the dictionary at the right spot. With practice, you will be able to find words quickly.

Exercises Alphabetical Order

A. Arrange each group of words in alphabetical order.

1	2	3	4
franc	elm	Sun	neck
peso	walnut	Mercury	arm
dollar	beech	Venus	head
rupee	pine	Earth	hand
pound	fir	Mars	heart

B. Working with a classmate, practice opening the dictionary as close as you can to a particular letter. Have your classmate say a letter. Try to open your dictionary to that letter. Then switch roles and say a letter for your classmate. Continue until you can open the dictionary close to a specific letter most of the time.

Part 2 Guide Words

In most dictionaries you will find **guide words** at the top of each page. These help you find a word more quickly. The guide word on the left tells you the first word on the page. The guide word on the right tells you the last word on the page.

On pages 18 and 19 you will find a reproduction of a dictionary page. The guide words for this page are *ridgepole* and *righteous*. Notice that all the other words on the page fall between these two in alphabetical order.

After you have opened to the right section of the dictionary for the word you want to find, you can find the exact page by following the guide words. Flip pages quickly until the guide words tell you that you are getting close. In your mind, compare the guide words and the word you are looking for.

Exercises Using Guide Words

A. Write the numbers 1 through 5 on a sheet of paper. Beside each of the following numerals you will find the guide words for a dictionary page. After the guide words is another word. Decide whether you would find that word on a page *before* the given one, *on* it, or *after* it. Write *before, on,* or *after* on your paper.

1. **bloodhound**	**blubber**	blowout
2. **career**	**caribou**	careful
3. **contact**	**content**	contest
4. **endive**	**engage**	endow
5. **frazzle**	**free lance**	freedom

B. See how quickly you can find these words in your dictionary. Copy the guide words from the page where you find each one.

eggplant	trampoline	shuffleboard	vulture
iguana	dolphin	emu	yak
moose	newt	anaconda	woodchuck

ridge·pole (rij′pōl′) *n.* the horizontal timber or beam at the ridge of a roof: also **ridge′piece′**

rid·i·cule (rid′i kyōōl′) *n.* [Fr. < L. *ridiculum*, a jest, ult. < *ridere*, to laugh: for IE. base see VERSE] **1.** the act of making a person or thing seem foolish, as by making fun, mocking, laughing, etc. **2.** words or actions used in doing this —*vt.* **-culed′, -cul′ing** to make fun of or make others laugh at; deride; mock

RIDGEPOLE

SYN.—**ridicule** implies a making fun of a person or thing by way of showing disapproval [*he ridiculed her new hat*]; **deride** suggests contempt for or a strong dislike of what is being made fun of [*to deride another's beliefs*]; **mock** suggests a ridiculing (the unkind imitation of another's manner-isms or habits [*it is cruel to mock his lisp*]; **taunt** implies insulting ridicule, esp. as shown by jeering at another and harping on something that makes him feel ashamed [*they taunted him about his failure*]

ri·dic·u·lous (ri dik′ye las) *adj.* deserving ridicule; absurd —see SYN. at ABSURD —**ri·dic′u·lous·ly** *adv.* —**ri·dic′u·lous·ness** *n.*

rid·ing[1] (rid′iŋ) *adj.* **1.** that rides **2.** of or for riders on horseback [*jodhpurs and boots are parts of a riding habit*] ☆**3.** designed to be worked by a rider [*a riding mower*] —*n.* the act of one that rides

rid·ing[2] (rid′iŋ) *n.* [OE. *-thrithing*, a third part] any of the three administrative divisions of Yorkshire, England

Ri·el (rē el′, rēl) *n.* [see RIAL, REAL[2]] *see* MONETARY UNITS, table (Cambodia)

Rif (rif) mountain range along the Mediterranean coast of Morocco: also **Er Rif** (er)

rife (rif) *adj.* [OE. *ryfe*] **1.** happening frequently or commonly; widespread [*gossip was rife*] **2.** *a)* abundant *b)* abounding; filled [*rife with error*] —see SYN. at PREVAILING —**rife′ness** *n.*

Riff (rif) *same as* RIF —*n., pl.* **Riffs, Riff′i** (-ē) a member of a Ber-ber people living in or near the Rif

☆**riff** (rif) *n.* [prob. altered < REFRAIN[2]] *Jazz* a short musical phrase played again and again — *vi. Jazz* to play a riff

to dress; clothe (usually with *out*) [*all rigged out in a cowboy suit*] —*n.* **1.** the arrangement of sails, masts, etc. on a vessel ☆**2.** equipment for a special purpose; gear [*a ham radio opera-tor's rig*] ☆**3.** equipment for drilling an oil well ☆**4.** *a)* a car-riage, etc. with its horse or horses *b)* a tractor-trailer or, sometimes, the tractor alone **5.** [Colloq.] dress or costume, esp. if odd or showy —**rig′ger** *n.*

Ri·ga (rē′gə) capital of the Latvian S.S.R.; seaport on the Baltic Sea: pop. 733,000

rig·a·ma·role (rig′ə mə rōl′) *n. var. of* RIGMAROLE

ri·ga·to·ni (rig′ə tō′nē; *It.* rē′gä tō′nē) *n.* [It., pl. < pp. of *rigare*, to mark with lines] short, ridged casings of pasta, often stuffed with ground meat, cheese, etc.

Ri·gel (rī′j′l, -g′l) [Ar. *rijl*, foot: in the left foot of Orion] a bright, bluish star, brightest in the constellation Orion

rig·ging (rig′iŋ) *n.* **1.** the chains, ropes, etc. used for support-ing and working the masts, sails, etc. of a vessel ☆**2.** equip-ment; gear

right (rit) *adj.* [OE. *riht*: for IE. base see REGAL] **1.** orig., straight: now only in mathematics [*a right line*] **2.** *a)* formed by a straight line perpendicular to a base [*a right angle*] *b)* having the axis perpendicular to the base [*a right cylinder*] **3.** in accordance with justice, law, morality, etc.; virtuous [*right conduct*] **4.** in accordance with fact, reason, etc.; correct; true [*the right answer*] **5.** fitting; suitable [*the right dress for a dance*] **6.** designating the side meant to be seen [*the right side of cloth*] **7.** *a)* physically or mentally healthy [*he doesn't look right*] *b)* in a satisfactory condition; in good order [*to make things right again*] **8.** *a)* designating or of that side of one's body which is toward the east when one faces north, the side of the more-used hand in most people *b)* designating or of the corresponding side of anything *c)* closer to the right side of a person facing the thing mentioned [*the top right drawer*] **9.** of the bank of a river on the right of a person facing downstream **10.** of the political right; conservative or reactionary —*n.* **1.** what is right, or just, lawful, proper, etc. [*to know right from wrong*] **2.** *a)* a power, privilege, etc. that a person has or gets by law, nature, tradition, etc. [*the right of free speech*] *b)* [*often pl.*] an interest in property, esp. incorporeal **3.** the true or correct report, as of a happening (with *the*) **4.** *a)* the right side [*the first door on the right*] *b)* a turn toward the right side [*take a right at the corner*] **5.** *Boxing a)* the right hand *b)* a blow delivered with the right hand **6.** [*often* **R-**] *Politics* a conservative or reactionary position, party, etc. (often with *the*): from the seating (on the right) of conservatives in some European legislatures —*adv.* **1.** in a straight line; directly [*go right home*] **2.** in a way that is correct, proper, just, favorable, etc.; well [*do it right*] **3.** completely [*soaked right through his coat*] **4.** exactly [*right here*] ☆**5.** immediately [*come right down*] **6.** on or toward the right hand or side **7.** very [*he knows right well*]: colloquial except in certain titles [*the right reverend*] —*interj.* agreed! I understand! —*vt.* **1.** to put in or restore to an upright position [*to right a capsized boat*] **2.** to correct [*to right an error*] **3.** to put in order [*she righted the room*] **4.** to make amends for [*to right a wrong*] —*vi.* to regain an upright position —**by right** (or **rights**) in justice; properly —**in one's own right** through one's own status, ability, etc. —**in the right** on the side supported by truth, justice, etc. —**right away** (or **off**) without delay; at once —**to rights** [Colloq.] in or into proper condition or order —**right′er** *n.* —**right′ness** *n.*

right·a·bout (rīt′ə bout′) *n. same as* RIGHTABOUT-FACE —*adv., adj.* with, in, or by a rightabout-face

right·a·bout-face (-fās′) *n.* **1.** a turning directly about so as to face in the opposite direction **2.** a complete turnabout, as of belief —*interj.* a military command to do a rightabout-face

right angle an angle of 90 degrees, made by the meeting of two straight lines perpendicular to each other

right-an·gled (rīt′aŋ′g'ld) *adj.* having or forming one or more right angles; rectangular: also **right′-an′gle**

right·eous (rī′chəs) *adj.* [altered < OE. *rihtwis*: see RIGHT &. -WISE] **1.** acting justly; doing what is right; upright; virtuous [*a righteous man*] **2.** morally right or having a sound moral basis [*righteous anger*] —see SYN. at MORAL —**right′eous·ly** *adv.* —**right′eous·ness** *n.*

RIGHT
ANGLE

---

see ROW′] ☆**1.** *a)* a shoal, reef, etc. in a stream, producing a stretch of ruffled or choppy water *b)* a stretch of such water, or a ripple on it **2.** the act or a method of riffling cards —*vt., vi.* **-fled, -fling 1.** to ruffle or ripple **2.** to leaf rapidly through (a book, etc.) by letting the edges of the pages slip lightly across the thumb **3.** to shuffle (playing cards) in a way like this by holding part of the deck in each hand

riff·raff (rif′raf′) *n.* [< OFr. *rif et raf* < *rifler*, to scrape + *rafle*, a raking in] **1.** those people regarded as worthless, low, coarse, etc.; rabble **2.** [Dial.] trash

ri·fle1 (rī′f'l) *vt.* **-fled, -fling** [Fr. *rifler*, to scrape < OFr. < MHG. *riffeln*, to scratch] **1.** to cut spiral grooves on the inside of (a gun barrel, etc.) ☆**2.** to hurl or throw with great speed —*n.* ☆**1.** a shoulder gun with spiral grooves cut into the inner surface of the barrel: see RIFLING **2.** [*pl.*] troops armed with rifles

ri·fle2 (rī′f'l) *vt.* **-fled, -fling** [< OFr. *rifler*, to plunder, orig. to scratch: see prec.] **1.** to ransack in order to rob; pillage; plunder [*to rifle a safe*] **2.** to take as plunder; steal —**ri′fler** *n.*

☆**ri·fle·man** (-mən) *n., pl.* **-men 1.** a soldier armed with a rifle **2.** a man who uses, or is skilled in using, a rifle

rifle range a place for target practice with a rifle

☆**ri·fle·ry** (-rē) *n.* the skill or practice of shooting at targets with rifles

ri·fling (rī′fliŋ) *n.* **1.** the cutting of spiral grooves within a gun barrel, to make the projectile spin when fired **2.** a system of such grooves

rift (rift) *n.* [Dan., a fissure < *rive*, to tear: see RIVE] **1.** an opening caused by splitting; fissure; cleft **2.** an open break in friendly relations —*vt., vi.* to burst open; split

rig (rig) *vt.* **rigged, rig′ging** [< Scand.] **1.** *a)* to fit (a ship, mast, etc.) with sails, shrouds, etc. *b)* to fit (a ship's sails, shrouds, etc.) to the masts, yards, etc. **2.** to fit (*out*); equip **3.** to put together or prepare for use, esp. in a makeshift or hasty way (often with *up*) [*to rig up a table out of old boxes*] **4.** to arrange in a dishonest way; fix [*to rig an election*] **5.** [Colloq.]

---

lease Turn Book Sideways

19

---

fat, āpe, cär; ten, ēven; is, bīte; gō, hôrn, tōōl, look; oil, out; up, fur; get; joy; yet; chin; she; thin; then; zh, leisure; ŋ, ring; ə for *a* in *ago*, *e* in *agent*, *i* in *sanity*, *o* in *comply*, *u* in *focus*; ′ as in *able* (ā′b'l); Fr. bal; ë, Fr. coeur; ö, Fr. feu; Fr. mon; ô, Fr. coq; ü, Fr. duc; r, Fr. cri; H, G. ich; kh, G. ich; ‡ foreign; ☆ Americanism; < derived from. See inside front cover.

Part 3 Finding a Word

You may have asked this question before: "How can I look up a word in a dictionary if I'm not sure how to spell it?" You can find a word even if you are not sure of the spelling. It will take you more time than it would if you knew the spelling, but you can do it.

Below you will find a "Word-Finder Table." This table shows many ways to spell the sounds you may hear at the beginnings of words. To use the table, first find the spellings for the sound you hear. Then check the dictionary under those spellings until you find the word you want.

Word-Finder Table

If the word begins with a sound like . . .	then also try the spellings . . .	as in the words . . .
a in care	ai	air
e in get	a	any
e in here	ea, ee	ear, eerie
f in fine	ph	phrase
g in go	gh, gu	ghoul, guard
h in hat	wh	who
j in jam	g	gym
k in keep	c, ch, q	can, chorus, quick
n in no	gn, kn	gnu, kneel
o in long	a, ou	all, ought
r in red	rh	rhyme
s in sew	c, ps, sc	cent, psychology, scene
sh in ship	s	sure
t in top	th	thyme
u in under	a, o	ago, onion
u in use	you, yu	youth, yule
ur in fur	ear	earn
w in will	wh	wheat
z in zero	x	xylophone

Exercise Using the Word-Finder Table

Use the Word-Finder Table to find each of the words described below. When you find the word, write its correct spelling.

1. the name for a small glass bottle that sounds like *file*
2. the name of an herb that sounds like *time*
3. the name for a wharf or dock that sounds like *key*
4. the name for an African antelope that sounds like *new*

Part 4 Word Division

The spelling of a word in the dictionary shows how the word is divided into syllables. Some dictionaries use space to show this. Others use a centered dot.

bub ble   bub·ble

Sometimes, when you are writing or typing a paper, you may find that a long word will not fit at the end of a line. Part of the word will have to run on to the next line. When that happens you should divide the word between syllables. Use a hyphen to show that the word continues on the next line.

RIGHT: bub-ble   WRONG: bu-bble, bubb-le

Exercises Word Division

A. Rewrite each of the following words. Show the syllables just as your dictionary does.

jellyfish	helicopter	nameless	connection
hammer	bottle	national	parade

B. Use a hyphen to show how you could divide each word.

gearshift	hacksaw	mallet	cricket
handlebars	chisel	butterfly	locust

Part 5 Pronunciation

Sometimes you will use a dictionary to find out how to pronounce a word. Most dictionaries give the pronunciation in parentheses. The pronunciation follows the word itself. As you read the explanation that follows, refer to the dictionary page reproduced on pages 18 and 19.

Accent Marks

In two-syllable words, one syllable gets a stronger emphasis than the other when the word is pronounced. You say **RID**ing and **RI**fle, putting a heavier emphasis on the first syllable in each word. Dictionaries show you where to put this heavier emphasis by using accent marks.

> rid·ing (rīd′iŋ)
> ri·fle (rī′f′l)

The mark (′) following a syllable tells you that the syllable is emphasized, or accented.

In words of more than two syllables, usually two syllables are emphasized. One of the two gets a stronger emphasis than the other. Dictionaries show the two emphasized syllables by using two accent marks. One accent mark is larger and heavier than the other. The syllable with the heavier accent mark gets the heavier emphasis.

> rid·i·cule (rid′i kyool′)

Respellings

Notice that the respellings of the words on pages 18 and 19 are not exactly the same as the normal spellings. The spelling of the pronunciation is a way of showing the sounds in the word. In the word *right*, the letters *igh* stand for the long *i* sound. The dictionary shows this sound as ī. In the word *ridgepole,* the letters *dge* stand for the same sound as *j* in *jam.* The dictionary shows this sound as *j.*

Most dictionaries use letters of the alphabet in respellings wherever possible. For instance, the letter *b* stands for the first sound in *bat.* Sometimes letters are used in pairs. Many dictionaries use *sh* for the first sound in *sure.*

Some sounds are shown by letters with special marks above them. These marks are called **diacritical marks.** A diacritical mark above a letter shows that it stands for a particular sound. The letter *a* with a short line above it, *ā,* stands for the long *a* sound. This is the sound you hear at the end of the word *pay.* The short line above *a* is a diacritical mark called a **macron.**

A few sounds are shown by special symbols. These symbols are not letters. They are used only to stand for sounds in dictionary respellings.

On page 24 is a chart showing respellings that most dictionaries use. After each respelling is a word that shows the sound that the respelling stands for.

Not all dictionaries use the same system for respelling words. Your dictionary will have a chart called a **pronunciation key.** This chart will show you the system that your dictionary uses. Most dictionaries print a short version of the pronunciation key at the bottom of every right-hand page. You should study the pronunciation key for your dictionary.

Exercise **Pronunciation**

Look up each of the following words in your dictionary. Copy the respelling. Be sure to copy the accent marks and diacritical marks and any special symbols that your dictionary uses. Pronounce each of the words.

bucket	difficult	foreign
jewel	masonry	oblique
phonograph	profession	rustle
slight	strawberry	thermometer
turmoil	vacant	weave

Respellings Used in Most Dictionaries

Sounds Shown by Letters of the Alphabet

a	ask	b	bat	n	not
e	ten	d	dip	p	put
i	it	f	fall	r	red
u	up	g	get	s	sell
		h	hat	t	top
		j	jump	v	van
		k	kick	w	wish
		l	let	y	yet
		m	met	z	zip

Sounds Shown by Letters in Pairs

oo	look	ch	chip
oi	oil	sh	she
ou	out	th	thin
		th	then
		zh	garage

Sounds Shown by Letters with Diacritical Marks

ā	ate	ō	go
ä	hot	ô	law
ē	meet	ōō	who
ī	bite	yōō	use

Sounds Shown by Special Symbols

ə	ago	ŋ	sing

'l (shows the sound between *b* and *l* in *bubble*: bub'l)

Part 6 Definitions

Most often, you will look up a word to find out what it means. Many words in English have more than one meaning. After you find your word, you will have to find the meaning that fits what you are reading.

Look at the definitions for the word *right* on pages 18 and 19. Notice that each different definition has a number. For most of the definitions a phrase or a sentence is given as an example. These examples show how the word is used with a particular definition.

Exercise Definitions

Refer to the dictionary entry for *land* below. On your paper, write the number of the definition that fits each sentence.

1. Flight 703 will arrive at 6 o'clock and land on runway 24.
2. She hopes to travel to a foreign land.
3. A peninsula is land bordered on three sides by water.
4. I want to leave the city and live out on the land.
5. Ogilvy Construction landed that big contract.
6. The package landed right side up.

---

land (land) **n.** [OE. < IE. base *lendh-*, heath] **1.** the solid part of the earth's surface not covered by water **2.** *a)* a country, region, etc. [a distant *land*, one's native *land*] *b)* a country's people **3.** ground or soil [rich *land*, high *land*] **4.** ground thought of as property [to invest in *land*] **5.** rural or farming regions [to return to the *land*] **6.** *Econ.* natural resources **—vt. 1.** to put on shore from a ship [the ship *landed* its cargo] **2.** to cause to end up in a particular place or condition [a fight *landed* him in jail] **3.** to set (an aircraft) down on land or water **4.** to catch [to *land* a fish] **5.** [Colloq.] to get or win [to *land* a job] **6.** [Colloq.] to deliver (a blow) **—vi. 1.** to leave a ship and go on shore [the tourists *landed*] **2.** to come to a port or to shore: said of a ship **3.** to arrive at a specified place [he *landed* in Phoenix after a long bus ride] **4.** to alight or come to rest, as after a flight, jump, or fall [the cat *landed* on its feet]

Part 7 Synonyms

As you learned in Chapter 1, **synonyms** are words that have similar meanings. The words *big* and *large* are synonyms. *Happy* and *glad* are also synonyms.

Look at the following dictionary entry for the word *story*. After the definitions you will find the abbreviation SYN. This abbreviation stands for the word *synonym*. A **synonymy** is a list of synonyms for a word.

Dictionary Entry for Story

sto•ry (stôr•e) **n.,** *pl.* **-ries** [< OFr. < L. < Gr. *historia:* see HIS-TORY] **1.** the telling of an event or series of events, whether true or made-up; account; narration **2.** an anecdote or joke **3.** a piece of fictional writing shorter than a novel; narrative; tale; specif., *same as* SHORT STORY **4.** the plot of a novel, play, etc. **5.** *a)* a report or rumor *b)* [Colloq.] a falsehood or fib **6.** romantic legend or history ☆**7.** a news event or a report of it, as in the newspapers **—vt. -ried, -ry•ing** to decorate with paintings, etc. of scenes from history or legend

SYN.—story is a general term for any informative or entertaining account, either oral or written, of something that really happened or that is partly or wholly made-up; **narrative,** a more formal term, is typically a prose account of a happening or series of happenings, either real or fictional; **tale** usually means a simple, leisurely story, more or less loosely organized, esp. one that is made-up or legendary; **anecdote** is a term applied to a short, entertaining, often instructive account of a single incident, usually personal or biographical

---

Notice that the synonymy for *story* does more than just list synonyms. Three words are given with meanings close to *story*. They are *narrative, tale,* and *anecdote.* The synonymy explains the special meaning and use of each of these words. Sometimes a synonymy will also give sample phrases or sentences to show how each synonym is used.

A synonymy can help you choose the best word for what you want to say. Did that disaster movie *scare, frighten,* or *terrify* the audience? A synonymy will tell you just what the differences among the three words are. Then you can choose the best one.

Exercise Synonyms

Find two synonyms for each of these words. Use each synonym in a sentence to show its specific meaning.

strong   neat   praise   sloppy   beautiful
mystery   talk   lean   impolite   support

Review Exercises Putting Your Dictionary
Skills Together

A. Arrange the following words in alphabetical order.

shout   cry   murmur   call
whisper   declare   grumble   chatter
announce   say   mutter   mumble

B. Below are the guide words for four dictionary pages. Write a word that you would find on each page.

cannon - - - - - - cantaloupe   himself - - - - - - - - - - - - hire
elephant - - - - - - - - - ellipse   mariachi - - - - - - - - - market

C. Divide each of the following words into syllables.

salmon   dachshund   mummy   nonresident
calabash   designate   gluttony specific

D. Write the pronunciation for each of the following words.

mountain   valley   desert   tundra
demonstrate prevention   freight   ladle

E. Use your dictionary to find the meaning of each italicized word.

1. He didn't win, but we all admired his *pluck*.
2. Fred's Diner isn't one of my favorite *haunts*.
3. The edges of a quarter are *milled*.
4. No *nostrum* will cure this disease.
5. The cows were *lowing* in the meadow.

Chapter 3

Sentence Combining

A sentence is a group of words that states a single main idea. However, some main ideas are made up of smaller ideas. If each smaller idea is stated in a sentence of its own, the result is often choppy. The writing may give the reader only a vague idea of how the smaller ideas are related. Study the following group of sentences:

> Phil sat in the dining room. He shredded his napkin. He was nervous.

The ideas can be combined in one sentence.

> Phil sat in the dining room, nervously shredding his napkin.

The new sentence has only one main idea, but that main idea has several parts. The new sentence flows smoothly and shows how the ideas are related. It is much more effective than the group of sentences. This chapter will give you practice in writing sentences that express ideas clearly and precisely.

Part 1 Joining Sentences

Two sentences may state similar ideas that are equally important.

Libby fed the animals. Sam cleaned all the animals' cages.

These sentences can be joined by a comma and the word *and*. Here is the combined sentence. It states both ideas.

Libby fed the animals, and Sam cleaned all the animals' cages.

The sentences could also be joined by a semicolon.

Libby fed the animals; Sam cleaned all the animals' cages.

Two sentences may state contrasting ideas of equal importance. The sentences usually can be joined by a comma and the word *but*.

The sound on this TV set is not working. The picture is clear.
The sound on this TV set is not working, but the picture is clear.

A pair of sentences may express a choice between ideas of equal importance. The sentences usually can be joined by a comma and the word *or*.

Should we go skating? Should we go for a bike ride?
Should we go skating, or should we go for a bike ride?

Exercise Joining Sentences

Join each pair of sentences. Follow the directions given.

1. The door was locked. The windows were boarded shut. (Join with **, and.**)
2. Shall we go by train? Would you rather take the bus? (Join with **, or.**)
3. The lights grew dim. The curtains parted. (Join with **;**)
4. Amy offered to lend me her running shoes. They didn't fit. (Join with **, but.**)

Part 2 Joining Sentence Parts

The ideas expressed by two sentences may be so closely related that words are repeated in the sentences. The ideas may be combined in one sentence, using only the important parts of each sentence. The repeated words can be eliminated.

When the sentence parts express similar ideas that are equally important, they usually can be joined by *and*. (The words in italics can be eliminated.)

> Anna designed the posters. *She designed* the pennants.
> Anna designed the posters and the pennants.

When the sentence parts express contrasting ideas, they usually can be joined by *but*.

> I burned the rolls. *I made* a delicious salad.
> I burned the rolls but made a delicious salad.

When the sentence parts express a choice between ideas, they usually can be joined by *or*.

> Shall we rake the leaves today? *Shall we rake the leaves*
>   Thursday?
> Shall we rake the leaves today or Thursday?

Exercise Joining Sentence Parts

Join the related parts in each pair of sentences by following the directions in parentheses. Eliminate the italicized words.

1. Lisa worried. Jon *worried*. (Join related parts with **and**.)
2. The dog may have eaten the steak. *The dog may have* buried it. (Join related parts with **or**.)
3. The conductor was busy. *He was* friendly, *though*. (Join related parts with **but**.)
4. The ball rolled around the rim once. *It* fell through the net. (Join related parts with **and**.)
5. Sherry lost the letter I sent her. *Sherry lost the* map *I sent her*. (Join related parts with **and**.)

Part 3   Adding Single Words

The ideas in a pair of sentences may not be equally important. Perhaps only one word in the second sentence is really important to the main idea expressed by the pair of sentences. The one important word can be added to the first sentence. The new sentence will be a tighter and more effective way of expressing the idea.

> Carol is an illustrator. *She's* good.
> Carol is a good illustrator.
>
> Benjamin arranged the wrenches. *He did it* carefully.
> Benjamin arranged the wrenches carefully.
>
> We couldn't help admiring the team. *The team was* losing.
> We couldn't help admiring the losing team.

You may be able to add several single words to a sentence. Adding several words will allow you to combine more than two sentences. You can combine more than two sentences if one of the sentences states a main idea, and each of the others adds only one important detail to the main idea.

> A book rested on the table. *The book was* heavy. *The table was* wobbly.
> A heavy book rested on the wobbly table.

Be careful to choose the right location in the first sentence for each word that you add.

You may have to use a comma when you add more than one word to a sentence.

> Sludge washed up on shore after the oil spill. *The sludge was* thick. *The sludge was* sticky.
> Thick, sticky sludge washed up on shore after the oil spill.

Sometimes you can join the words with *and*.

> Diana received a message. *It was* long. *It was* complicated.
> Diana received a long and complicated message.

Exercises Adding Single Words

A. Combine each of the following groups of sentences by adding the important words. Eliminate the italicized words and follow any special directions given in parentheses.

1. John had a parrot. *The parrot was* talkative.
2. Katy set the lamp on the table. *The lamp was* polished.
3. Lois slipped into the room. *She came in* silently. *The room was* darkened.
4. I realized I was standing in cement. *The cement was* wet.
5. The audience burst into applause after the finale. *The audience was* delighted. *The applause was* enthusiastic. *The finale was* rousing.
6. Paul spread a glaze over the ham. *The glaze was* thin. *The glaze was made of* apricot. (Do not use a comma.)
7. The book is in a drawer in the kitchen. *It is a* telephone book. *It is* new. (Do not use a comma.)
8. The starship sped through the asteroid belt. *The starship was* battered. *The asteroid belt was* dangerous.
9. The most popular performer was a juggler. *He was* Canadian.
10. Rose placed the coins in a box. *The coins were* shiny. *The box was* purple.

B. Combine each of the following groups of sentences by adding important words to the first sentence. Decide on your own how the sentences should be combined.

1. The experiment was a success. The success was complete.
2. Ellen adjusted the sails. The sails were flapping.
3. The curtains faded in the sunlight. The sunlight was dazzling.
4. The puppies scampered across the floor. The puppies were muddy. The floor was shiny.
5. The cyclists displayed a map of their trip. The map was hand-made. They displayed it proudly.

Part 4   Adding Words That Change Form

Before you add an important word to a sentence, you may have to change the form of the word. You may have to add -y.

>Don't sit on that chair. *It* wobbles.
>Don't sit on that wobbly chair.

Sometimes you will have to add -ing or -ed.

>Nate and I set up the chairs. *They would* fold.
>Nate and I set up the folding chairs.

>Trish smoothed the paper. *It had a* crease.
>Trish smoothed the creased paper.

At other times you will have to add -ly.

>Alan solved our electrical problems. *He was* quick.
>Alan quickly solved our electrical problems.

Often, the word ending in -ly can be placed in any of several positions in the sentence.

>Jean remarked that she had not seen Eve in years. Jean was sad.

>Sadly, Jean remarked that she had not seen Eve in years.
>Jean remarked sadly that she had not seen Eve in years.

Exercises Adding Words That Change Form

A. Combine each pair of sentences by adding the important word. Follow the directions given. Eliminate the italicized words.

1. Luis backed away from the snake. *The snake* hissed. (End the important word with **-ing**.)

2. I cleaned the shelves. *They were covered with* dust. (End the important word with **-y**.)

3. We arranged the turkey on a platter. *The turkey was in* slices. (End the important word with **-ed**.)

4. Alec whistled to tell us that he'd spotted the hawk. *His whistling was* soft. (End the important word with **-ly**.)

5. The cat stalked the chipmunk. *The cat's movements were* slow. (End the important word with **-ly**.)

B. Choose the important word from the second sentence in each pair. Add it to the first sentence. Decide on your own how to change its form.

1. That stack of dishes may fall. The stack leans.
2. Rob scrubbed the tub. The tub had dirt in it.
3. Charlie made a banner. The banner had stripes.
4. Michelle called my name. Her voice was loud.
5. We had to wash the rags. The rags had oil on them.

Part 5 Adding Groups of Words

You may find that one sentence contains a group of words that can add important information to another sentence.

Dad is fixing dinner. Dad is in the kitchen.
Dad is fixing dinner in the kitchen.

This part will show you ways to add groups of words from one sentence to another to create a tighter expression of an idea.

Adding Groups of Words Without Changes in Form

You may be able to add a group of words to a sentence without making any other changes. When the group of words gives more information about someone or something, add it near the words that name the person or thing.

The noise was startling. *The noise was* in the basement.
The noise in the basement was startling.

When the group of words describes an action, add it near the words that name the action.

Don was waiting. *He was* at the door.
Don was waiting at the door.

When the group of words adds more information to the entire main idea of the other sentence, you may add it at the beginning or at the end.

Mr. Yamada always sends his mother flowers. *He sends them* on his birthday.
Mr. Yamada always sends his mother flowers on his birthday.
On his birthday, Mr. Yamada always sends his mother flowers.

Exercises Adding Groups of Words Without Changes in Form

A. Combine each of the following pairs of sentences by adding a group of words to the first sentence. Eliminate the italicized words.

1. You will be sleeping in a bed. *The bed is one* with a canopy.
2. The red coat is mine. *The coat is* in the lost-and-found.
3. The pastries look delicious. *The pastries were* at Henson's Bakery.
4. Ms. Foster will be flying a red biplane. *She will be* in the air show.
5. My brother loves to talk. *He talks* about his archaeological studies.

B. Combine each group of sentences.

1. Mount Fuji is a volcano. The volcano is in Japan.
2. The blister began to hurt. The blister was on my heel.
3. Joy and Jeff stood poised. They were on the tightrope.
4. Tom stood. He was at the center of the stage.
5. Becky will mail the package. She'll mail it at noon.

Adding Groups of Words with Commas

In some cases, when you add a group of words to a sentence, you will have to separate it from the rest of the sentence with a comma or a pair of commas.

My favorite bread is challah. *Challah is* a soft yeast bread.
My favorite bread is challah, a soft yeast bread.
"Alligator on the Escalator" was written by Eve Merriam.
"Alligator on the Escalator" is a humorous poem.
"Alligator on the Escalator," a humorous poem, was written by Eve Merriam.

Exercises Adding Groups of Words with Commas

A. Combine each of the following pairs of sentences by adding a group of words to the first sentence. Follow the instructions given in parentheses. Eliminate the italicized words.

1. My dog is the world's worst watchdog. *My dog is* a dachshund. (Use a pair of commas.)
2. The man in the gorilla suit is George Appleby. *He is* our neighbor. (Use a comma.)
3. Stacy's alarm clock is loud enough to wake the whole household. *Stacy's alarm clock is* a small portable one. (Use a pair of commas.)
4. Neighbors of ours celebrate Bastille Day. *They are* the Legers. (Use a pair of commas.)
5. Patty Benoit is the only person I know who has made a parachute jump. *She is* my sister's roommate. (Use a pair of commas.)

B. Combine each of the following pairs of sentences.

1. On the table was my father's most famous creation. It was an artificial grapefruit.
2. Marilyn couldn't open the register. Marilyn was the substitute cashier.

3. We had cannoli for dessert. Cannoli is an Italian pastry.

4. Ms. Lorenzo organized our school's first science fair. She is our science teacher.

5. I saw Charles A. Lindbergh's plane in Washington. Charles A. Lindbergh's plane was the *Spirit of St. Louis*.

Adding Groups of Words with *-ing* and *-ed*

Sometimes when you add a group of words to a sentence, you will have to change the form of one of them. In its new form, the word will often end with *-ing* or *-ed*.

> The man must have been a spy. *The man* stood under the street lamp.
> The man standing under the street lamp must have been a spy.

> We keep the octopus in a tank. *We* fill *the tank* with salt water.
> We keep the octopus in a tank filled with salt water.

Occasionally, a group of words will already contain a word ending in *-ing, -ed*, or another appropriate ending. Then you can add the entire group to the other sentence without changes.

> The crow must have been injured. *The crow was* dragging its left wing.
> The crow dragging its left wing must have been injured.

> The lobsters were great. *The lobsters were* flown in from Maine.
> The lobsters flown in from Maine were great.

> Inspector Hale stared at the mattress. *The mattress was* filled with money.
> Inspector Hale stared at the mattress filled with money.

When the words add information about someone or something, be sure to place the group next to the words naming the person or thing.

Ashley thought she saw her missing neighbor. *Ashley was* peering through the bookstore window.

Peering through the bookstore window, Ashley thought she saw her missing neighbor.

Ashley thought she saw her missing neighbor. *Her missing neighbor was* peering through the bookstore window.

Ashley thought she saw her missing neighbor peering through the bookstore window.

Exercises Adding Groups of Words with *-ing* and *-ed*

A.   Combine each pair of sentences by adding a group of words to the first sentence. Follow any directions given.

1. The woman is my aunt. *The woman is* weaving a rug.

2. A man has left a large donation for the relief fund. *The man* calls himself "a friend." (Use **-ing.**)

3. The singers were nervous. *They were* going on stage.

4. My sister gives her baby a vitamin supplement. *She* dissolves *it* in orange juice. (Use **-ed.**)

5. P. J. was surprised to see hundreds of people. *They were* waiting outside the theater.

B.   Combine each pair of sentences by adding an important group of words to the first sentence. Decide how the sentences should be combined and what changes may have to be made.

1. The people could barely breathe. The people were packed into the tiny elevator.

2. Connie searched through the photographs. The photographs were spread out on the table.

3. The library doesn't have the book. The book was reviewed in yesterday's paper.

4. The library is holding an exhibit of pottery. People make the pottery in the local area.

Part 6 Combining Sentences by Substitution

You may be able to put a complete idea expressed by one sentence into another sentence. The *-ing* form of a verb can be used when substituting the idea of one sentence for the word *something* or the word *that* in another sentence.

> *Something* improved my grade in spelling. *I* memorized the word list.
> Memorizing the word list improved my grade in spelling.

Notice that the idea in the second sentence explains the word *something* in the first. The word *memorized* was changed to *memorizing*. Then *memorizing the word list* was substituted for *something* in the first sentence.

> *We* pounded the clay on the table. *That* helped us soften it.
> Pounding the clay on the table helped us soften it.

The word *pounded* was changed to *pounding*. Then *Pounding the clay on the table* was substituted for *That* in the first sentence.

Exercises Substitutions with *-ing*

A. Combine each of the following pairs of sentences by substituting with *-ing*. Eliminate the italicized words.

1. *People* water cactus plants too much. *That* can harm them.

2. Betty has always enjoyed *something*. *She* exercises as soon as she wakes up.

3. *I* wait in line for lunch. *That* makes me impatient.

4. *Jeff* started a quilting business. *That* was Jeff's best idea.

5. *Tony* practices the piano. *That* is Tony's favorite after-school activity.

B. Combine each of the following groups of sentences by substituting the idea in one sentence for the word *something* or the word *that* in the other sentence. Decide on your own what changes may have to be made.

1. Jack and Juanita began something. They mixed the pancake batter.
2. I wrote a report about the Middle East. That took a lot of work.
3. I ran for the presidency of the student council. That was not as easy as I had thought it would be.
4. Paul planned on something. He would join us after the game.
5. I said goodbye to Sol. That made me sad.

Part 7 Combining with *who*

A group of words that gives information about a person can sometimes be added to a sentence by using the word *who*.

The people are planning another trip for next year. *The people* organized the trip to St. Louis.

The people who organized the trip to St. Louis are planning another trip for next year.

In the example above, the group of words added to the first sentence is necessary to make it clear which people are meant. In some sentences, the added group of words is not absolutely necessary. The words merely add additional information. When the group of words merely adds additional information, combine with **, who.**

Mr. Stanley and Ms. Wilson are planning another trip for next year. *Mr. Stanley and Ms. Wilson* organized the trip to St. Louis.

Mr. Stanley and Ms. Wilson, **who** organized the trip to St. Louis, are planning another trip for next year.

Exercises Combining with *who*

A. Combine each of the following pairs of sentences by following the directions in parentheses. Eliminate the italicized words.

1. Julie Grimes hit the only home run. *She* came into the game as a pinch-hitter. (Combine with **, who.**)

2. Dulcie entertained my parents for hours. *Dulcie* really knows how to tell a story. (Combine with **, who.**)

3. Steve Adler directed this movie. *Steve Adler* is my second cousin. (Combine with **, who.**)

4. Mr. Goodwin has a huge collection of campaign buttons. *Mr. Goodwin* enjoys politics. (Combine with **, who.**)

5. The girl is Terry Jackson. *The girl* offered to fix your bike. (Combine with **who.**)

B. Combine each of the following pairs of sentences. Decide on your own whether to combine with **who** or **, who.**

1. Ed couldn't remember where he had put the masking tape. Ed likes to have a place for everything and everything in its place.

2. I called Frank. Frank is at home with a cold.

3. Sandy Miller does volunteer work at the animal shelter. Sandy wants to be a veterinarian.

4. The girl is visiting from Finland. The girl is standing beside Jack.

5. People should sign up before the end of the day. They want to try out for the variety show.

Part 8 Combining with *which* and *that*

At times, the information added to a sentence is joined to it by the word *which* or the word *that*. When the group of words added to the first sentence is necessary to make the meaning clear, combine with **that**.

> This is the record. I wanted you to hear *the record*.
> This is the record that I wanted you to hear.

When the group of words is not absolutely necessary, but just adds additional information, combine with **, which**.

> Lentil soup is not hard to make. *Lentil soup* is high in protein.
> Lentil soup, **which** is high in protein, is not hard to make.

The word *that* can sometimes be omitted without changing the meaning of the sentence.

> This is the record I wanted you to hear.

Exercises Combining with *which* and *that*

A. Combine each of the following pairs of sentences by following the directions in parentheses. Eliminate the italicized words.

1. These bricks came from the old city hall. The city plans to recycle *these bricks*. (Combine with **, which.**)
2. Steve repaired Lucy's pocket watch. *It* was given to her by her grandfather. (Combine with **, which.**)
3. I was upset because I had lost the new scarf. I had crocheted *it* myself. (Combine with **that.**)
4. Carrie fixed the radio. I found *it* in the attic. (Combine with **that.**)
5. The newspaper has just won a Pulitzer Prize. I read *that newspaper*. (Combine with **that.**)

B. Combine each of the following pairs of sentences. Decide on your own whether to combine **, which** or **that.**

1. The map helped us find the fairgrounds. Kent drew the map.
2. The typewriters were donated by local businesses. We use the typewriters for the school paper.
3. The shoes turned my feet red. I bought the shoes on sale.
4. Ingrid's shin guards fit me perfectly. They no longer fit her.
5. Have you ever eaten in the restaurant? Your sister recommended the restaurant.

Part 9   Combining To Show Causes and Effects

Often in your writing you will want to explain to your readers that something happened because of something else. If you do not make it clear that one thing caused another, your reader may not realize that one event was a cause and the other, an effect. The following example uses the word *because* to make the relationship clear.

> We moved closer to town. (**because**)
> I can walk to the movie theater now.
>
> Because we moved closer to town, I can walk to the movie theater now.

Notice that a comma separates the two sentences. The sentences might be combined in another order. Then the comma would not be needed.

> I can walk to the movie theater now because we moved closer to town.

The word *since* can also be used to show a cause-and-effect relationship.

We'll be having sandwiches for dinner.
The stove is broken. (**since**)

Since the stove is broken, we'll be having sandwiches for
   dinner.
We'll be having sandwiches for dinner since the stove is
   broken.

There is another way to combine sentences to show a cause-
and-effect relationship. Words can be added before the effect,
or result. If you use this method, you will also have to use a
semicolon **(;).**

We moved closer to town.
I can walk to the movie theater now. (**; as a result,**)
We moved closer to town; as a result, I can walk to the movie
   theater now.

The stove is broken.
We'll be having sandwiches for dinner. (**; therefore,**)
The stove is broken; therefore, we'll be having sandwiches
   for dinner.

You will find the following words useful for indicating causes in
your combined sentences.

because   since   for

You will find these words useful for indicating results in your
combined sentences.

so   as a result   thus
therefore   consequently

Exercise Combining To Show Causes and Effects

Combine each of the following pairs of sentences by using
the key words given in parentheses.

1. These shoes hurt my feet. **(since)**
   I don't wear them.

2. These shoes hurt my feet.
   I don't wear them. **(; so,)**

3. Dan has a wonderful voice. **(because)**
   He won the lead role in the musical.

4. Dan has a wonderful voice.
   He won the lead role in the musical. **(; therefore,)**

5. Eric lost his watch. **(because)**
   He has been asking me for the time all day.

Part 10   Applying Combining Skills

As you have learned, there are several ways to combine related ideas in your sentences. Your next step is to use these combining skills to eliminate choppiness and vagueness from your writing.

Notice how the following paragraph has been revised.

> Some sports require team play. Other sports depend on individual effort. Success in a team sport depends on something. Each player works for the good of the team. Success in an individual sport depends on one person alone. Some people prefer team sports. They are in a group of people. The people share a common goal. They enjoy that. Some people prefer individual sports. They like to be on their own. They rely only on themselves.

> Some sports require team play, but other sports depend on individual effort. Success in a team sport depends on each player's working for the good of the team, but success in an individual sport depends on one person alone. Some people prefer team sports because they enjoy being in a group of people who share a common goal. Some people prefer individual sports because they like to be on their own, relying only on themselves.

Read something that you have written. Think about how it might be improved. Remember that there are many ways to express any idea; one way may be more effective than another. Good writers choose the way that communicates an idea most clearly.

Exercise Applying Combining Skills

Combine the sentences in each of these groups into a single sentence. Write the combined sentences as a paragraph. Then, in your own words, complete the story.

1. I was sitting in a room.
   I was sitting alone.
   The room was dimly lit.
   I was watching the news.
   The news was on TV.

2. The newscaster was talking about a gorilla.
   The newscaster was Bobby Bunt.
   The gorilla was huge.
   The gorilla was kept at the zoo.
   The zoo was nearby.

3. The gorilla weighed four hundred pounds.
   The gorilla was so strong.
   It could pick up a car.

4. The zoo-keepers were worried.
   The gorilla could rip open its cage.
   The gorilla could escape.
   The escape would be easy.

5. I turned suddenly.
   I saw a hand.
   The hand was reaching through the window.
   The hand was large.
   The hand was hairy.

Review Exercises Sentence Combining

A. Join each pair of sentences by using **, and** or **, or** or **, but.**

1. Yesterday I flew in a plane. I saw five states in an hour.
2. The tickets went on sale this morning. By the time we got to the theater, they were all gone.
3. Pets are fun. They require care and attention.

B. Join the related parts of each pair of sentences by using **and** or **or** or **but.** Eliminate the italicized words.

1. Sir Gawain buckled his armor. *He* rode after the dragon.
2. Next summer, I may get a job as a paper carrier. *I may* babysit.
3. I saw Sam standing at the end of the hall. *I saw* Harry *standing at the end of the hall.*

C. Combine each group of sentences by adding important words. Follow the directions given in parentheses. Eliminate the italicized words.

1. Ron looked for the election results in the paper. *He was* anxious. (End the important word with **-ly.**)
2. My sweater shrank in the dryer. *My sweater was* wool.
3. A rainbow arched across the bay. *The rainbow was* pale. *The rainbow was* shimmering. (Use a comma.)

D. Combine each of the following pairs of sentences by adding an important group of words to the first sentence. Follow the directions given in parentheses. Eliminate the italicized words.

1. A local police officer taught the first-aid course. *The officer was* Mr. George Garcia. (Use a pair of commas.)
2. Two statues guarded the entrance. *The statues were* of monkeys. *It was the entrance* to the temple.
3. Did you see the recipe for fudge? *The recipe was* in Tuesday's paper.

E. Combine each of the following pairs of sentences by substituting with -*ing.* Eliminate the italicized words.

1. Dr. Hendricks is very good at *something. She* puts her patients at ease.
2. I comb my cat's long fur. *That* can be tedious.
3. *Something* became Judy's passion. *She* practiced tennis.
4. *People* parachute from planes. *That* requires training.

F. Combine each pair of sentences by following the directions in parentheses. Eliminate the italicized words.

1. Tracy Kidder has now joined a troupe of jugglers. *He* used to be very clumsy. (Combine with **, who.**)
2. The boy saved four families. *The boy* spotted the smoke. (Combine with **who.**)
3. Students limit their career choices. *Students* don't explore many areas of study. (Combine with **who.**)

G. Combine each of the following pairs of sentences by following the directions in parentheses. Eliminate the italicized words.

1. I can fix the lamp. *It* fell off the table. (Combine with **that.**)
2. I wanted someone to invent a pen. I would never be able to lose *it.* (Combine with **that.**)
3. This building was once a customs house. *The building* is now a museum. (Combine with **, which.**)

H. Combine each of the following pairs of sentences by using the key words given in parentheses.

1. Claire overslept.
   She missed the bus for the class picnic. **(; as a result.)**
2. Arthur's car ran out of gas. **(because)**
   We missed the first half of the movie.
3. Arthur's car ran out of gas.
   We missed the first half of the movie. **(; so,)**

Chapter 4

The Process
of Writing

Writing as often as you can helps you to write more easily. In addition to your writing assignments, you may want to keep a journal. Your journal could be a small book that you carry with you. In it you can jot down things you see or hear. You can write down ideas or feelings as they occur to you. You can then use your journal for topics for your writing assignments.

What you see or hear or think or feel belongs to you until you can share it with someone else in writing. Your experiences are different from anyone else's. Whenever you write, however, there will always be something that remains the same: the process of writing. There are steps you can follow: pre-writing, writing a first draft, and rewriting, or revising. These steps are important. They help you decide what to write about, how to organize what you write, and how to rewrite, or revise, what you have written. You will learn how to follow these three steps in this chapter.

1. *Possible Topics*
    moving day
    the soccer game
    my first airplane ride

2. *Selected topic*
    my first airplane ride

I was going to have
~~This would be~~ my first airplane
ride. I ~~was~~ invited to visit my grand-
mother's ~~house,~~ and my ~~Mom and~~
~~Dad~~ said I ~~could~~ fly there. I

I was going to have my first
airplane ride. I had been invited
to visit my grandmother, and
my parents said I was old

Part 1   Pre-Writing

Knowing what to write about often seems to be the hardest part of writing. Take your time at this point in the process of writing. Choose a subject that interests you. If you have jotted down ideas in a journal, page through your journal until you find something you would like to write more about. When you have chosen your topic, narrow it so that you can handle it in a given length.

Next, make a list of interesting details that you could use to develop your topic. Use all of your senses to make your topic come alive. List as many details as you can think of. You can always discard those that do not work.

Finally, jot down any notes or ideas related to your writing. You do not have to use all of them. If you need to learn more about your topic, do that, too.

Here is an example of pre-writing notes.

1. Possible Topics
    the balloon man
    my TV hero
    the county fair
    my friend's party
    the day I baked a pie

2. Selected Topic
    the county fair

3. Specific details
    hot weather
    sideshows
    dusty ground
    smells of hot dogs, peanuts,
      popcorn, cotton candy
    games of chance
    sword swallower, fat lady
    tattooed man
    penny arcade
    loud music
    Ferris wheel, roller coaster
    exhibit of crafts
    crowds of people
    merry-go-round

4. Notes
    use vivid sensory details
    descriptive paragraph?
    don't try to describe everything
    spatial organization?

Part 2 Writing the First Draft

At this point in the process of writing, you are ready to write. Do not fuss with the writing. Do not worry about spelling or punctuation. Do not be concerned about organizing ideas. Just write. Let whatever happens, happen. This is only your first draft. You will rewrite, or revise, later.

Here is an example of a first draft of a paragraph.

First Draft

The smell of peanuts was in the air as we waited in line at the gate of the county fair. We were listening to the noise and excitement around us. On our right, a red-shirted man was telling everyone to come to see the sword swallower. On our left was a yellow tent with a colored poster of a tattooed man. Soon we could hear the sound of the roller coaster. The people in it were screaming. The loud music of the merry-go-round, the smell of popcorn, and the crowds of people made us a little dizzy. Jan and I didnt know what to do.

Part 3 Rewriting, or Revising

Now read what you have written. At this stage of the process, you will need to work more carefully and thoughtfully. Do you need to use more precise words anywhere? Do you need to call upon your senses to create a more vivid scene? Do you *show* your reader what you want to say?

Is your topic sentence strong and interesting? Do your ideas flow smoothly from one sentence to another? Did you stick to your topic? Did you leave out unnecessary details? Do you like what you have written? Read your writing aloud. Do your ears catch what your eyes did not?

The *tantalizing* smell of *roasting* peanuts ~~was in the air~~ *hung over us* as we waited in *the hot, dusty* line at the *entrance to* ~~gate of~~ the county fair. *Once inside,* We were ~~listening~~ *caught up in* the noise and excitement around us. On our right, a *fat* red-shirted man was ~~telling~~ *calling* everyone to come to see the *amazing* sword swallower. *To* On our left ~~was~~ *stood* a *bright* yellow tent with a *vividly* colored poster of a tattooed man *in front of it*. *As we moved on,* Soon, we could hear the *roar* ~~sound~~ of the roller coaster *and screams of the* The people in it ~~were screaming~~. The *high pitched* ~~loud~~ music of the merry-go-round, the smell of *freshly popped corn* ~~popcorn~~, and the *swarms* ~~crowds~~ of people *around us* made us a ~~little dizzy~~ *bit giddy*. Jan and I didnt know *where to begin* ~~what to do~~.

Proofreading

It is important to make your writing correct, as well as clear and interesting. Check capitalization, punctuation, and spelling. Use whatever references you have available to check your work.

Finally, when you are satisfied that your writing is clear and correct, write your final copy. Write carefully. Make your copy as neat as possible. Make correct paragraph indentations. Leave good margins around your writing. Use whatever headings your teacher requires.

When you have finished your final copy, proofread your work. Read it aloud one final time.

Here is the final copy of the paragraph. Compare it with the two preceding paragraphs.

Final Copy

> The tantalizing smell of roasting peanuts hung over us as we waited in the hot, dusty line at the entrance to the county fair. Once inside, we were caught up in the noise and excitement around us. On our right, a fat red-shirted man was calling everyone to come to see the amazing sword swallower. To our left stood a bright yellow tent with a vividly colored poster of a tattooed man in front of it. As we moved on, we could hear the roar of the roller coaster and the screams of the people in it. The high-pitched music of the merry-go-round, the smell of freshly popped corn, and the swarms of people around us made us a bit giddy. Jan and I didn't know where to begin.

Guidelines for the Process of Writing

Pre-Writing
1. Choose a subject that interests you.
2. Make a list of possible topics.
3. Select a topic and narrow it.
4. Make a list of interesting details that you could use to develop your topic.
5. Jot down any notes or ideas related to your topic.
6. Learn more about your topic if you need to.

Writing the First Draft
1. Begin to write.
2. Continue to write. Do not stop to fuss over or correct anything at this stage. Let your thoughts flow freely.

Rewriting, or Revising
1. Read what you have written.
2. Did you include everything you wanted to?
3. Did you develop only one main idea?
4. Did you leave out unnecessary details?
5. Did you stick to your topic? Does your paragraph have unity?
6. Is your topic sentence strong and interesting?
7. Do your ideas flow smoothly from one sentence to another?
8. Are your ideas clearly expressed?
9. Did you organize your ideas in the best way?
10. Is each word the right word?
11. Did you use your senses to *show* your reader what you wanted to say?
12. Read your writing aloud. Do you like what you have written?
13. Rewrite, or revise, wherever necessary.

PROOFREADING
1. Read your rewritten, or revised, first draft.
2. Check for correct capitalization.
3. Check spelling. Use a dictionary, if necessary.
4. Check to see that all punctuation is correct.
5. Make a neat, final copy.
6. Read your final copy aloud, to yourself.

Chapter 5

Writing the Paragraph

The paragraph is the basic tool for organizing ideas in any kind of writing. If you can write a good paragraph, you can write a good composition, a good report, or a good letter. In this chapter, you will review the main parts of a paragraph. You will study the way that sentences are put together into well written paragraphs.

Part 1 What Is a Paragraph?

A **paragraph** is a group of sentences that work together to explain or support one main idea. That idea usually is stated in the first sentence. The rest of the paragraph contains several sentences that develop the main idea more fully. Following is an example of a well written paragraph.

> *Tom slept more soundly that night than he had in a long time.* His dreams were of the new friend he had found. He dreamed of the deer and himself running over the green meadows and up the gentle slopes of the hills. He dreamed beautiful dreams like these until the morning when the sun came through his window and woke him.—JENNY DEBOUZEK

The first sentence tells you that the paragraph is going to be about Tom's sound sleep. This is the one main idea of the paragraph. The rest of the sentences develop that idea. They give you a sense of Tom's long and peaceful rest.

Paragraph Unity

When all of the sentences in a paragraph relate to one main idea, the paragraph has **unity.** Sometimes a paragraph contains sentences that stray from the main idea. These "extra" sentences can be removed easily to create a unified paragraph.

Other paragraphs, like this one, have more serious problems.

> Driver's training should be a required course in every high school in the United States. Defensive driving means anticipating the actions of other drivers. Millions of people are killed in automobile accidents every year. Insurance statistics have not proved that teen-agers are unsafe drivers. Many insurance companies offer lower insurance rates to students who have completed driver's training courses.

The first sentence in this paragraph is about the need for a driver's training course in every high school. Each of the next three sentences introduces a different idea. The second sentence defines defensive driving. The third sentence makes a statement about automobile accidents. The fourth sentence gives a fact about insurance statistics. Only the last sentence relates directly to the opening sentence in the paragraph. It begins to explain why driver's training should be required.

The sentences in this paragraph do not develop one main idea. They are, therefore, a series of unrelated sentences, not a unified paragraph.

Paragraph Length

"How long does a paragraph have to be?" is a question asked by many beginning writers. The answer is easier than you might suppose: *A paragraph should be long enough to develop a main idea.* For example, the following paragraph is too short to explain the topic sentence clearly:

> Almost all of us agreed that Jack was the luckiest boy in town. To our envious eyes, he had everything a boy could ever wish for.

Why was Jack lucky? What did he have? The question can be answered only by adding more sentences.

> Almost all of us agreed that Jack was the luckiest boy in town. He had his own minibike and lots of space to ride it in. When he was tired of that, Fallah, his black mare, stood waiting patiently in the stable. No matter what he asked his dad for, it miraculously appeared the next day. He even had his own pool table. Furthermore, he didn't have to do chores like the rest of us. The gardener and the stable hand took care of the chores. To our envious eyes, he had everything a boy could ever wish for.

The detailed information in the longer paragraph explains clearly and completely why Jack was considered the luckiest boy in town.

Exercise Studying Paragraph Unity

In each of the following paragraphs, one or more sentences do not relate to the main idea of the paragraph. Pick out the "extra" sentences. Then decide whether the remaining sentences give enough information about the main idea to make a fully developed paragraph.

1

Deep-sea diving requires more than putting on a wet suit and an iron mask. Treasures lie buried at the bottom of the sea. Jacques Cousteau has spent most of his life filming undersea life. Divers must be knowledgeable about their equipment.

2

All animals have senses, but not all animals use them in the same way. Many people have lost their sense of hearing. A frog, for instance, does not see a fly as we see it—in terms of legs, shape of wings, and number of eyes. In fact, a frog won't spot a fly at all unless the fly moves. Frogs are amphibious animals. Put a frog into a cage with freshly killed insects, and it will starve.

3

My cousin and I learned most of our family's history by playing in Grandmother's attic. Grandmother lived in a little town in Ohio. In one corner stood a brass-bound trunk, filled with forgotten dolls once treasured by aunts and mothers. Grandfather's World War I uniform hung proudly on a metal rack, along with once-stylish dresses. The clothing now is much more comfortable than it was thirty years ago. When we dressed up in the old-fashioned clothes, we felt that the past was truly part of our lives.

4

Jeff Daniels is deaf, yet he knows when his telephone rings or his alarm clock goes off. His "hearing ear" dog, Rags, tells him. Rags, who was trained by the American Humane Association, alerts his master whenever there is a knock on the door or a phone call and leads Jeff to the source of the sound. Seeing-eye dogs are used by blind people.

Part 2 The Topic Sentence

The topic sentence is usually the first sentence in a paragraph. It tells what the rest of the paragraph is going to be about. The topic sentence is the key to paragraph unity. It states the one main idea that must be developed by the other sentences. If a sentence relates directly to the topic sentence, it belongs in the paragraph. If it relates only indirectly or not at all, it does not fit and should be removed.

The topic sentence is important from the point of view of both the writer and the reader. It helps the writer to focus on the one idea that gives direction to the paragraph. It helps the writer to stay on the track so that he or she does not bring in ideas that are unrelated to the main idea. For the reader, the topic sentence acts as a guide by letting him or her know immediately what the entire paragraph is going to be about.

To understand more clearly what a topic sentence does, look at the following paragraph.

> My husband had very definite opinions about raising children. He believed that parents should provide proper models for their children and should give them guidelines as to what they can and cannot do. He thought that children should be taught to face reality, to accept themselves, to be able to function under supervision, to seek some formal training and education, and to realize that it was their duty to help oppressed people. He believed that children should have a belief in a tradition and that this should come originally from the home. He did not believe in spoiling children.
> —BETTY SHABAZZ

The topic sentence says: "My husband had very definite opinions about raising children." This is the main idea of the paragraph. The sentences that follow describe the opinions. These sentences relate directly to the topic sentence. The paragraph, therefore, has unity.

The topic sentence of the paragraph is a general statement. It presents the idea of definite opinions without giving any specific information about them. The other sentences in the paragraph explain the opinions in some detail. The same arrangement can be found in most paragraphs. The topic sentence gives an idea that covers, or takes in, the specific ideas in the rest of the paragraph.

Exercises Working with Topic Sentences

A. Each of the following groups has five sentences about one topic. Choose the one sentence in the group that would work best as the topic sentence.

1. a. Living things are organic matter.

b. Things that were never alive, such as minerals and glass, are inorganic matter.

c. Lumber, wood, and cotton were once alive, so they are organic matter.

d. Anything that takes up space is called "matter."

e. Matter can't be destroyed, but it can be changed into energy.

2. a. Jack drinks so much milk that Dad jokes about buying a cow.

b. Jack's standard question after school is, "What's for dinner?"

c. When Jack packs his school lunch, it looks like a grocery bag.

d. My brother Jack claims that his hobby is eating.

e. Mom is threatening to put a padlock on the refrigerator.

3. a. The bare branches of the maple trees were outlined in shimmering white.

b. Our yard looked magically different after the heavy winter snow.

c. The bushes in front of the garage drooped, heavy with snow blossoms.

d. The old garage wore a fresh white coat of snow-paint.

e. The bird bath near the house had become a frosty snow-cone.

4. a. Sometimes a giraffe's height can lead to its death.

b. Every time a giraffe takes a drink of water, it is in danger.

c. A giraffe can't drink easily because it can't kneel down.

d. A giraffe takes a long time to bend its legs apart.

e. While a giraffe is drinking, it is helpless if a lion or tiger attacks.

5. a. When my little brother had the measles, Mrs. Paulson played checkers with him every day.

b. Mrs. Paulson often bakes cookies for us.

c. Mrs. Paulson bandages our scraped knees without scolding us for being careless.

d. I guess every child on the block has had her for a babysitter at one time or another.

e. Bespectacled Mrs. Paulson is like a grandmother to everyone in the neighborhood.

B. Select one of the groups of sentences from Exercise A, and work the sentences into a paragraph. Begin the paragraph with the topic sentence. Arrange the rest of the sentences in the order you think is best. If necessary, revise the sentences or add words and phrases so that your finished paragraph reads smoothly.

Part 3　Writing Topic Sentences

The topic sentence of a paragraph has two main jobs:

1. It must state the main idea of the paragraph, which is the idea developed by the rest of the sentences.
2. It must capture the reader's attention so that he or she wants to find out more about the main idea.

Stating the Main Idea

In Part 2 you learned that a topic sentence is a general statement. It presents an idea that can be developed with details.

Sometimes, in writing a topic sentence, a writer may express an idea that is *too general* to be developed in a single paragraph. Following is an example of such a sentence:

> *There are many kinds of dogs.*

This subject is so broad that about all the writer could do is list the different dog breeds. The paragraph would probably be as dull to write as it would be to read.

Suppose the topic sentence were revised like this:

> *The poodle has played a starring role in the history of dogdom.*

The writer narrowed her main idea so that it could be developed in one paragraph. She went on to supply more details.

> *The poodle has played a starring role in the history of dogdom.* The breed is believed to have originated in Russia, where black standard-sized poodles were used as water retrievers for bird hunters. The Russians called the dog "pudel," which literally means "splashing in water." The breed spread to northern Germany, where the brown color was introduced. German artists as early as the fifteenth century depicted the poodle, and the great Spanish artist, Goya, used this breed in several of his paintings. The first evidence of a toy poodle's existence came from England, where the "White Cuban" breed,

said to have begun in Cuba, became an English favorite. Queen Anne had several poodles during her reign in the early eighteenth century.—EVELYN MILLER

The writer was able to explain her main idea in one paragraph. She gave sufficient details within that paragraph to leave the reader feeling satisfied.

Writing Interesting Topic Sentences

Any writer who puts time and effort into a paragraph wants it to be read. If the topic sentence is dull and uninteresting, however, the reader may not read the entire paragraph.

Look at the following topic sentence:

> *I'd like to tell you about the use of teaching machines in the schools of the future.*

This sentence makes clear what the rest of the paragraph is going to be about. It is a general statement that is narrow enough to be developed in one paragraph. The sentence, though, is flat and unimaginative.

Now, look at this topic sentence:

> *In the world of tomorrow, teaching machines will take into account different learning rates, working as fast (or as slowly) as the students using them.*

Your response to the sentence might be, "Gee, that sounds interesting. Tell me more." The writer has caught your attention. You want to find out more about teaching machines.

In the world of tomorrow, teaching machines will take into account different learning rates, working only as fast (or as slowly) as the students using them. They will offer the child individual attention. They will possibly offer more patience than could be expected from the average teacher. They will offer immediate feedback so that the children know how well they are doing and can take pride in their progress. More than that, the machines will help make learning fun.

Writing a Topic Sentence

When writing a paragraph, begin by jotting down some ideas about what you might want to say. Study your notes and cross out those ideas that do not seem to fit well with the others. Then write a topic sentence.

Guidelines for Writing Topic Sentences

1. Does the sentence clearly state the main idea that you plan to develop in the paragraph?
2. Does the sentence present an idea that is narrow enough to be explained or supported in a single paragraph?
3. Does the sentence express the main idea in such a way that the reader will want to read the entire paragraph?

Exercises Writing Good Topic Sentences

A. Here is a list of poorly written topic sentences. They are either too broad, too uninteresting, or both. Decide what is wrong with each sentence. Then rewrite the sentence so that it would be an effective topic sentence for a paragraph.

1. In this paragraph I am going to explain several ways of conserving energy.
2. Summer is the best time of the year.
3. Each year Mother invites my teacher to dinner.
4. This story about a blind deer made me very sad.
5. There are many ways to raise money when you need it.
6. Younger brothers take advantage of their sisters.
7. My favorite sports are basketball and soccer.
8. This literary masterpiece is going to be about someone I've known for years—me.
9. I like all kinds of music.
10. America's history is filled with heroes.

B. In the following paragraphs, the topic sentences have been removed. Read each paragraph carefully. Then write a good topic sentence. Be sure that it does the things listed on page 68.

1. _____(topic sentence)_____. In cities, all deliveries were by horse and wagon. Horses moved urban local passengers by carriage, omnibus, and horse-drawn streetcars. Stagecoaches bore passengers, mail, and baggage across rough and dusty Western roads, negotiating steep grades and fording unbridged streams. After 1840, teams of fast trotting horses for light coaches became popular in the East.

2. _____(topic sentence)_____. He was a husky, long-legged chap, to me a perfect physical specimen. I asked him where he'd been, and he replied that he had been climbing the foothills north of town. I asked him why he did it. He told me that his doctor had advised it; that he was trying to correct certain difficulties following an illness. He was climbing the foothills every day to develop his lungs and legs.

3. _____(topic sentence)_____. The dynamite had been frozen and thawed many times. Its paper covering had absorbed the nitroglycerine, making it dangerous no matter how carefully it was handled. In fact, dynamite like that sometimes explodes when two sticks of it are pulled apart, as the ghosts of a good many miners could tell you.

4. _____(topic sentence)_____. There they were—thirty-six whales pulled up on the shore. Every one of them weighed up to 4,000 pounds and measured nearly twenty feet long. They were the true monsters of the deep, the "black-fish" in Melville's famous story, *Moby Dick*.

5. _____(topic sentence)_____. They took him into a room where there were only some boxes and three bananas hanging from the ceiling. They wanted to see how long it would take the chimp to pile up the boxes and climb on them. The chimp did not touch the boxes. He pushed one of the men under the bananas, crawled up on his back, and brought the bananas down in two minutes.

Chapter 6

Developing the Paragraph

In writing, just as cooking, you may have available all the ingredients for a good product. The trick lies in selecting the right ingredients from those on hand and in putting them together correctly and creatively.

For a paragraph, the "right ingredients" are ideas that develop the main idea. Supporting ideas can take a variety of forms. They might be details that appeal to the senses. They might be facts, figures, or examples. They might be definitions of things or concepts. This chapter discusses how different kinds of supporting ideas can be used to develop paragraphs.

Part 1 Using Specific Details

Details are items of information that work together to create a clear impression in a reader's mind. To better understand the nature of details, let's examine five lines written by Geoffrey Chaucer, an early English poet.

> His beard was broader than a shovel, and red
> As a fat sow or fox. A wart stood clear
> Atop his nose, and red as a pig's ear
> A tuft of bristles on it. Black and wide
> His nostrils were.

The details in these lines of poetry are visual details. They appeal to the reader's sense of sight, with phrases such as these:

broader than a shovel	red as a pig's ear
red as a fat sow or fox	tuft of bristles
atop his nose	black and wide

By choosing such vivid details, Chaucer succeeds in communicating a clear picture of a person's appearance in just a few lines.

Using Visual Details

Visual details can be used to build a paragraph that describes a place or a thing. In the following example, the writer tells about a camp on the outskirts of a village.

> That summer we camped along the railroad tracks on the outskirts of a village. Our tent was next to the last in a row of several others just like it—a square of brown canvas curtains with a roof sloped like a pyramid, held up by a pole that peeped through a vent at the top. The plank floor of the tent was set up on bricks, the ends of the timbers sticking out in front, making a shelf that we used for a porch. The roof was held down by ropes staked down at the four corners and along the sides. Between the tents there were lean-to's where the women cooked and washed clothes in iron tubs, heating

the water over stone fire pits. The swamp came up close in back, and in front spilled into a ditch, making a moat that separated the camp from the tracks just beyond. Over this ditch there was a catwalk of planks leading to the tracks, the main street of the neighborhood.—ERNESTO GALARZA

The writer opens the paragraph with a general statement about the camp. He then expands this idea with details about the location of his family's tent, about the way the tent was constructed, about the lean-to's between the tents, about the swamp behind and in front of the campsite, and about the tracks beyond the ditch. Each detail is carefully selected to give the reader a good idea of what the camp looked like.

Writing About a Person

Suppose you want to describe a person. Each person has some special distinction—something in the way he or she looks, or dresses, or acts—which makes that person an individual. These are the specific details you would include in your description of that person. Some of the details would be visual details about the person's appearance. Others might be details about the person's behavior, moods, and outlook on life.

Notice, in the following paragraph, how the writer combines different kinds of details.

She was a black child, with huge green eyes that seemed to glow in the dark. From the age of four on she had a look of being full-grown. The look was in her muscular, well-defined limbs that seemed as though they could do a woman's work and in her way of seeing everything around her. Most times she was alive and happy. The only thing wrong with her was that she got hurt so easily. The slightest rebuke sent her crying; the least hint of disapproval left her moody and depressed for hours. But the other side of it was that she had a way of springing back from pain. No matter how hurt she had been, she would be her old self by the next day.—JEAN WHEELER SMITH

The writer first gives specific details about the child's outward appearance; for example: "a black child," "huge green eyes," and "muscular, well defined limbs." She then describes the child's sensitivity and resilience. The writer develops the paragraph with details that help us to see a unique individual.

Developing a Paragraph

When you sit down to write a paragraph that is to be developed with many details, keep these five steps in mind.

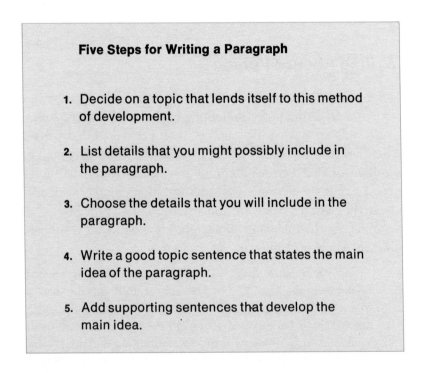

Five Steps for Writing a Paragraph

1. Decide on a topic that lends itself to this method of development.

2. List details that you might possibly include in the paragraph.

3. Choose the details that you will include in the paragraph.

4. Write a good topic sentence that states the main idea of the paragraph.

5. Add supporting sentences that develop the main idea.

Exercise Developing a Paragraph with Details

Each of these topic sentences may be expanded into a paragraph by using specific details. Choose two sentences. Use your imagination to develop each into a well written paragraph.

1. Old Rob was certainly an unusual dog.
2. Not a breath stirred over the open prairie.
3. Walking from the marble terrace, we entered the central hall of the mansion.
4. The visitor from Neptune looked nothing like a human.
5. Sam was in his early fifties, and the hair that showed under his hat was iron gray.
6. The old peddler's cart was piled high with fruit.
7. The landlord had moved enough stuff into the room to furnish three rooms its size.
8. The bird watcher waited patiently on the park bench.
9. The first light of dawn glowed faintly on the horizon.
10. Every day I explored a little more of the river.
11. At night I dreamed of nothing but the cat.
12. I shall never forget the guest who arrived at our house one afternoon last September.

Part 2   Using Facts or Figures

A topic sentence sometimes makes a statement that is best supported with facts or figures. Following is an example of this method of paragraph development. Notice that the writer has used a few figures along with many facts.

A most enchanting part of Puerto Rico is El Yunque Rain Forest, named after the 3496-foot-high mountain El Yunque. This 28,000-acre stretch of jungles, hills, streams, and waterfalls, a bare hour's drive from San Juan, is the only rain forest in the West Indies and the only tropical preserve of the United States National Park Service. Here, giant ferns unfurl feathery branches up to 30 feet. Orchids in pastel shades cling to their host trees. Among the 200 species of trees are hardwoods which, elsewhere, were cut down centuries before to build Spanish cathedrals, forts, monasteries, and homes. One of these is the mighty *ausubo*, called the bullet wood tree because of the toughness of its wood.—ROBIN McKOWN

In the opening sentence, the writer introduces the subject of the paragraph—the El Yunque Rain Forest. She follows with facts and figures about the forest.

1. It is a 28,000-acre stretch of jungles, hills, streams, and waterfalls.
2. It is an hour's drive from San Juan.
3. It is the only rain forest in the West Indies.
4. It is the only tropical preserve of the National Park Service.
5. Giant ferns there grow up to 30 feet.
6. Orchids grow there also.
7. In the forest are 200 species of trees.
8. Some of the forest's trees are hardwoods.
9. The *ausubo* is called the bullet wood tree because of its hard wood.

Together, these facts and figures develop the idea that the El Yunque Rain Forest is an enchanting part of Puerto Rico.

Using Figures

In some paragraphs, like the following, figures are used to give weight to the main idea.

> Until the 1930's, many Americans believed that anyone who couldn't find work was lazy and shouldn't be helped by the government. The experience of the Great Depression (1929–1939) changed that. From 1931 to 1940, the unemployment rate was never less than 14 percent of the total work force. In 1933, the worst year of the Depression, 25 percent (one out of every four persons) couldn't find a job—any job.
> —MARC ROSENBLUM

The writer tells us in his topic sentence that "Until the 1930's, many Americans believed that anyone who couldn't find work was lazy...." He then explains that the Great Depression changed that idea and presents dates and unemployment statistics. The figures in this paragraph emphasize the idea that there can be reasons other than laziness for a person's not working.

Exercise Developing a Paragraph with Facts or Figures

Each of the following topic sentences can be expanded into a paragraph by using facts or figures. Choose two of the sentences. Then develop each into a well written paragraph. You may have to do some outside reading to gather facts and figures for your paragraphs. Be sure, though, that your paragraphs are your own work. Do not copy them from other sources.

1. The 55 m.p.h. speed limit saves lives.
2. Our wild animals are disappearing rapidly.
3. The (name of team) is made up of individual champions.
4. The future looks bright for careers in technical fields.
5. Father penguin "babysits" with his children.
6. Each year, fires destroy great tracts of valuable land.
7. The Catskill Mountains are a popular vacation area.
8. It's easy to spot poison ivy if you know what to look for.
9. The platypus is one of the world's oldest animals.
10. George Washington Carver helped to make peanuts big business.

Part 3 Using Examples

A topic sentence may express an idea that is best developed through the use of examples. Following is such a sentence.

Poverty can be measured by more than income.

The writer could have supported this idea with facts and figures like the following:

1. The percentage of American families whose income falls below the official poverty line
2. The percentage of American families that do not have indoor plumbing
3. The number of complaints received each winter from tenants who do not have sufficient heat in their apartments
4. The number of rat bites treated each year at one hospital

Instead, the writer gave several examples from the experience of one family. The facts and figures in the paragraph relate to that family rather than to poor people in general.

Poverty can be measured by more than income. There are five people in Cass Tanner's family. They live in a one-bedroom apartment. The building they live in violates at least fifteen city building-code regulations. It has exposed electrical wiring. The plumbing does not work properly. In January, during five days of subfreezing weather, the heat did not go above fifty-five degrees. Cass wakes up each night to make sure that his brothers and sisters are not bothered by rats. Mr. Tanner's take-home pay from a part-time job is $380 per month. The rent is $165 per month.—WILLIAM F. SAALBACH

In this paragraph, the idea that "Poverty can be measured by more than income" becomes drastically clear through a series of examples. By focusing on the living conditions of one poor family, the examples make a stronger emotional impact on the reader than impersonal facts and figures would have done.

Exercise Developing a Paragraph with Examples

Each of the following topic sentences can be developed into a paragraph by using examples. Choose two of the sentences. Then support each main idea with three or four specific examples.

1. Many American Presidents have served only one term.
2. Violence has increased both on and off the playing field.
3. You can add just about anything to a basic hot dog.
4. Not everything that glitters is as valuable as gold.
5. Clothing that looks stylish may feel far from comfortable.
6. Some healing drugs come from unlikely sources.
7. Young animals play in ways similar to human children.
8. (Name of town or city) has interesting museums.
9. Life in the wilderness was hard for the pioneers.
10. Some animals make better pets than others.

Part 4 Using an Incident

A topic sentence might lend itself to development with an incident. Following is an example of such a sentence:

Life in this electronic age is tough on kids.

The writer could have supported this topic sentence with several examples of how the electronic age is "tough on kids." Instead, he chose to relate an incident that illustrates the main idea of the paragraph.

> Life in this electronic age is tough on kids. Two sixth-graders felt the call of the fishpole one afternoon and took along their walkie-talkies. Word of this got to the teacher, who borrowed a walkie-talkie from another student. The teacher tuned in and, sure enough, heard the truants. He promptly cut in to suggest that they appear in the classroom post-haste. They did.—JOHN BROWN

An incident, like the one in this paragraph, can be drawn from personal experience or from a writer's imagination. Whatever its source, though, the characteristics and function of an incident remain the same. It is a brief "story" that illustrates the general idea in the topic sentence.

Exercise Developing a Paragraph with an Incident

Each of the following topic sentences may be expanded into a paragraph by using an incident. Choose two of the sentences and develop each into a well written paragraph.

1. A practical joke can backfire.
2. You're never too old to learn to ride a bike.
3. I never believed in ghosts.
4. My dog taught me the meaning of loyalty.
5. One today is worth two tomorrows.
6. Running away never solved a problem.
7. You're never too old to cry.

Part 5 Using a Definition

When developing a paragraph, a composition, or a report, a writer may wish to use a word or phrase in a very specific way or to use a term that may be unfamiliar to the reader. To make certain that the term will not be misunderstood, the writer will provide a definition.

Every good definition has three parts:

1. The term to be defined
2. The general class to which the term belongs
3. The particular characteristic that sets the term apart from the other members of the general class

Study the following examples:

Term To Be Defined	General Class	Particular Characteristic
Hypnotism is	a kind of sleep	induced by motions of the hands or other suggestions.
A tariff is	a tax	placed on certain goods brought into a country.
A pilgrim is	a person	who travels to a sacred place.
A quarterback is	a football player	who directs the team.
Sorrow is	a feeling of grief	that comes from suffering, loss, or regret.
Geography is	a science	dealing with the earth and its life.
A granary is	a building	in which grain is stored.

Avoiding Errors

In defining a term, a writer must be careful not to make the following errors:

1. Defining the word or phrase by using *where* or *when*. For example:

   "Sorrow is when a person feels grief," or "A granary is where grain is stored." *Sorrow* is not a "when"; it is a feeling. A *granary* is not a "where"; it is a building.

2. Defining the term with the same word or a variation of the same word. For example:

   "Hypnotism is the process of hypnotizing."

3. Putting the term into too large a general class. For example:

   "A granary is a place where grain is stored."

Expanding a Definition

A basic definition can be accompanied by an explanation, an illustration, or both. The definition then becomes a paragraph, as in the following examples.

1

Water that is fit to drink is called *potable water*. It must be clear and colorless, pleasant-tasting, free of harmful bacteria, and fairly free of dissolved solids. Although distilled water is pure, it does not make the best drinking water. Small amounts of mineral matter and air in the water make it taste better, unlike distilled water which has a "flat" taste.—TRACY, TROPP, AND FRIEDL

2

Empathy is a feeling of positive regard for others—being able to sense how the other person is feeling and the emotion

taking place. It also takes in the ability to communicate the feeling back to that person in the receiver's own words. It means "the ability to walk in another person's moccasins."
—GWEN MOJADO

3

A pueblo was a type of village built by the Indians of the Southwest. Its buildings were placed in a receding terrace formation and each one housed a number of families. The houses were flat-roofed and built of stone or clay. They were America's first apartment houses. Some of the houses were four stories high, and some had over five hundred rooms. The people reached their homes by climbing up ladders placed on the outside of the larger buildings. When other tribes raided a village, the Pueblo Indians pulled up the ladders and the enemy had a hard time getting in. A room below the ground was special. It was called a kiva and was used for religious ceremonies and social meetings.—ROSEBUD YELLOW ROBE

In these three paragraphs, the basic definitions function as topic sentences. Each sentence contains the three necessary parts of a definition.

Term To Be Defined	General Class	Particular Characteristic
Potable water is	water	that is fit to drink.
Empathy is	a feeling	of positive regard for others.
A pueblo was	a village	built by the Indians of the Southwest.

The other sentences in each paragraph give additional details about the word or phrase being defined. The reader comes away with a clear understanding of what the term means.

Exercises Developing a Paragraph with a Definition

A. Each of the following sentences presents a faulty definition. A part of the definition may be missing. The general class may be too large. The term may have been defined by using *where* or *when*. The word may have been defined with the same word.
Divide a sheet of paper into three columns. Head the columns "Term To Be Defined," "General Class," and "Particular Characteristics." Then write the correct three-part definition for each.

1. A good friend is a special person.
2. Play is activity.
3. A novel is written in prose.
4. Studying is when you read and think.
5. A dog is a kind of animal.
6. A fly has two wings.
7. A bicycle is a machine with two wheels.
8. Quarantine is where you're isolated because you're sick.
9. The sun is something that gives off light and heat.
10. Anthropology is all about people.
11. A lyric is a song.
12. Graduation is the act of being graduated.
13. R.S.V.P. is when you must answer someone's invitation.
14. A hat is a thing people wear on their heads.
15. Passing a course is when you get above a certain grade.

B. Following is a list of words that may be defined in paragraph form. Choose two of the words. Write a topic sentence containing a three-part definition for each word. Then expand the topic sentences into well written paragraphs.

motorcycle	snob	carburetor
sorceress	elevator	friend
honor	energy	leaf
rectangle	conservation	helicopter
minnow	equality	nitrogen
loyalty	fad	love

Chapter 7

Different Kinds of Paragraphs

Before you begin to make a cake, you must decide on the kind of cake you want to produce. Your choice will determine the ingredients you use and the way you blend those ingredients together.

Similarly, when you are going to write a paragraph, you must first decide on your purpose for writing. Do you want to tell a story? Do you want to describe something? Do you want to explain an opinion or an idea? Your answers to these questions will determine the kind of paragraph you will write.

Three major kinds of paragraphs are examined in this chapter: the narrative paragraph, the descriptive paragraph, and the explanatory paragraph. Each has a different purpose and is, therefore, put together in a slightly different way.

Part 1 The Narrative Paragraph

When you tell a friend what happened on the way to school, or about a program you saw on television, or about your friend's experience at camp, you are telling, or narrating, a story. A paragraph that does the same thing is called a narrative paragraph. Narrative paragraphs relate events in the order in which they took place. This type of organization is called time sequence or chronological order.

The First-Person Narrative Paragraph

Your first reaction to an assignment requiring you to write a narrative paragraph might be, "What can I possibly write about?" Think for a minute about all the things that have happened to you—funny things, serious things, exciting things. Then think about the things you imagine happening, either in the future or in a made-up world where anything is possible.

As you do your preliminary thinking, you will most likely discover several possible subjects for your paragraph. All of these subjects relate to your own real and imagined experiences. Each idea could be developed as a first-person narrative. This is the kind of paragraph in which a writer tells a story using first-person pronouns such as I, we, us, me, my, mine, and our.

Studying an Example

One writer chose as a subject her first ride on a motorcycle. Before she began to write, she took a few minutes to plan her paragraph. First she asked herself the following questions: How did I feel about taking the ride? Was I enthusiastic? Was I frightened? Whose motorcycle was it? How did I get the chance for a ride? She wrote down the answers to these questions so that she would remember to include the ideas in the opening of her paragraph.

Next she thought about how she felt when she was actually on the motorcycle. She asked herself these questions: Was it like riding a roller coaster? a fast bicycle? How did I feel at the beginning of the ride? Did my feelings change? How did I behave during the ride? She added these ideas to her list. Then she wrote the following paragraph:

> I was torn between panic and pleasure when Pete offered to drive me to school on his new motorcycle. Suppose I fell off? My hands felt clammy-cold at the thought. Bravely, I managed a weak smile. With fingers shaking, I buckled on the helmet Pete offered and hoisted myself behind him. With a roar like a jet, we took off down the street. Gradually, I relaxed my knuckle-white grip and looked around. It was like skimming over the streets on a sleek, two-wheeled space ship. By the time we reached school, all my fears had been blown away by the force of the wind around us. The motorcycle seemed like an old friend, and I had been the first girl in school to ride on it.

From the first sentence on, the writer involves the reader in her experience. She vividly describes her reactions with phrases such as "torn between panic and pleasure," "hands felt clammy-cold," "with fingers shaking," and "my knuckle-white grip." By doing so, she allows the reader to see life, for a few minutes, through her eyes.

Exercise Writing a First-Person Narrative Paragraph

Following is a list of topic sentences that may be developed into first-person narrative paragraphs. Choose one of these sentences, or write one of your own. Then develop the sentence into a well written paragraph that relates a real or imaginary experience.

1. Something exciting happened when I least expected it.
2. I still blush when I think of my most embarrassing experience.

3. It was the funniest April Fool trick I had ever played.

4. I knew something was going to happen the moment I woke up.

5. It was a baby-sitting job I'll never forget.

6. It was my first speech, and I tried not to show how nervous I felt.

7. I learned to like being the _____ child in the family.

8. Last summer, I did something I've never done before.

9. I was determined to succeed at _____.

10. The day I broke my arm began like any other day.

The Third-Person Narrative Paragraph

In a first-person narrative, the writer has a part in the action. In a third-person narrative, the writer mentally steps back from the action and relates something that happened to someone else. The subject of a third-person narrative can be a real or an imaginary event. As in all narrative paragraphs, the story in a third-person narrative unfolds in chronological order, the order in which it happened.

Following is an example of a third-person narrative paragraph. Notice the use of the third-person pronouns *he, she, his, her,* and *him.*

Grace watched the cobra, waiting for a chance to master the deadly snake. Suddenly the cobra's head hit Grace's hand, but he did not bite. He struck with his mouth closed. As rapidly as an expert boxer drumming on a punching bag, the snake struck three times against Grace's palm, always for some incredible reason with his mouth shut. Then Grace slid her open hand over his head and stroked his hood. The snake hissed again and struggled violently under her touch. Grace continued to caress him. Suddenly the snake went limp and his hood began to close. Grace slipped her other hand under the snake's body and lifted him out of the cage. She held the reptile in her arms as though he were a baby. The cobra raised his head to look Grace in the face; his dancing tongue was less than a foot from her mouth. Grace braced her hand against the curve of his body and talked calmly to him until he folded his hood. He curled up in her arms quietly.—DANIEL MANNIX

The writer of this paragraph uses strong, specific verbs throughout the paragraph; for example: *hit, bite, struck, slid, stroked, hissed, struggled, caress, slipped, lifted, raised, braced, folded,* and *curled.* These action words help the reader to visualize the encounter between Grace and the cobra. The reader "sees" the events as they were seen by the writer.

Exercise Writing a Third-Person Narrative Paragraph

Choose one of the sentences suggested below, or write a topic sentence of your own. Then use your imagination to develop the sentence into a third-person narrative paragraph.

1. When Jack awoke, he found that he had become invisible.
2. Gloria tried to run, but her legs had turned to water.
3. The two boys had been marooned on the island for a month.
4. Jenny was determined to win first prize.
5. Steve was in the bank when the robbers entered.
6. The bicycle lay upside down, its wheels still turning.
7. The search for the lost child continued through the night.
8. When Tom learned that his uncle had left him a million dollars, he began to make plans.
9. Jean had always wanted to be an actress.
10. Darlene's childhood had been filled with hardships.

Part 2 The Descriptive Paragraph

The purpose of a descriptive paragraph is to paint a picture with words. A description appeals to one or more of the five senses—sight, hearing, smell, taste, or touch. Of these senses, sight and hearing are the most highly developed. Therefore, most descriptive paragraphs appeal mainly to either sight or hearing or to a combination of the two.

Choosing Words and Details Carefully

The success of a descriptive paragraph is judged by the clarity of the picture created in the reader's mind. This picture depends on the specific words and details used by the writer.

Suppose, for example, that a writer described a new girl in class as "pretty." The reader would have only a vague idea of what the girl looks like. On the other hand, if the writer used details such as "curly jet-black hair," "creamy skin," and "clear blue eyes with long black lashes," the reader would have a good mental image of the girl.

Specific nouns, strong verbs, adjectives, adverbs, and descriptive phrases all help to create a clear picture in a reader's mind. Without them, descriptive writing is lifeless and ineffective. Read, for example, this sentence: "The bird sang in the tree." The nouns *bird* and *tree* are general. The verb *sang* does not give the reader a clue about how the bird sounded. The sentence lacks adjectives, adverbs, and descriptive phrases.

Compare the sample sentence in the preceding paragraph with this revised version: "The fat old bluejay chattered angrily in the blackened pine tree." In place of the general noun *bird* is the specific noun *bluejay*. The general verb *sang* has been replaced with the specific verb *chattered*. The adjectives *fat*, *old*, *blackened*, and *pine* and the adverb *angrily* have been added to the sentence. The reader can now see and hear the bluejay in the same way that the writer did.

Appealing to the Sense of Sight

Many descriptions appeal to the sense of sight. The details in these paragraphs describe size, shape, color, appearance, position, and movement. Together, they create a visual image in the mind of the reader.

Following is an example of a descriptive paragraph that includes many sight details.

> By the time the boy had got to the house, the walking man was only halfway down the road, a lean man, very straight in the shoulders. Jody could tell he was old only because his heels struck the ground with hard jerks. As he approached nearer, Jody saw that he was dressed in blue jeans and a coat of the same material. He wore clodhopper shoes and an old, flat-brimmed Stetson hat. Over his shoulder he carried a gunny sack, lumpy and full. In a few minutes he had trudged close enough so that his face could be seen. And his face was as dark as dried beef. A mustache, blue-white against the dark skin, hovered over his mouth; and his hair was white, too, where it showed at his neck. The skin of his face had shrunk back against the skull until it defined bone, not flesh, and made the nose and chin seem sharp and fragile. The eyes were large and deep and dark, with eyelids stretched tightly over them. Irises and pupils were one, and very black, but the eyeballs were brown. There were no wrinkles in the face at all.—JOHN STEINBECK

The paragraph is a vivid and interesting word picture of an old man. The writer carefully painted the picture with specific words and details, such as "heels struck the ground with hard jerks," "dressed in blue jeans and in a coat of the same material," "clodhopper shoes and an old, flat-brimmed Stetson hat," "a gunny sack, lumpy and full," "a mustache, blue-white against the dark skin," "shrunk back against the skull," and "sharp and fragile." In addition, he drew the comparison that "his face was as dark as dried beef." Comparisons like this help to create a clear image in the reader's mind.

By changing specific details, a writer can change completely the picture drawn in a paragraph. The following paragraph is basically the same as the first paragraph about a walking man. The details, though, are different.

By the time the boy had got to the house, the walking man was only halfway down the road, a short, fat man, very round-shouldered. Jody could tell he was young only because his heels struck the ground with short, quick jerks. As he approached nearer, Jody saw that he was dressed in white duck pants and a coat of the same material. He wore dusty white shoes and a new black derby hat. In his right hand he clutched a bright red and black carpetbag, plump and full. In a few minutes he had walked close enough so that his face could be seen. And his face was as white as blackboard chalk. A thin mustache, black against the white skin, drooped over his mouth, and his hair was black, too, where it showed at his neck. The skin of his face was puffed out so that it was difficult to define bone, and the nose and chin seemed lost in rolls of flesh. The eyes were small and pale blue, with thin black eyebrows arched above them. There were no wrinkles in the face at all.

Now, rather than seeing a lean, hard old man, the reader sees a short, fat young man.

To better understand the importance of details in descriptions, study the following paragraph. In it, an unskilled writer attempts to describe an old man.

By the time the boy had got to the house, the walking man was only halfway down the road. Jody could tell he was old; and, as he approached nearer, Jody saw that he was dressed in old jeans and a coat. He wore old shoes and an old hat. Over his shoulder he carried a sack. In a few minutes he had walked close enough so that his face could be seen. His face was very dark. He had a white mustache and white hair, dark eyes, and thin nose. There were no wrinkles in the face at all.

The paragraph is dull, uninteresting, and too general to evoke much of a picture in a reader's mind.

Following Spatial Order

The ideas in a descriptive paragraph must be arranged in some kind of logical order. In paragraphs that appeal to the sense of sight, the order usually is spatial order. Things are described in relation to other things in the same area or space.

Some descriptions are organized in loose spatial order. The first paragraph about the old man, for example, presents details in three groups: 1. the details noticed from a distance; 2. the details Jody noticed as the man approached; and 3. the details Jody saw at close range. Within these groups, the details are given in the order that they caught Jody's attention. The writer does not bother to explain that the shoes are on the man's feet or that the hat is on top of his head. The space relationships are clear.

In some descriptions, particularly in descriptions of places, information about space relationships is essential. The following paragraph describes a scene at the edge of a river.

> The river ran smooth and shallow at our feet, and beyond it a wide sandy beach sloped upward gently to the edge of the forest, against which the rocks shone as white as weathered bones. The red soil bank on our side of the river, the silver sheet of water in front of us, the wet browns and greys of the sandbars, the whitewashed ramp of rocks on the opposite shore, the green forest front and the pale purple of the Sierra Madre were like stripes of water colors. Across them strings of mules and donkeys moved with their loads, fording the river with their bellies awash. The drivers followed, their white *calzones* rolled above their thighs and the water up to their waists.—ERNESTO GALARZA

In this paragraph the writer uses specific space, or direction, words to show the relationship of one thing to another. The words and phrases are: "at our feet," "beyond," "upward," "to the edge," "on our side," "in front of," "on the opposite shore," "across," "above," and "up to." These direction words allow the reader to picture the scene.

Appealing to the Sense of Hearing

The second most common kind of description appeals to the sense of hearing. The details in these paragraphs describe sounds rather than sight, as in the following example.

> The sound of a strange song floated in the air and seemed to be coming right out of the trunk of the tree. I stood there, turning my ears around in search of the source. The voice was light and unstrained, like some bird, and with a melancholy, human note. The sounds of the frantic children screaming for me to hurry with the ball faded into the background. My heart drummed fiercely, as I felt the presence of an unknown force.—J. E. FRANKLIN

The writer of this paragraph captures the quality of a sound with words such as "strange," "floated," "light," "unstrained," "melancholy," and "human." He also describes the screaming of the children and the drumming of his own heart, sounds whose sharpness and realism contrast with the strange sound. These details help the reader to share the writer's uneasiness.

Paragraphs that appeal to the sense of hearing are not necessarily organized in spatial order. The details, however, must be arranged in some logical order that is easy to follow.

Combining Sense Details

The word picture created in this paragraph makes you feel that you are actually in the kitchen described by the writer.

> I close my eyes and remember my mother's kitchen. The cocoa steamed fragrantly in the saucepan. Geraniums bloomed on the window sills, and a bouquet of tiny yellow chrysanthemums brightened the center of the table. The curtains, red with a blue and green geometrical pattern, were drawn, and seemed to reflect the cheerfulness throughout the room. The furnace purred like a great sleepy animal; the lights glowed with steady radiance. Outside, alone in the dark, the wind battered against the house.

Most of the details in the paragraph appeal to the sense of sight; for example: "tiny yellow chrysanthemums brightened," "red with a blue and green geometrical pattern," and "lights glowed." Two details appeal to the sense of hearing: "purred like a great sleepy animal" and "battered against the house." One phrase, "cocoa steamed fragrantly," appeals to a third sense, the sense of smell. The writer weaves these details together to recreate a scene from her past.

Exercises Writing Descriptions

A. In each pair of sentences, choose the sentence that creates a more vivid image in your mind. Then write a sentence that gives different details about the same subject.

1. a. The branch clicked against the window with the sound of snapping fingers.
   b. The branch made little noises as it hit the window.

2. a. My mother made a delicious dessert last night.
   b. My mother baked a juicy apple pie last night.

3. a. Tom's sunburn felt as though his back were on fire.
   b. Tom's sunburn was painful.

4. a. Dad gave Mother some beautiful flowers.
   b. Dad gave Mother a dozen long-stemmed red roses for her birthday.

5. a. The steak was as tough as shoe leather.
   b. The steak was not as good as I had expected.

6. a. She had a voice that sounded like chalk squeaking against a blackboard.
   b. She had an unpleasant voice.

7. a. The night wrapped us in black velvet.
   b. The night was extremely dark.

8. a. The sandwich filling tasted like old library paste.
   b. The sandwich filling tasted awful.

B. Following is a list of topic sentences. Choose two—one describing sight, and one describing sound—or write sentences of your own. Then, using either your personal experience or your imagination (or both), develop the two sentences into descriptive paragraphs. In the paragraph that appeals to the sense of sight, arrange the details in spatial order. Be sure to use specific details in both paragraphs.

1. On Sundays, I hear the peal of church bells.
2. My room was on the second story above the garage.
3. After the storm, a rainbow appeared.
4. From the sound of her voice, I knew she was frightened.
5. In the distance, cars rumbled over the bridge.
6. My aunt gave me a lovely Japanese doll for my birthday.
7. My favorite painting is _____.
8. At sunup, construction on the building across the street began again.
9. The sounds of the awakening city intruded on the pre-dawn stillness.
10. The Golden Gate Bridge is beautiful at sunset.
11. Overhead, geese flew south for the winter.
12. The rock group seemed more concerned with quantity of sound than with quality of sound.
13. He was the oldest man I had ever seen.
14. I awoke at midnight to the sound of a fire engine.
15. Nefertiti was a gorgeous Siamese cat.

C. Choose one of the ideas below, or use an idea of your own. Write a good topic sentence. Then develop a one-paragraph description of at least six sentences that appeals to two or more senses.

1. A garden	6. A hospital room
2. The kitchen before dinner	7. Cows grazing in a pasture
3. A laundromat	8. A circus or carnival
4. A barbecue or picnic	9. A gas station
5. Your street at night	10. A busy shopping center

Part 3   The Explanatory Paragraph

The explanatory paragraph is one of the most important kinds of paragraphs that you must learn to write. This is because you will probably do more explanatory writing throughout your life than any other kind. In an explanatory paragraph, you explain, as clearly as possible, *how*, *what*, or *why*.

The "How" Paragraph

Imagine this situation. You are standing on the corner of 5th South and State Street. A stranger asks you for directions to the VA Hospital. You give the person these instructions.

> We're on the corner of 5th South and State Street, about a half-hour walk from the VA Hospital. Fifth South isn't a through street, so to get to the hospital the easiest way, you'll first have to go south one block to 6th South. At 6th South, turn to your left and go east. Go straight east until you reach 13th East, then turn north. Go north on 13th East for one block until you reach Foothill Drive. Turn right, or east, on Foothill Drive and continue going east for about a mile. You'll see the hospital on the south side of the street.

These directions, written as they are in paragraph form, are an example of an explanatory paragraph. In this kind of paragraph, a writer explains, in chronological order, how something is done. He or she tells what to do first, what to do next, and so on.

After reading an explanatory paragraph, the reader should be able to do or make something. Consider, for example, the following situation. You have been invited to a Chinese banquet, where you will be expected to eat with chopsticks. A friend who is experienced in using chopsticks gives you these written directions.

Eating with chopsticks adds an extra something to any Chinese meal. Learning to use chopsticks properly is not hard; after all, even a Chinese toddler can do it. First, hold the sticks in your right hand, one on top of the other. Grip them about a third of the way from the ends. Next, place the lower stick at the base of your thumb. Rest it also on the tip of your fourth (or ring) finger. Then, place the second stick between the tip of your thumb and the tips of your index and middle finger. Hold the lower stick steady, but move the upper stick so that together they act like "tongs." Remember to keep your hand relaxed and to hold the chopsticks lightly but firmly.

These instructions are detailed and well organized. They tell you exactly what to do and how to do it. After practice, you will be able to eat with chopsticks at the banquet.

Exercise Writing a "How" Paragraph

Following is a list of topic sentences, each of which may be developed into a "how" paragraph. Choose one of the sentences, or write one of your own about something that you do well. Then expand your topic sentence into a well written paragraph.

1. One of the first things you have to learn in archery is how to string the bow.
2. Do you know how to get a cranky two-year-old to take a nap?
3. Changing a bike tire is easy.
4. Finger painting can be taught to a three-year-old.
5. You, too, can make ice cream the old-fashioned way—in a crank freezer.
6. Housebreaking a puppy requires a week of hard work.
7. To pass a test, you first have to learn how to study.
8. Water conservation begins at home.
9. Hiking is fun—if you know how to do it right.

10. Do you know the easiest way to learn to play the guitar?
11. Taking good photographs is fun.
12. You can teach your parakeet to talk.
13. Part of the fun of swimming is learning how to dive.
14. Learning to dance the _____ is a real challenge.
15. Tying a shoelace is as easy as one, two, three.

The "What" Paragraph

A "what" paragraph explains what something is and what it does. In other words, it defines a word or phrase.

In Chapter 6, Part 5, you studied paragraphs developed by expanding a definition. You learned that the topic sentence of this kind of paragraph contains three parts: the term to be defined, the general class to which the term belongs, and the particular characteristic that sets the term apart from the other members of the general class. Together these three parts form the basic definition of the term. Study the following examples.

Term To Be Defined	General Class	Particular Characteristic
A zebra is	an animal like a horse	with wide black-and-white stripes.
A snorkel is	a breathing tube	that can be used only on the surface of the water.
A hurricane is	a strong, swirling storm	that usually measures several hundred miles in diameter.

In Chapter 6 you also learned that the remainder of this kind of paragraph is made up of supporting details. The details further explain the basic definition, as in the example on the next page.

A hurricane is a strong, swirling storm that usually measures several hundred miles in diameter. The eye of the hurricane, often measuring 20 miles wide, is usually calm and has no clouds. Around the eye, winds blow at 75 miles an hour or more. Death and destruction, unfortunately, are too often part of the hurricane's story.

This paragraph, developed by definition, is a "what" paragraph. It explains what a hurricane is and what it does.

Exercise Writing a "What" Paragraph

Choose one of the following topics. Write a topic sentence that gives a three-part definition of the term. Then expand the topic sentence into a well written "what" paragraph.

1. hang-glider	6. celebrity	11. hockey
2. gossip	7. hamburger	12. civil war
3. rose	8. popularity	13. loneliness
4. tadpole	9. battery	14. lizard
5. courage	10. giraffe	15. circle

The "Why" Paragraph

The "why" paragraph gives reasons to explain the idea in the topic sentence. Some "why" paragraphs open with statements of fact; for example:

Beavers do a lot of good when they build their dams in the right places.

This sentence raises the questions: What good do beavers do? Why can the writer make this statement? The rest of the paragraph answers these questions.

Beavers do a lot of good when they build their dams in the right places. Beaver dams slow down the rush of water in brooks and streams. Brooks that otherwise would dry up in the summer flow all year 'round if a beaver dam is built across them. The trees and bushes near the brooks have enough moisture to grow well. Their roots hold the soil so that it does not wash away. Also, wells that usually go dry in summer hold water all year when beavers are put to work on nearby streams.

The writer gives three reasons to support his topic sentence.

1. Beaver dams slow down the flow of water so that brooks do not go dry in the summer.
2. Trees and bushes near beaver dams grow well; they prevent soil from being washed away.
3. Wells near beaver dams do not go dry in the summer.

These three reasons develop the idea that beavers do a lot of good. The reasons are specific facts that explain the more general fact stated in the topic sentence.

A second kind of "why" paragraph begins with a statement about something that happened; for example:

I didn't do my homework last night.

The reader most likely would respond to this sentence by asking, "Why didn't you do your homework?" The rest of the paragraph answers that question.

I didn't do my homework last night. Right after school, I had softball practice, and we practiced for about two hours. Just before we finished the last inning, I was playing catcher. John threw a fast ball. I tried to jump aside, but the ball hit me in the stomach and knocked all the wind out of me. When I got home, I was so tired and so sick to my stomach, I just didn't feel like doing homework.

The writer of this paragraph relates an incident that explains why she didn't do her homework. She presents one detailed reason to explain her opening statement. Another writer might have developed the same idea by giving several individual reasons. Either approach works, as long as the body of the paragraph explains why the event described in the topic sentence happened.

A third type of "why" paragraph opens with an opinion, an idea that the writer believes to be true. Following is an example of this type of topic sentence.

The frontier woman was, indeed, a special breed.

The writer develops this idea with strong supporting reasons.

The frontier woman was, indeed, a special breed. She proved her ability to uphold her end of the load even where physical endurance was required. She bore the children, cared for them when they were sick, and often taught them to read and write. She tended the garden, cooked the family's food, and preserved what she could for the winter. And when danger from wild beasts threatened, she proved herself capable of defending her family.—JANET HARRIS

In this paragraph, the writer explains why she thinks the frontier woman was a special breed. She presents these reasons:

1. The frontier woman held up her end of the load.
2. She bore and cared for the children.
3. She often taught the children to read and write.
4. She grew, cooked, and preserved the food.
5. She defended her family from wild beasts.

These facts support the opinion in the topic sentence.

Exercise Writing a "Why" Paragraph

Following is a list of topic sentences that can be expanded into "why" paragraphs. Choose one of these sentences or write one of your own. Then develop the sentence with reasons.

1. Physical training is more important than mental training.
2. All students should learn cooking in school.
3. Young people should be given a regular allowance.
4. Our country has a great need for more vocational schools.
5. Baby-sitting is a job that requires training.
6. The cost of electrical energy in our country is growing.

Checklist for Writing Paragraphs

This Checklist will help to remind you of the qualities necessary for good paragraphs. You should also follow the steps in the Guidelines for the Process of Writing on page 57.

1. Is the paragraph a group of sentences that work together to explain or support one main idea?

2. Does the paragraph have unity? Does each sentence relate to one main idea?

3. Does the paragraph have a topic sentence that states one main idea? Does the topic sentence capture the reader's interest?

4. If the paragraph is developed by using specific details, do the details work together to create a clear impression for the reader?

5. If the paragraph is developed by facts or figures, do they fully develop the main idea?

6. If the paragraph is developed by examples, are there enough examples to develop the paragraph fully? Do they all relate to the main idea?

7. If the paragraph is developed by using an incident, is the incident drawn from first-hand experience? the writer's imagination?

8. If it is a paragraph of definition, are the three basic parts of a definition expanded by explanation or illustration?

9. If it is a narrative paragraph, is it developed in chronological order?

10. If it is a descriptive paragraph, does it use vivid sensory details? Does it describe in a logical order? Does it use space words and phrases?

11. If it is an explanatory "how" paragraph, does it give instructions in logical order? If it is a "what" paragraph, does it use supporting details to expand the basic three-part definition? If it is a "why" paragraph, does it give reasons to explain the main idea?

Chapter 8

Writing Compositions and Reports

In the preceding three chapters, you have spent time mastering paragraphs. You have studied the structure of the paragraph. You have learned to develop paragraphs in a variety of ways. In this chapter, you will learn to express ideas in a form of writing that is based on the paragraph. You will study and write compositions, groups of paragraphs that communicate a writer's own feelings and ideas. You will also study and write reports, which present information learned by the writer from outside sources.

Part 1 Parts of the Composition

A composition is a group of closely related paragraphs that develop a single idea. Usually, a composition begins with an introduction that tells the reader what the composition will be about. This opening paragraph introduces the main idea of the composition, just as the topic sentence of a paragraph introduces its main idea.

The middle, or body, of a composition develops the idea introduced in the first paragraph. For example, if a student wrote a composition about what animals do in the winter, he or she might include a paragraph on animals that hibernate, another on birds that migrate south, and a third paragraph on animals that must struggle to stay alive during cold weather. Together, these paragraphs would develop the main idea of the composition.

The final paragraph, or conclusion, of a composition signals "the end" to the reader. It might do this by restating the main idea of the composition, by summarizing the supporting ideas, or by presenting one last thought on the subject.

Following is an example of a five-paragraph composition with a well developed introduction, body, and conclusion.

THE PERFECT DAY

Introduction   July 27th was no ordinary summer Saturday. After a week of cloudy, rainy weather, the day was absolutely perfect. I didn't even mind cleaning my room that morning because it gave me a chance to plan my afternoon. After considering options such as swimming, bike riding, and baseball, I decided that the day was made for tennis. I called my friend Ron to set up a match.

Body   Ron agreed to play, but explained that he had to deliver some cookies to his uncle first. He suggested that I come with him so we could play at a nearby park afterwards. We were halfway there when Ron told me that we were on our way to a nursing home. With visions of gloomy sick people clouding my perfect day, I was ready to head for home. Inside a nursing home was the last place I wanted to spend such a glorious day.

I was still protesting when Ron steered me up the steps, through a hallway, and into an old-fashioned living room. Ron's uncle was sitting in a wheelchair by the window. A half dozen other patients sat around the room. It smelled like cough medicine, and the sight of wheelchairs made me uncomfortable. I could feel my precious day slipping away. As I edged toward the door, I tripped over someone's feet. A quiet old man mumbled apologies. I noticed then an unusual set of wooden chess figures on the table beside the man. He invited me to examine a piece. He explained that he had carved the complete set by hand and that he had never played with it because he had no visitors and no one at the home played chess.

I couldn't believe it when I heard myself offering to play chess with him. I could see that Ron was still talking to his uncle, so I planned to play a quick game before setting off for the tennis court. Three hours later I was still playing chess! Mr. Watson was the best player I had ever seen. He beat me seven straight times. Then we took a break, and he showed me how to begin carving. I became disgusted when I found I was no better at carving than at chess. Mr. Watson explained that both take patience and practice. We laughed when he reminded me that he had several years' head start.

Conclusion   It was almost supper time when Ron and I finally left. Ron was shocked that we had stayed so long. He apologized for causing me to miss my afternoon of tennis and offered to play next Saturday. I suggested that, since we couldn't really depend on the weather to be fine enough for tennis, we should plan to visit his uncle again. After all, the weather is always perfect for chess!

The first paragraph of this composition introduces the topic "no ordinary summer Saturday." The three body paragraphs develop this idea. The second paragraph discusses Ron's errand and the writer's reaction to it. The third paragraph relates what happened inside the nursing home and the writer's encounter with the old man. The fourth paragraph describes the experience of playing chess and of taking time out to try carving. The conclusion of the composition shows the result of that one summer afternoon. It suggests that the writer discovered a new enthusiasm and a new friend.

Part 2 Finding a Subject

When you talk with your friends, you probably have no problems deciding what to say. Words almost trip over one another in your haste to communicate your ideas. However, when you are faced with a blank sheet of paper and told to write a composition, you may feel that you have absolutely nothing to say.

When you are in this situation, try using yourself as a subject. Imagine that your best friend, who has been away for several months, asks you what has been happening lately. What would you tell him or her? Maybe you would describe the spaghetti dinner that your class sponsored or a trip you have taken. Perhaps you would share a funny or frightening experience.

These kinds of subjects come from personal experience. They are developed with ideas drawn from your own memory.

Not everything you write about will reflect your own experiences, however. For example, let's say you choose to report on Navajo sand painting, the European Common Market, or termites. These subjects do not involve you personally. They must be developed with information from outside sources, such as books, magazines, and newspapers. The information you gather from these sources becomes part of your memory. These ideas are different from those related to personal experiences, yet they can be just as familiar. In other words, no matter what subject you select, you will eventually be writing about something you know well.

Exercise Listing Possible Subjects

Study the following list of subjects. Choose five that you think might be interesting subjects for a composition or a report and write them on a sheet of paper. Then add five subjects of your own. Review your entire list of ten subjects. Write *P* after the subjects that are based on personal experience, and *S* after those that will need to be developed with information from outside sources. *Keep your list for future reference.*

1. A Perfect Party
2. How Bats Use Radar
3. How To Budget Your Allowance—Sort of
4. Jonas Salk's Discovery of the Polio Vaccine
5. My Pet Peeves
6. When My Mother/Father Went to School
7. The Night I Told My Little Brother/Sister a Ghost Story
8. How My Dog Trained Me
9. The Planet Saturn
10. The Social Life of a Beehive
11. My Collection of _____
12. My Least Favorite Chore and Ways To Avoid It
13. The Legend of St. Valentine
14. Teen-Age Blues
15. How To Sail a Boat
16. Sunrise/Sunset
17. Smart Answers Are Not Always "Smart"
18. Scouting
19. Conquering Mt. Everest
20. Don't Be Afraid of Your Feelings

Part 3 Planning the Composition or Report

A composition begins with a general idea of a subject. Inexperienced writers often treat this general idea as a well defined idea, without giving it further thought. They begin to write immediately. Then, after a few sentences, they find that they have nothing more to say. The problem is that they did not first work out a plan for writing.

Planning takes time, but the time spent is worthwhile. The end product is a clear, well organized composition or report that communicates ideas effectively from writer to reader.

Narrowing the Subject

The first thing you must do in planning a composition or report is to decide on a general subject. Then you must decide how far to narrow the subject so that it can be developed in five paragraphs.

Study the following subjects:

1. The Ape That "Talks" with People
2. The Geography of Latin America

The first subject—The Ape That "Talks" with People—focuses on one particular ape. A writer could easily develop this idea in a short composition. Therefore, the subject is acceptable as is and does not have to be narrowed.

The second subject, however, would most likely present problems. Latin America, which includes all the countries from Mexico to the tip of South America, is a huge area with many different kinds of geography. The writer could give only the briefest and most general information within the limits of a few paragraphs. The reader would end up knowing very little about the subject.

The subject "The Geography of Latin America" must be narrowed. The easiest way to do this is to choose one area or one country in Latin America; for example, Mexico. A writer would be able to develop the new topic, "The Geography of Mexico," with enough specific information to make the report interesting and meaningful to the reader.

Exercise Choosing and Narrowing Your Subject

From the list of subjects you made in the preceding exercise, choose the one subject you would like to write about. Study it carefully. Decide if it is narrow enough to be covered in five paragraphs. If it is too general, narrow it so that it is a workable topic. You may wish to check your final topic with your teacher.

Putting Down Ideas

You have decided on a general subject, then narrowed it to the point where it can be easily covered in a few paragraphs. The next step is to write down the ideas you want to include.

If your subject is a personal experience, the ideas will come to you as you think about the subject. Simply jot down the ideas on 3″ × 5″ note cards, putting only one idea on each card. The important thing is to get all your ideas on paper.

Your subject might be the kind that needs to be developed with information from sources outside yourself. Now is the time to gather the necessary information. Many writers first make a list of questions about their subjects. They use these questions as a general guide to their reading.

The writer who decided on the topic "The Geography of Mexico" listed these five questions.

1. Does Mexico have seasons like the United States?
2. Does Mexico's climate differ among its many regions?
3. What is the overall shape of the country?
4. Does the country have mountains?
5. Does Mexico have any unusual features?

She then wrote down what she already knew about the geography of Mexico. She recorded the ideas on $3'' \times 5''$ note cards, writing one idea on each card.

Next, she searched the card catalog and the *Abridged Readers' Guide to Periodical Literature* for the titles of books and articles on Mexico and Mexican geography. She also looked over the reference shelves for books that might contain useful information. She read about her subject in several sources. As she read, she wrote facts on note cards. Again, she put only one fact on each card. She was careful to record each fact accurately and completely and to write it in her own words.

The writer also noted on each card the source of the fact written on that card. She followed these guidelines.

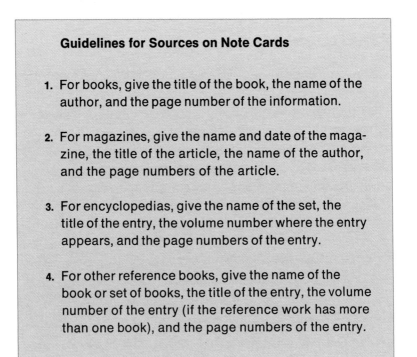

Guidelines for Sources on Note Cards

1. For books, give the title of the book, the name of the author, and the page number of the information.

2. For magazines, give the name and date of the magazine, the title of the article, the name of the author, and the page numbers of the article.

3. For encyclopedias, give the name of the set, the title of the entry, the volume number where the entry appears, and the page numbers of the entry.

4. For other reference books, give the name of the book or set of books, the title of the entry, the volume number of the entry (if the reference work has more than one book), and the page numbers of the entry.

To review the skills for finding information in books, magazines, and reference works, turn to Chapter 12.

Exercise Taking Notes

Write the ideas you want to include in your composition or report on 3″×5″ cards (or on pieces of paper cut into 3″×5″ rectangles). If you take ideas from books, magazines, or reference works, be sure to note the source of the idea. Follow the guidelines given in this lesson.

Grouping Ideas

Once you have written down your ideas, your next step is to group them together. Put into one group the ideas that are closely related to one part of your topic. Put into a second group the ideas that have to do with another part, and so on. You may find that some of your ideas do not relate to any part of your topic. These ideas should be set aside.

As an example, let's continue with the topic "The Geography of Mexico." On the writer's cards were these ideas:

Mexico is a long triangle pointing to South America.
Cold mountain roads
Warm, humid valleys with groves of bananas, guavas,
    mangoes, mameys, and sapotes
The mountains are breathtakingly steep and high.
Mexico is wide at the top and narrow at the bottom.
Paricutin, a new volcano
The people of Mexico love to sing and dance.
Strange plants and fruits on the lowlands; hedges of cactus
Some peaks are wild and rugged.
Wet season in summer; dry season in winter
In the dry months, no rain falls.
In the wet months, the rain is so heavy that it carries the soil
    from the mountains.
The first Europeans in Mexico were the Spaniards.
One village now lies at the bottom of a lake.
Some mountains are planted in orderly plots.
Mexico is a land of beauty, violence, and the unexpected.

As the writer studied these ideas, she began to see a pattern. Most of the ideas fell into four main groups: shape, climate, mountains and lowlands, and the unexpected. She listed the ideas in these four groups, as shown here.

Shape
1. Mexico is a long triangle pointing to South America.
2. Mexico is wide at the top and narrow at the bottom.

Climate
1. Cold mountain roads
2. Warm, humid valleys with groves of bananas, guavas, mangoes, mameys, and sapotes
3. Wet season in summer; dry season in winter
4. In the dry months, no rain falls.
5. In the wet months, the rain is so heavy that it carries the soil from the mountains.

Mountains and Lowlands
1. The mountains are breathtakingly steep and high.
2. Some peaks are wild and rugged.
3. Some mountains are planted in orderly plots.
4. Strange plants and fruits on the lowlands; hedges of cactus

The Unexpected
1. Mexico is a land of beauty, violence, and the unexpected.
2. Paricutin, a new volcano
3. One village now lies at the bottom of a lake.

The writer discovered that two of her original ideas did not have anything to do with the geography of Mexico and, therefore, did not belong in the report. She set aside the cards on which these two ideas were written:

The people of Mexico love to sing and dance.
The first Europeans in Mexico were the Spaniards.

Exercise Grouping Your Ideas

Put your own ideas into three or four related groups. Set aside any cards with ideas that do not develop your topic directly.

Organizing Ideas

The final step in planning is to organize your ideas into some kind of logical order. For compositions about personal experiences, the most common order is chronological. The events are recounted in the order in which they happened. Compositions that describe places often are organized in spatial order. The writer moves smoothly from one part of the scene to another.

Reports are frequently organized in order of importance. Usually, the least important ideas are presented first; the most important ideas are given last. The report thus builds to a climax and holds the attention of the reader right to the end.

The writer of the report "The Geography of Mexico" arranged her ideas in order of importance. She began with general information about the shape of the country and ended with the idea that Mexico is a land of the unexpected. Notice that she presents her idea groups in outline form.

THE GEOGRAPHY OF MEXICO

I. Shape
   A. Mexico is a long triangle pointing to South America.
   B. Mexico is wide at the top and narrow at the bottom.

II. Mountains and lowlands
   A. The mountains are breathtakingly steep and high.
   B. Some peaks are wild and rugged.
   C. Some mountains are planted in orderly plots.
   D. Strange plants and fruits grow on the lowlands.
   E. Hedges of round cactus appear on the lowlands.

III. Climate
   A. Cold mountain roads rise above warm, humid valleys.
   B. Groves of bananas, guavas, mangoes, mameys, and sapotes grow in the valleys.
   C. Summer is the wet season; winter is the dry season.
   D. In the dry months, no rain falls.
   E. In the wet months, the rain is so heavy that it carries the soil from the mountains.

IV. The unexpected
   A. Mexico is a land of beauty and violence.
   B. Paricutin is a new volcano.
   C. One village now lies at the bottom of a lake.

The writer will build on this outline when writing the five paragraphs of her report.

Exercises Organizing Ideas

A. Following are four groups of ideas. Rearrange each into logical order. Be ready to explain which order you followed—chronological, spatial, or order of importance.

1 The Value of a Good Novel
1. It sharpens understanding of human character.
2. It provides relaxation and entertainment.
3. It introduces readers to different kinds of societies.
4. It can lead to changes in law, education, politics, and social attitudes.
5. It is an aid to the study of history and geography.

2 Cleaning the Basement
1. I piled the giveaways into clean boxes and labeled the boxes.
2. I carried home boxes from the grocery store.
3. I swept and washed the basement floor.
4. I sorted the various stacks of junk into three piles: throwaways, giveaways, and things to keep.
5. I admired the completed job.
6. I stuffed the throwaways into large garbage bags and hauled the bags to the alley.
7. I neatly stacked the things to keep on shelves.

3 Our Rooftop Deck
1. Rows of tomatoes, beans, peppers, onions, and carrots grew in long planters set into the deck.

2. Scattered among the tables and chairs were trees and flowering bushes planted in large wooden pots.
3. Colorful flowers surrounded the bases of some of the trees.
4. At the other end of the deck, away from the tables and chairs, was the vegetable garden.
5. At one end of the deck were tables and chairs.
6. Redwood covered the entire rooftop.

4   How To Make Yourself Popular

1. Don't take offense easily.
2. Avoid arguing over differences.
3. Don't attack the beliefs and opinions of others.
4. Don't expose the weaknesses of others needlessly.
5. Follow the golden rule.
6. Don't betray secrets.

B.   Organize your own list of ideas into a logical order. Then make an outline, which you can use when writing your composition or report.

Part 4   Writing the Composition or Report

The plan for your composition is now finished. You have chosen your topic, gathered and recorded your information, grouped your ideas, and arranged the groups of ideas in logical order in an outline. You are now ready to begin writing the first draft of your composition or report.

At the beginning of this chapter, you learned that a good composition has an introduction, a body, and a conclusion. The first step in writing your composition is to write the introduction, or opening paragraph.

Writing the Introduction

As you learned earlier, the introduction of a composition or report is the paragraph that tells what the composition is going to be about. The introduction must do more than that, however. It must also catch the reader's attention so that he or she will want to finish reading what you have written.

When writing your introduction, you will certainly want to avoid such dull, uninteresting paragraphs as these:

> When my father was in the Army, we lived in Germany. Germany is a pretty neat place to live. In my composition, I will try to tell you what it's like to live in Germany, and why I think it's so neat.

> I'd like to tell you about the geography of Mexico. Mexico is a very interesting country. Its geography is very interesting, too, because it's so different.

Both of these introductions tell the reader what the compositions are going to be about, but both of them are so boring that no one would want to read further. Compare these two paragraphs with the following example:

> Mexico is a long triangle, pointing to South America. In the North it is a wide land, with many miles of cactus country between the Gulf of Mexico and the Pacific Ocean. In the South the country narrows as it meets the Central American states.

This paragraph covers the ideas listed under point I. of the outline for "The Geography of Mexico." It introduces the reader to the topic of the report with facts about the overall shape of the land. The writer of this paragraph treats factual material with a fresh approach. For example, instead of merely stating that Mexico is wide at the top, she notes the "many miles of cactus country between the Gulf of Mexico and the Pacific Ocean." With details such as these, she captures the reader's interest in the geography of Mexico.

Exercises Working with Introductory Paragraphs

A. Following are five paragraphs. Read them carefully. Decide which are good introductory paragraphs because they are interesting and tell what the composition is going to be about. Be prepared to explain why you think the others are not good.

1

The first English settlers arrived in India about the same time that the English arrived at Plymouth Rock and at Jamestown, in what is now the United States. Those long-ago settlements were very interesting.

2

There's something about Halloween night that always frightens me, even though I'm too old to believe in ghosts and goblins. The black always seems blacker and the shadows more eerie. Even the familiar howl of a neighbor's cat sounds different, somehow.

3

I think that the government ought to make every citizen vote. If I were President, I would introduce a law stating that every citizen had to cast a ballot in every election. Voting is important, so everyone should vote.

4

Many of us open our ears to compliments, yet close them to criticisms. Yet, criticism can teach us more than the most well meant compliment. It is from criticism that we learn our mistakes and how to do better next time.

5

There are many different kinds of pollution. Among them are noise pollution, water pollution, and air pollution. Pollution is a problem that we should all try to solve.

B. Write the introductory paragraph to your composition or report. Cover point I of your outline, or write a short paragraph that leads into the idea in the outline.

Writing the Body

The body is the most important part of a composition or report. It is in these paragraphs that the main idea presented in the introduction is supported or explained. The specific ideas in the body may take the form of descriptive details, events, facts and figures, examples, incidents or definitions, whatever information helps to develop the topic.

To better understand the role of the body paragraphs, let's return to the sample report on "The Geography of Mexico." The introduction to that report is as follows:

> Mexico is a long triangle, pointing to South America. In the North it is a wide land, with many miles of cactus country between the Gulf of Mexico and the Pacific Ocean. In the South the country narrows as it meets the Central American states.

This paragraph tells the reader that the report is about Mexico —not its people or its customs, but its geography. The paragraph describes the shape of the country, which is the first main topic of the outline for this report. The body paragraphs will cover the ideas listed under the next three main topics:

II. Mountains and lowlands
III. Climate
IV. The unexpected

The writer has changed the working title "The Geography of Mexico" to a catchier one, "Mexico: A Land of Contrasts."

MEXICO: A LAND OF CONTRASTS

Mexico is a long triangle, pointing to South America. In the North it is a wide land, with many miles of cactus country between the Gulf of Mexico and the Pacific Ocean. In the South the country narrows as it meets the Central American States.

Mexico is a country of ups and downs. The mountains are

breathtakingly steep and high. Some of the great peaks are wild and rugged, while others are planted in orderly plots so far up that they look like patchwork patterns against the sky. Along the lowlands, the earth grows strange plants and fruits. The cactus appears as round as a barrel, in great, fierce hedges.

The climate is up and down, too. From a cold mountain road, where pines recall Canadian forests, one may look down on warm, humid groves of bananas, guavas, mangoes, and soft mameys and sapotes, sweet and sticky. Mexico has a wet season in summer and a dry season in winter. In the dry months no rain falls, and the steep slopes become brown and gray. When the rains come, water pounds the roofs of mud huts like drumbeats and washes down the mountainsides through deep ravines in a rushing roar. The high slopes grow green, and flowers spring out all over them. The rains carry away soil from the mountains, however, and run so fast through the ravines that they do the lower slopes little good.

Mexico is a land of beauty and violence. It is a land of flowers and color, of song and brilliant birds. Snow-topped volcanoes glitter against a sky of vivid blue. Mexico is serene and beautiful, but it can also be unexpectedly violent. Only a few years ago a volcano, called Paricutin, thrust up abruptly through a farmer's field. It quickly buried a village under lava and ashes. A lake once covered a town, and the church spire may be seen by looking straight down into the water from a boat. Mexico is a land where anything can happen.

This example illustrates two important points concerning the body of a composition or report.

1. **A composition or report is always divided into paragraphs.** These divisions relieve the monotony of the page and make the composition easier to read.

Each paragraph in a composition or report deals with a new idea. The indentation at the beginning of a paragraph, therefore, signals that the composition is moving from one idea to another. The indentation acts like a rest stop on a road.

2. **Each paragraph in a composition or report begins with a topic sentence.** The topic sentence tells what the para-

graph is about. The supporting details in the paragraph relate to the topic sentence. Each paragraph in turn relates to the introductory paragraph. Thus, the composition has *unity*.

Exercise Writing Your Body Paragraphs

Write the three body paragraphs of your composition, following your outline. Begin each paragraph with a topic sentence.

Writing the Conclusion

You have almost finished the first draft of your composition or report. One step remains—writing the conclusion.

The conclusion presents the last idea the reader will take away from your composition or report. Therefore, it should be as clear and interesting as the introductory paragraph. The final paragraph should tie everything together in a way that clearly indicates "The End" to a reader.

A conclusion can be a sentence that makes a final comment:

I vowed never again to go near a cemetery at night.

A conclusion can also be a paragraph that summarizes the ideas in the composition or report, as in this example:

Mexico is truly a land of contrasts. It is a land of mountains and valleys, of hot and cold, of droughts and drenching rains. It is a land of bright green mountains and gray-brown deserts. Above all else, Mexico is a land where one learns to expect the unexpected. —MAY McNEER

Exercise Finishing Your Composition

Write the conclusion of your composition or report. Then reread, revise, and proofread the paragraphs, using the guidelines on page 123. Make a final neat copy.

If you have used information from books or magazines, list your sources at the end of your report.

Checklist for Writing Compositions and Reports

As you write a composition, follow the steps in the Guide-lines for the Process of Writing on page 57. Use this Checklist after you have written your composition.

1. Has the subject been narrowed to a topic that can be covered in a few paragraphs?

2. Does the composition deal with a single topic or idea?

3. Does it have an introduction, a body, and a conclusion?

4. Does the introduction present the main idea? Does it catch the reader's interest?

5. Does the body explain or support the main idea?

6. Does the conclusion restate the main idea, summarize the information, or comment upon it?

7. Do the paragraphs work together to develop the single topic or idea that is the subject of the composition?

8. Is the composition appropriate for the audience for which it is intended? Is the purpose clear?

9. Are the ideas presented in a clear, logical order?

10. Does the composition have unity? Are the supporting ideas in each paragraph related to the topic sentence? Is each paragraph directly related to the main idea in the introductory paragraph?

11. Are there transitional devices that tie the paragraphs together?

12. Is the title meaningful and interesting?

Chapter 9

Kinds of Compositions

Before writing a composition, you must make two important decisions. First, you must decide on a subject. Second, you must decide how to treat the subject. Suppose, for example, that you know a great deal about gerbils. You select this subject for a composition. Then you ask yourself: Do I want to tell a story about an experience I had with my gerbils? Do I want to describe the way they look and act? Do I want to explain how to care for gerbils?

If you decide to tell a story about the time your gerbils were lost in the classroom, you will write a narrative composition. If you want your reader to "see" your pet gerbils, you will write a descriptive composition. If you want to give instructions about how to care for gerbils, you will write an explanatory composition. These three kinds of compositions—narrative, descriptive, and explanatory—are examined in detail in this chapter.

Writing any kind of composition requires that you follow the steps described in the preceding chapter. These are the steps:

Steps for Writing a Composition

1. Choose a subject that is already familiar or one that will become familiar through reading and study.

2. Narrow the subject so that it can be developed easily in a five-paragraph composition.

3. List the ideas you want to cover on 3″×5″ note cards.

4. Group your cards according to related ideas.

5. List your ideas in groups.

6. Arrange your idea groups in logical order.

7. Make an outline.

8. Write an introduction that tells what the composition is going to be about; make sure that it is interesting enough to catch the reader's attention.

9. Write the body of the composition, making sure that each paragraph has a topic sentence and relates to the introduction.

10. Write the conclusion of the composition.

11. Revise and proofread the composition.

12. Make a final copy.

13. If necessary, give credit to outside sources.

Part 1 The Narrative Composition

Narrative compositions tell stories. These stories differ widely in their content, yet they have several things in common. First of all, they relate events in chronological order; that is, the time sequence in which the events took place. Each story has a beginning, a middle, and an end. As a rule, the beginning leads up to the main events in the story, the middle describes the events, and the end tells what happened as a result of the events.

The purpose of a narrative composition is to interest and entertain the reader. Specific details are essential, for they help the reader to become involved in the action of the story.

Narrative compositions fall into two basic categories. They are first-person narratives in which the writers relate events that happen to them or that they imagine happening to them. Or they are third-person narratives in which the writers recount events that happened or might have happened to others. In the following sections are examples of a first-person and a third-person narrative.

First-Person Narrative

I WASHED THE DISHES

When my brother enlisted in the Navy, I inherited his record player, his lower bunk on the bed we shared—and his job of doing the dishes. Now, I don't mind taking out the trash or raking leaves, but I hate doing dishes. A gloomy future of dishpan hands stretched before me unless I could convince Mom that I was the wrong person for the job.

The day after Will left for boot camp, Mom handed me a bottle of detergent. She pointed to the dirty dishes waiting on the side of the sink and ordered me to get busy.

I moaned and complained and offered to mow the lawn or to shovel the walks instead. (I was pretty safe in doing this because there was snow on the ground and the walks had already been shoveled.) Next I tried appealing to Mom's reason. I pointed out that school work is far more important than dishes and that, unless I got busy *immediately*, I couldn't possibly finish my homework before midnight. Mom's resolve didn't waver. She explained coolly that washing the dishes would take only a few minutes.

I realized that I was getting nowhere fast, so I decided to try a new angle. I filled the sink with cold water, squirted in a splash of detergent, and began to wash dishes. I put all the plates, glasses, silverware, and utensils into the sink at the same time. I didn't bother to scrape the plates beforehand, and bones, scraps of meat and vegetables, and soggy bread crusts floated to the top of the water like survivors of a miniature shipwreck. I rescued a few plates from the murky water and set them on the drainboard. Small flecks of food still clung to them. Then I took a misfit glass that wasn't too important, and dropped it on the floor. It broke with a crash that brought Mom directly to the kitchen. Right away she noticed the dishes on the drainboard and the mess in the sink. From the look on her face, I could tell my scheme was working.

With a pained smile, Mom urged me to run along and do my homework. As I left the room, I commented innocently, "Why thanks, Mom. I'm glad you'd rather have a scholarly son than a dumb one with dishpan hands."—ALLAN SMART

The first paragraph of the composition introduces the problem: how to avoid doing the dishes. In the body paragraphs, the writer relates, in chronological order, the steps he took to accomplish his goal. He first describes his unsuccessful attempts:

1. He offered to do other chores.
2. He tried to use homework as an excuse.

Then he tells how he carried out his successful plan.

1. He filled the sink with cold water and added detergent.
2. He put all the plates, glasses, silverware, and utensils in the sink together.

3. He didn't bother to scrape the dishes.
4. He stacked plates that were still dirty on the drainboard.
5. He dropped a glass on the floor.

As a conclusion, the writer tells us the "clever" remark he made to his mother after winning his battle.

Third-Person Narrative

THE WISE KING

Once there ruled in the distant city of Wirani a king who was both mighty and wise. He was feared for his might and loved for his wisdom.

Now, in the heart of that city was a well, whose water was cool and crystalline, from which all the inhabitants drank. Even the king and his courtiers drank from this well, for there was no other.

One night when all were asleep, a witch entered the city, and poured seven drops of strange liquid into the well, and said, "From this hour he who drinks this water shall become mad."

Next morning all the inhabitants, save the king and his lord chamberlain, drank from the well and became mad, even as the witch had foretold. During that day the people in the narrow streets and in the market place did naught but whisper to one another, "The king is mad. Our king and his lord chamberlain have lost their reason. Surely we cannot be ruled by a mad king. We must dethrone him."

That evening the king ordered a golden goblet to be filled from the well. When it was brought to him he drank deeply and gave it to his lord chamberlain to drink. There was great rejoicing in that distant city of Wirani, because its king and its lord chamberlain had regained their reason.—KAHLIL GIBRAN

In the opening paragraph, the writer introduces his main character, a wise and mighty king. In the next paragraph, he draws you a little farther into the story by telling you about the city's only well. You begin to wonder what is going to happen to the king and what it has to do with the well. The writer then tells you, in chronological order, what happened.

1. A witch put into the well a strange liquid that would make people go mad.
2. All the people except the king and the lord chamberlain drank from the well.
3. The people went mad and decided that the king and the lord chamberlain should be dethroned because *they* were mad.
4. The king and the lord chamberlain drank water from the well and became mad.

The writer gives an interesting twist to the ending by telling you that in the eyes of the people the king and the lord chamberlain "had regained their reason."

Exercise Writing a Narrative Composition

Following are two lists of ideas for narrative compositions. Choose one, or use an idea of your own, and write either a first-person or a third-person narrative. In writing the composition, be sure to follow the steps presented in the preceding chapter.

FIRST-PERSON NARRATIVE	THIRD-PERSON NARRATIVE
1. The Day I Broke the Neighbor's Window	1. Crisis at the Zoo
2. My New Job	2. Sam Makes Breakfast
3. When My Mother Visited School	3. Some People Were Born To Make Trouble
4. The Experiment That Failed	4. A Dog That Loves Everybody
5. My Shopping Spree	5. She Didn't See the "Wet Paint" Sign
6. One Day I Would Like To Forget	6. The Sad Clown
7. I Lost My Temper	7. The Creature Appeared Unexpectedly
8. My Secret Ambition	8. He Took the Wrong Road

Part 2   The Descriptive Composition

No two people experience things in exactly the same way. When you write a descriptive composition, you share a little of your own way of perceiving reality with your reader. For a short time, your reader sees, hears, touches, tastes, and smells through your senses.

Like the descriptive paragraph, the descriptive composition relies on specific details to communicate mental images to the reader. These details can be organized in spatial order. This arrangement is common for compositions that appeal mainly to the sense of sight. Compositions that appeal to one of the other senses or to a combination of senses are organized in a variety of ways, depending on content and on the writer's approach.

Following is an example of a descriptive composition that appeals to three senses—sight, hearing, and smell.

BY DAWN'S EARLY LIGHT

The dawn is the freshest, most beautiful part of the day. The traffic has just started. One car at a time goes by, the tires humming almost like the sound of the brook behind the hill. The sound carries not because it is sound, but because everything else is still.

It isn't exactly a mist that hangs over the thickets, but more nearly the ghost of a mist. It will be gone three minutes after the sun comes over the treetops. The lawns shine with a dew not exactly dew. There is a rabbit bobbing about on the lawn. If it were truly a dew, his tracks would shine black on the grass, and he leaves no visible track. Yet there is something on the grass that makes it glow a depth of green it will not show again all day. Or is it something in the dawn air?

And now the sun is shining in full. The leaves of the Japanese red maple seem a transparent red-bronze when the tree is between me and the light. This is the only tree I know whose leaves let the sun through in this way—except when the fall colors start. Green takes sunlight and holds it; red and yellow let it through.

I hear a brake squeak and know that the newspaper has arrived. I sit on the patio and read until the sun grows too bright on the page. Suddenly a hummingbird the color of green crushed-velvet hovers in the throat of my favorite lily, a lovely high-bloomer. The lily is a crest of white horns with red dots and red-velvet tongues along the inside of the petals and with a fragrance that drowns the patio. The humming-bird darts in and out of each horn, then hovers an instant and disappears.

Even without the sun's glare, I have had enough of the paper. I'll take the hummingbird as my news for this dawn. It is over now. It's time to call it a day.—JOHN CIARDI

The writer of this composition has chosen an unusual arrangement for a description. He moves in chronological order from just before dawn, to dawn, to after dawn. The details that recreate each specific time for the reader appeal to the different senses; for example:

sight	the ghost of a mist
	shine with a dew not exactly dew
	glow a depth of green
	transparent red-bronze
	the color of green crushed-velvet
	a crest of white horns with red dots and red-velvet tongues along the inside of the petals
	the sun's glare
hearing	tires humming . . . like the sound of the brook
	everything else is still
	a brake squeak
smell	a fragrance that drowns the patio

Indirectly, the composition also appeals to a fourth sense, the sense of touch. The reader can almost feel the cool pre-dawn mist and the growing warmth of the sun. This careful choice of words and details enables the author to share his favorite time of day.

Exercise Writing a Descriptive Composition

Have you ever seen storm clouds forming or a cat sleeping peacefully under a porch? Perhaps you remember an especially beautiful sunset or your back yard after a violent rainstorm. Maybe you know an interesting-looking person. Choose a topic from your own experience that you think you can describe for your classmates. Then write a five-paragraph descriptive composition, following the steps summarized on page 126. Try to use details that appeal to two or more senses. Consider arranging the details in spatial order, especially if your details appeal mainly to the sense of sight.

Part 3 The Explanatory Composition

The explanatory composition, like the explanatory paragraph, explains something to the reader. It may explain *how* something is done, *what* something is, or *why* something is so or is believed to be so.

The "How" Composition

The "how" composition explains how something is done. Most "how" compositions give instructions in a direct, straightforward style. The instructions are written in chronological order, telling the reader what should be done first, what should be done next, and so on. Compositions explaining how to construct a tree house, how to modify a pattern, or how to use a potter's wheel are examples of this kind of composition. The model on the next page is also an example of a composition with a step-by-step instructional approach.

KEFTA: A BURGER WITH A DIFFERENCE

America is the hamburger capital of the world. Yet the hamburger was not an American invention, nor is America the only place where this food is served. Although their burgers may not always look like a ground meat patty on a bun, people in Asia, Africa, and Europe have enjoyed their own versions of hamburgers for many years. People in the land of the Sahara, for example, eat a kind of round burger called Kefta.

To make Kefta, first get your ingredients and equipment ready. You'll need one pound of ground lamb or ground beef, one egg, one quarter cup of chopped onion, a dash of pepper, and a dash of salt. You'll also need a skillet or outdoor grill, a spatula, a large mixing bowl, and a pot holder.

Using your clean hands, mix and shape the ingredients. First mix the meat, egg, onions, and seasonings thoroughly. Then, if you wish, add any or all of the following: chopped cucumbers, chopped tomatoes, or chopped green peppers. Roll the meat mixture into seven or eight balls, each about the size of a golf ball.

Fry the Kefta in a skillet or barbeque it on an outdoor grill. If you use a skillet, adjust the flame of the stove to medium high. After about ten minutes, turn the meat over and cook it another ten minutes. On an outdoor grill, the cooking time probably will be shorter. You'll want to watch the meat closely and turn it often to prevent burning.

Kefta is delicious alone or served with rice. Try it the next time you're bored with the same old burger on a bun—it's an African treat that's great to eat!—GAY SELTZER

In the second type of "how" composition, the instructions are less direct. They often include general "hints" and suggestions about ways to apply a technique in different situations. As a rule, the subjects of these compositions are not developed in chronological order, because the steps involved do not necessarily follow one after another. In the following composition, for example, the writer describes clues that do not have to be noted in any particular order.

READING THE WATER

If you want to catch more fish, learn how to read the water. Your favorite lake, pond, or stream is full of clues that point to fish. If you look for the clues before you start casting, your chances of catching fish are sure to improve.

Anglers who like to wade streams for bass or trout read the water carefully. Riffles where water bubbles over the rocks and flows into a quiet pool are good fishing places. Especially during the mornings and evenings, fish gather around riffles to feed. They lie pointed upstream, waiting for the current to carry food to them. Cast a bait or lure above the riffles, and let the current carry it into the pool with the natural foods. Do this carefully at the right time of day, with the right bait, and you'll learn that reading the water means more fish.

In the warmer, brighter times of day the fish, especially the bigger ones, may be hiding in deep holes. Fish like to rest in shady places. This may be beside a rock or beneath a half-sunken log. It may be along a rocky ledge dropping off into the stream or lake. It may even be a hole so deep that the light is dim near the bottom. Also, watch for weedy places. Fish may be resting under submerged weeds, and a spinner or plastic worm worked along the edge of a weed bed can bring them out. Find where the smaller streams feed into a river, and you have located another fishing spot worth exploring.

Lakes, like fishing streams, can also be read by the fisherman who knows what to look for. Every lake has some fishing spots that are better than others. You can learn a lot just by looking at the surface of the lake. Are logs lying partly submerged on the edge of the lake? These are good hiding places for bass and other fish. Look around for other signs. The mouths of streams emptying into the lake, rocky ledges reaching into the water, old roads buried when the lake was filled, and fields of stumps sticking from the water are all good places to fish.

The more you study a lake or stream, the more fish you are going to catch. That is the best reason for learning to read the water.—GEORGE LAYCOCK

135

In the opening paragraph, the writer tells you that you can "read" clues in the water that will help you catch more fish. The three body paragraphs describe in a clear, interesting way the signs to look for. The paragraphs contain traces of chronological order. However, the structure of the entire composition is tailored to its content, not to strict time sequence. The last paragraph of the composition restates the idea that reading the water will result in catching more fish. This conclusion lets you know that the writer has finished what he had to say.

Exercise Writing a "How" Composition

You learn how to do something new almost every day. Sometimes you learn from reading, sometimes from another person's explanation or example. Think of something you know how to do well, something your classmates might enjoy learning about. Then write a five-paragraph composition that clearly explains how to do it. Arrange your ideas in chronological order, if this order fits the content of your composition. Be sure to follow the Steps for Writing a Composition summarized on page 126.

Ten suggested topics are given here, in case you have trouble thinking of a topic of your own.

1. How to win at _____(game)_____
2. How to build a birdhouse
3. How to budget your time
4. How to paint a bicycle
5. How to make bread
6. How to drive a minibike
7. How to stretch your money
8. How put up a tent
9. How to plan a party
10. How to raise bees successfully

The "What" Composition

The "what" composition, like the "what" paragraph, defines a word or phrase. The definition in the composition has the same three parts as in the paragraph: (1) the term to be defined, (2) the general class to which the term belongs, and (3) the particular characteristic that sets the term apart from the other members of the general class.

The remainder of the composition is made up of supporting ideas, usually arranged from the least to the most important, that further explain the definition. Following is an example of a "what" composition.

THE FEAST OF LIGHTS

For most Americans, the big winter festival is Christmas, but for American Jews, this season is the time for an important winter festival called Hanukkah. Hanukkah is also called the Feast of Lights because it is observed by lighting candles each day for eight days. Hanukkah also is observed by religious services in the temple, by parties at home, and by gift giving. Like Christmas, Hanukkah is a joyful family holiday.

Hanukkah celebrates an event that took place more than 2,100 years ago. Then, the land that is now Israel was ruled by the Seleucid Empire. The Seleucids worshipped the gods of ancient Greece and insisted that the Jews worship their gods too. For nearly twenty years, the Maccabees, or Jewish soldiers, fought for freedom and independence. The decisive battle occurred in 165 B.C., when the Maccabees returned to Jerusalem and destroyed the Greek statues. Then they repurified the temple and dedicated it to their God. In Hebrew Hanukkah means dedication.

A legend explains that, when the Maccabees were ready to light the oil lamps in the temple, they found enough oil for only one day. By a miracle, however, the lamps burned for eight days, and that is why Hanukkah lasts for eight days.

In Jewish homes today, the main feature of the Hanukkah

celebration is the lighting of the candles at dusk each evening. On the first night, one candle is lighted. The number of candles lighted is increased by one each succeeding evening until all eight candles are lighted. These candles are kindled each night by another candle, popularly known as the "shamos." A special blessing is said before each lighting and gifts are exchanged.

However it is celebrated, Hanukkah is a time of joy for every Jew.

In the first paragraph, you learn that Hanukkah is a Jewish family holiday, observed by candle lighting, religious services, parties, and gift giving. The body of the composition explains why Hanukkah is celebrated and more about the lighting of the Hanukkah candles. The ideas are organized from past to present, the order of importance for the writer. The conclusion restates the idea of Hanukkah as "a time of joy."

Exercise Writing a "What" Composition

Suppose that an amazing time machine has carried you back to the days before the Revolutionary War, when there were none of the conveniences that you take for granted today. Write a five-paragraph "what" composition, explaining a modern-day invention for a man or woman living in the days of George Washington. Remember to include the general class to which your subject belongs and its special qualities. Be sure to follow the Steps for Writing a Composition.

The "Why" Composition

The "why" composition explains why something is so, why something happened, or why something should be done. The opening paragraph states a fact or an opinion. The body paragraphs give reasons to explain why the fact stated is true or why the writer holds that particular opinion. Generally, the reasons are presented in their order of importance.

Following is an example of a "why" composition.

ONE FAMILY'S FAILURE

Last night I told the family the bad news. I had monitored and graded our use of energy for a week. Our family got an F.

Every day Mom drove twenty-eight miles back and forth to work alone, though two co-workers live nearby. So far, all three of them have ignored the chance to carpool. I was guilty of wasting gas, too. I had pestered Dad to pick me up after baseball practice on three afternoons, although I could easily have ridden the bus home.

Tuesday night was a disaster. My brother watched the same movie on the basement TV set that the rest of us watched in the den. Dad ran a dishwashing cycle for three cups, six glasses, four plates, and three little spoons. Also, several lights burned all evening without anyone's being in the rooms.

We wasted heat. The thermostat was lowered only three nights out of seven. We left the front door open much longer than necessary when coming and going. Wednesday afternoon, Mom even left the door ajar while she searched for change to pay for a postage-due letter. The furnace worked overtime for the next half hour to warm the house.

This country is consuming energy at a shocking rate. Unless every person cuts down on energy use, the future looks dim.

In the opening paragraph, the writer states that she gave her family an F for their use of energy. She then describes some of the activities that led her to this conclusion. She gives two examples of gas wasting, focuses on one wasteful night, and mentions an area in which the family is especially careless. These reasons explain why the family received a failing grade. The writer concludes by emphasizing the importance of conserving energy. She thus leaves the reader with a strong final comment on the problem.

Exercise Writing a "Why" Composition

Choose a problem that you feel strongly about. Write a "why" composition in which you state an opinion about the problem and then explain why you think the way you do.

Chapter 10

Writing Social and Business Letters

Writing letters is a good way to keep friendships alive. It is also a good way to obtain information, to order products, and to express your opinions. If you are like most people, you enjoy receiving letters. In order to receive them, however, you must also write them yourself.

There are three basic types of letters: friendly letters, social notes, and business letters. Each type has its own form. Having a form to follow can make letter writing a much easier and more pleasant task, because each form is a guide to what to say.

Part 1   Writing Friendly Letters

In a friendly letter, your writing can be casual, just as if you were talking. The purpose of a friendly letter is to let your friend know what you have been doing and how you feel about what has been happening. Letter writing is an enjoyable sharing of experiences between friends, but even casual letters need a standard form to keep them organized and easy to read. The following example of the form for a friendly letter will help you review the five parts of a friendly letter.

Heading   267 Palm Drive
Cruz, California 95063
July 18, 1982

Salutation
Dear Terry,

Body

Love,   Closing

Beth   Signature

The **heading** is written in the top right-hand corner. It consists of three lines. The first line is your street address. The second line is your city, state, and zip code. The third line is the date of the letter. In the heading, pay particular attention to punctuation and do not abbreviate, especially on the date line.

The **salutation,** or greeting, is the way you say "hello" to your friend. It can be as casual or personal as you wish. Here are some examples:

Dear Todd,   *Greetings Pal,*
Hi Manuel,   *Hello Good Buddy,*

The salutation begins at the left margin. The first word and all other nouns are capitalized, and the last word in the salutation is followed by a comma.

The **body** of a friendly letter is where you communicate your message. Since you are writing to someone you know well, your writing can be conversational, just as if you were talking. In this way, your personality will show through, and your writing will be more interesting. Remember to indent each paragraph in the body.

The **closing** is a simple way of saying "goodbye" to your friend. Capitalize only the first word of the closing and use a comma at the end of the closing. Usually the closing lines up with the first word in the heading. Some closings are common, and some are more personal. Here are some suggestions for closings:

Love,   *Your friend,*   *Missing you,*
Sincerely,   *Still waiting,*   *Confused,*

The **signature** in a friendly letter is written below the closing. Only your first name is needed. Keep your letter personal by always writing your signature by hand, even if you have typed the rest of the letter.

Guidelines for Writing Friendly Letters

What you do every day may not seem particularly interesting to you, but remember that a friend enjoys just keeping in touch. A friendly letter gives you the chance to write about events and feelings that are meaningful to you and interesting to your friend. The following guidelines will help you.

Guidelines for Friendly Letters

1. In the first paragraph, make comments about the last letter you received from your friend.

2. Write one or more paragraphs about people and events that interest both you and your friends.

3. Use specific words for descriptions and action.

4. Ask questions so that your friend has something to write back about.

5. Make your handwriting neat and legible.

6. Use the proper letter form.

Read the sample of a friendly letter on page 145. See how each part is developed.

Exercises Writing Friendly Letters

A. Choose one of the following ideas and rewrite it. Develop each situation more specifically, and use vivid details.

1. We bought a puppy last week. It's really cute, but it's always getting into trouble, and it's very hard to train.

2. When my brother left for college, he said I could use his CB. I have set it up in my room. It's a lot of fun.

3. Last weekend I babysat for a family of six kids. You wouldn't believe how busy they kept me. What a mess!

318 Laurel Road
Bexley, Ohio 43209
October 28, 1982

Dear Julie,

I was so glad to get your letter at last.
I guess I just couldn't wait to see the pictures.
Boy, are they fantastic! I especially like
the one of you and Andy in the sailboat.
Of course, Jim's favorite is the one where we're
all standing there like drowned rats holding
up our fish. That's just like a brother,
especially since he caught the biggest fish.
Anyway, it was a great family reunion, and
already I can't wait until the next one.

You'll never guess what I'm doing in school.
I actually tried out for the girl's basketball
team and made it! Our first game is
next week so I'll be writing again soon to
let you know how it went. I'm really
excited.

I really have to get to my homework
now. Say "hi" to your family for me and
write soon.

Miss you,
Suzanne

B. Write a friendly letter to one of your best friends. You may write about events that have actually happened to you, or you may want to use some of those suggested in the following list. Follow the guidelines on page 144. Use your best handwriting.

> Student Council elections at school
> How your cat destroyed your science project
> The movie you saw last weekend
> How you redecorated your bedroom
> Your friend's surprise birthday party
> Your recent camping trip

Part 2   Social Notes

Social notes are written for a specific purpose, such as to invite someone to a party, to thank someone, or to accept an invitation. Social notes have the same form as a friendly letter, but they are much shorter. Sometimes only the date is used in the heading instead of the writer's whole address.

Social notes are a form of courtesy that people appreciate. The following kinds of social notes are the ones you will write most often.

The Thank-You Note

Usually a thank-you note is written after you have received a gift. Even if you don't particularly like the gift, it is still important to thank the person for thinking of you.

Another form of thank-you note is called a "bread-and-butter" note. You write this note when you have stayed overnight at someone's house.

Both forms of thank-you notes express your appreciation for someone else's thoughtfulness toward you. On the next page are samples of the two types of thank-you notes.

A Thank-You Note

2217 Massachusetts Avenue
Lawrence, Kansas 66044
June 5, 1982

Dear Aunt Alice,

The sweater you knitted for me for graduation is soft and warm and beautiful. It matches perfectly the skirt Mother made for me. How thoughtful both of you were. Thank you so much.

Mother and Dad and Grandmother were able to come to the ceremony, and we went out to dinner afterwards. I wish you and Uncle Fred could have been there too.

Love,
Cindy

A Bread-and-Butter Note

4950 North Marine Drive
Chicago, Illinois 60640
April 14, 1982

Dear Mr. and Mrs. Pacini,

Thank you very much for letting me spend last weekend at your house while my parents were out of town. I had a great time at the baseball game.

I really enjoyed myself. I hope that Tom can spend a weekend with me soon.

Sincerely,
Matt Brendan

Notes of Invitation, Acceptance, and Regret

Invitations have to be written carefully to make sure that all the necessary details are included. Use the following checklist:

Guidelines for Writing Invitations

1. Specify the type of the activity.
2. Tell the purpose of the activity.
3. Give the address of the place where the activity will be held.
4. Give the day, date, and time of the activity.
5. Tell how the person should reply to the invitation.

Include directions or transportation suggestions if needed.

The abbreviation R.S.V.P. stands for a French phrase that means "please respond." The person sending the invitation would like to know how many people are going to attend the party. Sometimes there will be a phone number next to the R.S.V.P. so that all you have to do is call. Usually, however,

> 417 Monroe Avenue
> Mapleton, Iowa 51034
> June 1, 1982
>
> Dear Juanita,
> You are invited to attend a graduation party at my house on Friday, June 14. The party will start immediately following our graduation ceremony, at approximately 10:00. Your parents are welcome, too.
> I sure hope you can be there.
>
> Sincerely,
> Carla
>
> R.S.V.P.

you should send a note of acceptance or regret. Always answer an invitation as soon as possible.

A Note of Acceptance

June 5, 1982

Dear Carla,
    After graduation is a great time to have a party. Being at your house is always lots of fun. My parents will be coming, too. Thanks for the invitation.

Your friend,
Juanita

A Note of Regret

June 5, 1982

Dear Carla,
    I wish I could attend your graduation party. I know it will be lots of fun. Unfortunately my parents have already invited several of our relatives over for a celebration.
    Ask if you can spend the night on Saturday so you can tell me all about the party.

Your friend,
Juanita

Exercise Writing Social Notes

Choose two of the following situations and write the appropriate notes on plain paper.

1. Write a note to your uncle thanking him for helping you with a project. You select the project.

2. Write an invitation to a surprise birthday party.

3. Write a note thanking a friend's parents for taking you on vacation with them.

4. Write a note to a neighbor apologizing for crushing her flowers. You decide how it happened.

5. Write a note accepting an invitation to join a club.

6. Write a note of regret for a barbecue you are unable to attend.

Part 3   Writing Business Letters

When you want to request information, or order a product, or even complain about a product, you will need to write a business letter. A business letter is written for a specific purpose and requires a different style of writing from that of a friendly letter. A business letter should be brief, clear, and to the point. It should follow the required form.

Business Letter Form

When writing a business letter, always use 8½" × 11" unruled white paper. If possible, type your letter. If you do not type well, write your letter with blue or black ink. Leave equal margins on both sides, and at the top and bottom of the paper, and use only one side of the paper.

The form for a business letter is similar in many ways to the form for a friendly letter. There are two types of business letter forms: **block form** and **modified block form.**

The block form for a business letter is to be used only when the letter is typewritten. Notice that all parts of the letter begin at the left margin. There is a double space between paragraphs, and the paragraphs are not indented.

920 South Lake Avenue
Greenville, South Carolina   29602
November 23, 1982

The Danbury Mint
47 Richards Avenue
Norwalk, Connecticut   06856

Dear Sir or Madam:

Sincerely,

Valerie Hayward
Valerie Hayward

The modified block form is always used when the letter is handwritten. In this form, the heading remains in the upper right-hand corner, as in a friendly letter. Notice that in this form the paragraphs are indented, and the closing and signature line up with the heading.

Modified Block Form

Heading

920 South Lake Avenue
Greenville, South Carolina 29602
November 23, 1982

Inside Address

The Danbury Mint
47 Richards Avenue
Norwalk, Connecticut 06856

Dear Sir or Madam: Salutation

Body

_____

_____

_____

_____

_____

Yours truly,   Closing
Valerie Hayward   Signature
Valerie Hayward

Parts of a Business Letter

The parts of a business letter are similar to the parts of a friendly letter except that they are written more formally. Follow these suggestions for writing the parts of a business letter:

1. **Heading.** The heading of a business letter is the same as the heading for a friendly letter. Check capitalization and punctuation and do not abbreviate.

2. **Inside Address.** The inside address consists of the name and address of the firm or organization to which you are writing. This address follows the same capitalization and punctuation rules as the heading. The inside address always begins at the left margin.

3. **Salutation.** The salutation begins two lines after the inside address and ends with a colon (:). If you are writing to a specific person, use *Dear* and then the person's name, such as *Dear Mr. Reed:*. If you do not know the name of the person to whom you are writing, use a general greeting, such as *Dear Sir or Madam:* or *Ladies and Gentlemen:*.

4. **Body.** The body of a business letter is brief, courteous, and to the point. State clearly the purpose of your letter.

5. **Closing.** The closing appears on the first line below the body. Here are common closings for a business letter:

   Sincerely yours,   Yours truly,   Respectfully yours,

   Notice that *only* the first word of the closing is capitalized and that the closing is followed by a comma.

6. **Signature.** Type or print your name four spaces below the closing; then write your signature in the space between. Even if your signature is not clear, your name can be clearly read.

Make a copy of each of your business letters so you will have a record of what you wrote and when you wrote it. You can do this by using carbon paper. Always mail the original.

Part 4   Types of Business Letters

There are three basic types of business letters, each with its own specific purpose: the letter of request, the order letter, and the letter of complaint or adjustment. Each of these business letters follows the same basic business letter form and includes the same parts of a letter. The only differences appear in the information you include in the body of the letter.

The Letter of Request

This type of business letter is particularly useful for getting first-hand information for reports, for receiving catalogs and pamphlets, and for researching a product before you buy it. In a letter of request, be sure to include the following information:

Guidelines for Letters of Request

1. Identify yourself.

2. Tell why you are contacting the person or company.

3. Tell what specific information you need.

4. Tell why you need the information.

Notice how these guidelines are followed in the letter of request on the next page.

58 Eagle Road
La Crosse, Wisconsin 54601
February 10, 1982

Action for Children's Television
46 Austin Street
Newtonville, Massachusetts

Dear Sir or Madam:

Our language arts class at Winston Junior High School is studying television and advertising. Our teacher listed your organization as a good resource for information on this subject. My particular report concerns advertising for Saturday morning papers. I would appreciate your sending me any information you have on this subject. It is necessary that I receive this information by March 1 for my report.

Yours truly,
David Stewart
David Stewart

Exercise Writing Letters of Request

Write a letter of request dealing with one of these situations. Use correct business letter form. (Do not send the letter.)

1. You have just started backpacking as a hobby and would like to join a group or club. Write to International Backpackers Association, P.O. Box 85, Lincoln Center, ME 04458.

2. Your uncle has given you his stamp collection. You would like to add to it, but you need more information. Write to *National Stamp News*, Box 4066, Anderson, SC 29622.

3. Your family is moving to Texas, and you want to learn all you can about the state. Write to Texas Tourist Development Agency, Box 12008, Dept. NW, Austin, TX 78711.

The Order Letter

In the order letter, you must include many specific details to make sure you receive the exact merchandise you want to buy.

Guidelines for Order Letters

1. Give the name of the product and how many you want.

2. Give the name of the publication in which you saw the ad.

3. Give the catalog number, size, and/or color.

4. Compute the price of the item(s).

5. Include the cost of the postage and handling.

6. Compute the price of the total order.

7. State any item you are enclosing, such as a check or money order, or a picture, etc.

8. Restate any important terms that are a part of the ad, such as delivery time.

The following is a sample of an order letter.

163 Poinsetta Drive
Tampa, Florida 33684
October 14, 1982

Masterwork
1708 17th Street
Santa Monica, California 90404

Dear Sir or Madam:

Please send me the photo belt buckle advertised in the September issue of <u>Better Homes and Gardens</u>. I am enclosing $7.95, plus $1.00 postage.

I am enclosing the black and white photo to be used. I understand that my photo will be returned and that delivery will take four to six weeks.

Yours truly,
Robert Takamoto
Robert Takamoto

Exercise Writing Order Letters

Choose two of the following situations. Write an order letter for each. Include all of the ne....s..ry information. Use correct business letter form. (Do not send the letter.)

1. Order one sports equipment caddy, Style Q–56, $8.50 ppd., from Spear Engineering Company, Dept. 3053, Box 7025, Colorado Springs, CO 80933, as seen in the September issue of *Better Homes and Gardens.*

2. Order two sets of 14 personalized pencils, each with your full name. $1.00 per set with 25¢ handling per set, from Atlas Pencil Co., Dept. BHG, Hallandale, Florida 33009, as seen in the July issue of *Boys' Life.*

3. Order the following plans as seen in *Popular Mechanics:* PL–1715, $5.95; PL–1406, $14.95; PL–1401, $6.95; PM Catalog, 50¢; ppd. from Popular Mechanics Plans Library, Box 1014, Radio City Station, New York, NY 10019.

The Letter of Complaint or Adjustment

When you have spent time and money ordering or buying a product, you naturally want to be a satisfied customer. The manufacturer of the product usually wants you to be a satisfied customer. If you are not totally satisfied, write directly to the company and courteously state your problem.

Guidelines for Letters of Complaint or Adjustment

1. Give the specific name of the product.

2. Tell when and where the item was purchased.

3. Describe the specific nature of the problem.

4. Tell how you want to have the problem corrected or state that you are returning the merchandise either to be fixed or for a refund.

_____ Avenue
Seattle, Washington 98124
August 18, 1982

Holiday Gifts
Department 409-8H
Rock Ridge, Colorado 80034

Dear Sir or Madam:

When I received my personalized sweat-shirt in the mail, I noticed that my name was misspelled.

I have already waited four weeks and I am very disappointed.

I am returning the sweatshirt to you and would like to have the mistake corrected as soon as possible. If delivery will take another four weeks, please refund the $4.95 that I have already paid.

Respectfully,
Frank Steiner
Frank Steiner

Exercise Writing Letters of Complaint or Adjustment

Choose one of the following situations and write an appropriate letter of complaint. Use correct business letter form. Use your local telephone directory or a product you own as a resource for an appropriate address.

1. Write to a candy company complaining about the freshness of a candy bar you bought.

2. The magazine subscription you ordered cost $8.00 for a year's subscription. When you received the bill, it read $80.00.

3. The catalog you ordered still has not arrived. The ad stated 3–4 weeks' delivery. It has now been 6 weeks and you have already paid $3.00 for the catalog.

4. The new 10-speed bike you bought is missing a part. The store can't replace it, so you must write to the company.

5. Write to your local city or village government complaining about a particularly dangerous intersection.

Part 5 Preparing Your Letter for the Mail

Once you have taken the time to write a friendly letter or a business letter, it is important to fold the letter correctly so that it can be read easily. It is also important to address the envelope carefully so that the letter will reach its destination.

Folding Your Letter

If your friendly letter is written on writing tablet paper, which is generally 6″ × 8″, you should first fold the paper in half. If the letter is still too large for the envelope, fold it in thirds beginning from each side, as shown in the following diagram.

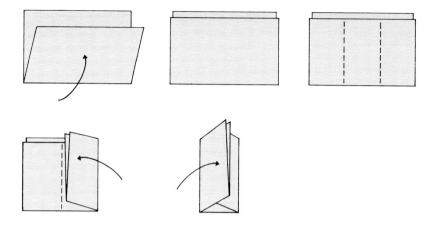

A business letter that is written on standard 8½″ × 11″ paper should be folded into thirds. First, fold from the bottom up and then fold the top third down, as shown below.

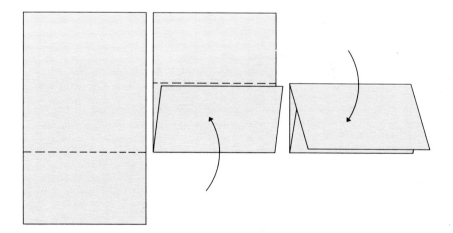

Addressing the Envelope

The following steps should be taken when addressing your envelope:

Guidelines for Addressing Envelopes

1. Make sure the envelope is right-side up.

2. Always put your return address on the envelope.

3. Double-check all numbers to make sure they are in the proper order.

4. Include the correct zip code.

Addressing Envelopes for Friendly Letters

Envelopes for friendly letters are usually small, such as $6\frac{1}{2}'' \times 3\frac{1}{2}''$ or $5'' \times 5''$.

Miss Annette Johnson
7562 North Hoyne
Chicago, Illinois 60645

Mr. James Speare
2013 St. James Street
Philadelphia, Pennsylvania 19111

When you write out the name of the state, you must place a comma between the city and the state. However, when you use the two-letter abbreviation for the state, capitalize both letters in the abbreviation.

Addressing Envelopes for Business Letters

When addressing a business envelope, follow the same procedure you did for a friendly letter, but always include your return address on the front of the 9½″ × 4″ envelope that is used for business letters. In addressing a business envelope, you may need an additional line if you are writing to a particular person in the company or if you want the letter to go to a specific department in the company.

Mrs. Joan Caedmon
856 Burke Avenue
Mission, KS 66202

Mr. Lawrence Laski, Sales Manager
Heraldica Imports, Inc.
21 West 46th Street
New York, NY 10036

Exercise Addressing Envelopes

Address an envelope for each of the following addresses. Use your own address as the return address. Draw a 9½″ × 4″ space on your paper for a business envelope and a 5″ × 5″ space for a friendly letter or invitation.

1. Ms. Maria Talbot, Personnel Director, Ventura Industries, Inc., 1700 4th Ave., Portland, Oregon 97201
2. Mr. W. L. Young, 2600 Vista Blvd., Fresno CA 93717
3. Casual Designs, 325 S. Washington, Dept. BHG 9, Royal Oak MI 48067
4. Ms. Caroline Bexley, 2308 Algonquin Rd., Bay Minette, Alabama 36507

Chapter 11

Clear Thinking

Clear writing begins with clear thinking. Think about your ideas carefully. Be sure that they are clear and make sense. Then you will be well on your way to making yourself understood.

When you can recognize faulty thinking in yourself, you will be better able to recognize it in others. You will be able to spot faulty thinking behind what others say and write.

In this chapter you will learn how to recognize clear and faulty thinking. You will learn how to correct faulty thinking in yourself, so that it does not weaken what you say or write.

Part 1 Fact or Opinion?

What Is a Fact?

A fact is a piece of information that can be shown to be true. The following sentence is a statement of fact.

The Lincoln Memorial is in Washington, D.C.

A person who reads the statement can check to see if it is true. The reader could go to Washington to find out if the Lincoln Memorial is there. The reader could also find an encyclopedia article on Washington or on the Lincoln 'Memorial.

A fact may be true in one of two ways:

1. A fact may be true by definition, as the following sentence is.

Trout are fish.

That sentence is a statement of fact. You can check it in a dictionary. You will find that the word *trout* is the name given to one kind of fish. Therefore, the statement "Trout are fish" is true by definition.

2. A fact may be true by observation, as this sentence is.

Trout cannot live out of water.

You can check that statement by performing an experiment. You can get a trout, keep it out of water, and observe it to see if it lives. Scientists have already made this observation, so you don't have to make it yourself. You can look in an encyclopedia or in a book about fish to find out if the statement is true. The statement is true by observation.

What Is an Opinion?

An opinion cannot be shown to be true. The following sentence is a statement of opinion.

Fried trout is delicious.

That statement is not a statement of fact. You may agree with it. You may not. If you were to ask everyone in your neighborhood whether fried trout is delicious, some would say that it is. Some would say that it is not. The statement cannot be proven. It cannot be checked, either by definition or by observation. It is a statement about the way someone *feels* about fried trout, not a statement of a fact about fried trout.

Examples of Facts and Opinions

Following are two sets of statements. In each set, the first two statements are statements of fact. The third is a statement of opinion.

> The moon is a satellite of the earth.
> The moon takes more than twenty-seven days to orbit the earth.
> The full moon is a beautiful sight.

> Spinach is a vegetable.
> Spinach contains Vitamin A.
> Spinach makes a tasty salad.

We all have opinions. Some of us like city life, others prefer the country or the suburbs. Some of us like to eat fish. Some don't. Our opinions are some of the things that make us different from each other. You are entitled to your opinions, but don't try to make people think that your opinions are facts.

Exercise Fact or Opinion?

Read each of the following pairs of statements. Identify each statement as *fact* or *opinion.*

1. Children spend too much time watching television.

The average child between the ages of two and five spends more than thirty-one hours a week watching television.

2. Franklin D. Roosevelt was elected to four terms as President of the United States.

Franklin D. Roosevelt was an outstanding President.

167

3. The average humidity in Phoenix, Arizona, is 37 percent.
Phoenix, Arizona, has a dry, uncomfortable climate.

4. In 1976, doctors in the United States earned an average of $62,799.
Doctors are overpaid.

5. Americans conduct more than 633 million telephone conversations every day.
People waste money on telephone calls when they could write letters.

6. One American in ten lives in a big city with a population of a million or more.
Big cities are exciting places to live.

7. Ty Cobb was the greatest hitter in baseball.
Ty Cobb had a lifetime batting average of .367.

8. More than forty million foreign tourists visited the United States last year.
We should be doing more to attract foreign tourists.

Part 2   Judgment Words

Judgment words are words that express opinions rather than give facts. Often they are adjectives, as in the following examples.

a *lazy* person   a *luxurious* home   a *clever* idea

The words *lazy, luxurious,* and *clever* are all judgment words. They give us someone's opinion of the person, the home, and the idea. They do not tell us facts about them.

Watch and listen for judgment words. Ask yourself whether the facts would support the opinions that the judgment words express. In your writing, be careful of the adjectives you use. Ask yourself whether your facts can be checked.

Following is a list of judgment words. Be especially careful of these words and their synonyms.

sensible	foolish	valuable	worthless
beautiful	ugly	good	bad

Exercise Judgment Words

Find the judgment word in each of the following statements.

1. Test-drive the beautiful new Hurricane Six.
2. Senator Hearst is doing an excellent job.
3. Dan wastes his allowance playing electronic games.
4. Sudsy Satin gives your hair a lovely shine.
5. Here's the tastiest coffee money can buy!

Part 3 Connotations of Words

Many words have two kinds of meanings. One kind of meaning is clear-cut and direct. This kind of meaning is given in a dictionary. It is called a word's **denotation** or **denotative meaning.** The other kind of meaning is not clear-cut. It is a meaning that is only suggested by the word. This kind of meaning comes from the ideas or feelings that a word brings to a person's mind. This suggested meaning is called a word's **connotation** or **connotative meaning.** The following pairs of examples show how important connotation can be to meaning.

fortified with essential nutrients
vitamins added

passenger-restraint system
seatbelt

living room with view
living room with one window

The connotations of words can make them work like judgment words. If vitamins are added to a cereal, the cereal has been fortified with essential nutrients. However, the word *fortified* suggests strength and well-being, and the words *essential nutrients* emphasize the idea of good health and nutrition.

A seatbelt is a passenger-restraint system. It is something that holds a passenger in place. However, the phrase *passenger-restraint system* sounds very technical, suggesting that a lot of engineering research went into development of the product.

If you were looking for an apartment, would you be more attracted by one that was described as having a *living room with view* or one that had a living room with one window?

Exercises Connotations of Words

A. Football teams are often named for animals. Following are twelve possible names for football teams. Think about the connotations of each name. Explain why the connotations of each make it a good or bad choice as a name for a football team.

The Poodles	The Mice	The Guppies
The Hawks	The Stallions	The Mammoths
The Sharks	The Panthers	The Goats
The Hippos	The Pigeons	The Grizzlies

B. Each of these statements contains at least one word or phrase with strong connotations. Find them. Replace them with words or phrases that do not have strong connotations.

1. Johnson admitted that he had not attended last week's meeting.

2. Neighborhood residents begged to be heard.

3. Are you ready to put up with Governor Nelson for four more years?

4. Let's stop giving handouts to people who don't work.

5. Nancy boasted that she had finished in twenty minutes.

6. With this policy you will feel secure in knowing that your loved ones will never lose their home.

7. Dallas crushed the Eagles, 24–10.

8. Supporters of the tax cut have spread this propaganda all over the state.

9. We'll help you find a rewarding position with a good firm.

10. At The Country Shoppe you will find selected antique furnishings for gracious living.

Part 4 Slanting

Writing that uses the power of connotation and judgment words to influence a reader's opinions is called **slanted writing.** The term *slanting* comes from the idea that the writer "leans" toward one side of an issue. Read the following sentences. Notice that the first one states facts. The second and third are slanted in different directions.

1

A hundred people tried Sunburst toothpaste and Mintgreen toothpaste. Sixty-six thought that Sunburst tasted better. Sixty-four thought that Mintgreen cleaned teeth better.

2

A hundred people tried Sunburst toothpaste and Mintgreen toothpaste. An overwhelming majority praised new Sunburst's fresh, bright, wake-up flavor. Of course, we knew that new Sunburst had great taste. What made us especially proud was the number of people who said that Sunburst cleaned their teeth better.

3

Let's talk about Mintgreen, the toothpaste for people who really care about their teeth. In a recent test, a hundred people tried Sunburst toothpaste and Mintgreen toothpaste. An overwhelming majority thought that Mintgreen really did the job, leaving their teeth truly clean and germ-free.

If you come across such statements in reading—or if you write them yourself—ask yourself which words are judgment words and which words have been chosen for their connotations. In the examples, *overwhelming, great, really,* and *truly* are judgment words. The words *fresh, bright, wake-up,* and *germ-free* have been chosen for their connotations.

Exercise **Slanting**

Following are three reports. Two are slanted. One is neutral. It is not slanted; it reports only the facts. Find every example of slanting in the two slanted reports. Explain how each is an attempt to influence the reader.

1

Striking school bus drivers met with the school committee today to discuss two issues. First, the drivers say that twelve buses should be replaced. Each of these buses is more than ten years old. Second, bus drivers would like to be covered by the retirement plan for other city workers. School attendance was off by 50 percent in this fourth day of the strike.

2

Striking school bus drivers hit the school committee with their demands today. First, they want the committee to spend your tax dollars on twelve luxurious new buses. Second, the drivers are calling for an enormous increase in their retirement benefits. For four long days now, they have brought education in this community to a virtual standstill.

3

Striking school bus drivers today asked the school committee to consider two proposals. First, twelve old buses that need frequent repair should be replaced with newer models, which feature improved safety devices. Second, the drivers asked that they be covered by the city retirement plan, so that they will be able to enjoy their golden years without undue financial worry. School attendance has declined somewhat during the brief strike.

Part 5　Checking the Facts

Facts can be checked. As a writer and speaker, you owe it to your reader or listener to check your facts before you present them as true. An incorrect fact can embarrass you as a writer. You may base an opinion on an incorrect fact, only to have someone point out to you that your information is wrong.

Most readers are willing to give a writer the benefit of the doubt. They accept the writer's information as it is presented— as true information. An honest and careful writer makes certain that it *is* true.

Do not take facts for granted. Let's suppose that you are going to write about transportation needs in your city. You are about to write that bus fares have doubled in the last five years. Where did you get that information? Did you read it in a newspaper? Did a friend mention it to you? Do not assume that the information is correct. If you are going to state it as a fact, check it.

Before accepting information as true, ask yourself:

> What is the source of this information?
> Is the source reliable?

If you cannot remember the source for some information, do not think of it as a fact.

A reliable source is one that is widely recognized, qualified, and unbiased.

1. A source will be widely recognized if many people have used its information and found it to be correct. Which is likely to be a better source of information about a local election—a newspaper or a conversation you overhear while riding on a bus?

2. A source is qualified if care has been taken to learn about the subject in depth and check the facts in advance. Which is likely to be a better source of information about nutrition —a booklet written by a dietitian or a book written by a movie star?

3. A source is unbiased if it has nothing to gain from presenting inaccurate facts. Which is likely to be the less biased source of information about a new car—a road test in a consumer magazine or a television advertisement for the car?

As a reader or listener, you owe it to yourself to check the facts in what you read or hear before you accept them as true.

You can check facts in two ways. One way is to collect first-hand information. If someone says "Snow is falling," you can check the statement by stepping outside. Another way to check a fact is to collect second-hand information from reliable sources. If someone says, "The Indian elephant has smaller ears than the African elephant," you don't have to go to India and Africa to check the statement. You can go to the reference section of your local library. There you will find encyclopedias, almanacs, atlases, and dictionaries that will answer most of your needs in checking facts.

Exercise Checking the Facts

Following are ten statements. Check the facts in each statement. Use reliable sources. Tell what source you used to check each. Correct the statements that are incorrect.

1. Benjamin Franklin was born in Philadelphia in 1706.
2. Philadelphia lies on the Delaware River.
3. The Delaware River forms the border between Pennsylvania and New Jersey.
4. Pittsburgh is the capital of Pennsylvania.
5. The population of Pittsburgh in 1970 was 1,000,000.
6. The United States Bureau of the Census was established in 1902.
7. In 1902, the Wright Brothers made the first successful airplane flight.
8. The Wright brothers made their first flights at Kitty Hawk, Georgia.
9. Georgia is bordered on the east by the Atlantic Ocean.
10. The Atlantic is the largest of the world's oceans.

Part 6 Making the Facts Clear

The work that goes into checking your facts will be wasted if your reader can't understand the facts you write. To make them clear, choose the most specific words you can. However, choose your words carefully. Do not choose words that say more than you can prove.

Be Specific

Words refer to people and things. A general word refers to a great number of things. A specific word refers to a small number of things. A general word may mean different things to different people. A specific word is more likely to be clear to most readers. Think about the following pairs of sentences.

> Last year Bay City grew enormously.
> Last year the population of Bay City increased by 20 percent.

> Executive suitcases have sturdy handles.
> Executive suitcases have handles that can support six times the weight of the suitcase.

In each pair of sentences, the second is more specific than the first. The phrase *grew enormously* leaves the reader wondering how much the city grew. Did it double in size? Writing that the population increased by 20 percent tells the reader just how much the city grew. The word *sturdy* may mean one thing to a person who packs shirts and socks in a suitcase. It may mean something else to a traveling salesperson who packs a suitcase with samples of plumbing supplies.

A general statement may be much like a judgment. Compare the following sentences.

> The mayor announced some small budget cuts.
> The mayor announced that the salaries of all city employees would be cut by 10 percent.

A 10-percent cut in the salaries of all city workers may be

small in the opinion of the writer. However, it is not likely to seem small to the workers who face it.

When you use specific words to state your information, your reader will have an exact idea of what you mean. You will be sure that you have said something that you can prove. Compare the following four statements.

1. Fifty-five percent of the students who buy lunch in our school cafeteria do not eat spinach when it is served.
2. Most students in our school do not eat spinach.
3. The students in our school don't eat green vegetables.
4. Teenagers don't like vegetables.

The first statement is the most specific. It tells us about a group of students who are clearly identified and a behavior that can be observed. The statement can be proved.

Think about ways that the other statements could be challenged.

The second statement is less specific than the first. The word *most* does not tell us how many as specifically as *fifty-five percent* does. The statement does not limit the student's behavior to the school cafeteria. Perhaps some of the students like to eat spinach at home. This statement would be harder to prove.

The third statement is still more general and would be even harder to prove. First, it suggests that all students in the school do not eat green vegetables. Second, *green vegetables* includes everything from lettuce to pickles.

The last statement would be hardest to prove. The word *vegetables* names a great many foods. Entire cookbooks have been devoted to vegetables. The word *teenagers* names more than twenty million people in the United States alone.

Give Your Source

Tell your reader where you got your information. If you do, you will show that you have gone to the trouble of checking your facts. Your reader will be able to judge whether your information is from a reliable source. Your reader will also be able to check your facts.

Each of the following statements gives a source for the information it contains.

> According to the Bureau of the Census, the population of Bay City increased by 20 percent last year.

> The school dietitian has reported that 55 percent of the students who buy lunch in our school cafeteria do not eat spinach when it is served.

Exercise Making the Facts Clear

Choose the more specific statement from each pair.

1. Phoenix, Arizona, has a dry climate.
On the average, only fifteen inches of rain falls in Phoenix in a year.

2. Nature Bread contains flour, water, yeast, and salt.
Nature Bread contains only natural ingredients.

3. Hernandez's campaign has received frequent coverage in the media recently.
The local paper has run stories about Hernandez's campaign for five days in a row.

4. The new four-cylinder Chipmunk will save you money.
The new four-cylinder Chipmunk uses less gas than last year's model.

5. The average salary for a professional football player is over 55,000 dollars.
Professional athletes earn more money than most people.

6. A person can learn useful information from television.
Last night I saw a television show about whales, and learned that some whales can hold their breath for an hour.

7. Foreign travel in the United States is increasing.
The number of foreign visitors to the United States doubled from 1977 to 1978.

Part 7 Generalizing

When you see something happen many times, you may find a pattern. Finding a pattern in what you observe is called **generalizing.** Once you spot the pattern, you have made a **generalization.**

Public opinion polls depend on generalizing. A pollster may ask questions of a thousand people in a city of a million. The answers that the thousand people give will be taken to represent the answers that all the people would have given if they had been asked.

Suppose that you have started a small business of your own. You sell T-shirts that you have designed and made. You have two designs. One has a cartoon of a smiling cat; that other has a cartoon of a smiling dog. In the first week of selling, you sell twice as many cat shirts as dog shirts. In the second week of selling, you again sell twice as many cat shirts. The results for the third week are the same. When it is time to make some new shirts, will you make more cat shirts or more dog shirts? You will make more cat shirts, of course. You have made a generalization: "Cat shirts are twice as popular as dog shirts."

Errors in Generalizing

Mistakes in generalizing usually occur in one of two ways.

1. There may not have been enough cases for a true pattern to show up. Suppose that the public opinion poll had been based on only ten people. Would that have been enough to predict what the other 999,990 thought? Probably not.

2. The generalization may be too broad. It may try to take in more occurrences than the facts will support. Think about each of the following generalizations.

Everybody loves a parade.

April is always rainy.

These generalizations are too broad. There are people who don't like parades. There is a possibility that an area will have a very dry April. Farmers and fruit growers know that they have to be prepared for dry weather that may come when they least expect it.

Qualifying Generalizations

Generalizations become too broad when you try to make them cover *all* cases. The following words can push your generalizations too far.

always	never	nobody	all the time
everyone	every	everybody	no one

Qualifying a generalization means telling how many cases it applies to. You might qualify a generalization with words like:

sometimes	some	a few	frequently	many
rarely	most	often	infrequently	

If you do not use a qualifying word, your generalization may seem too broad even if you don't use words like *always* and *never*. Compare the sentences in each of the following pairs. Which one is an accurate generalization?

Lefty Cortez never bunts.
Lefty Cortez has tried to bunt only three times this season.

People like to drive big cars.
Some people like to drive big cars.

Jill visits her grandmother every Friday.
Jill visits her grandmother on Friday whenever she can.

Giving Evidence for a Generalization

Generalizations are useful. Without them we would see only details. We wouldn't see the patterns in life and in the way people behave. However, generalizations can be dangerous if we think of them as rules or as true statements that apply to every case. You can avoid this danger by telling your reader how you made your generalization. Consider the following:

> Most students in our school prefer salad to cooked vegetables at lunch. I have worked in the school cafeteria for six weeks. During that time, salads were served on twelve days. Cooked vegetables were served on eighteen days. As students turned in their dishes, I counted the number of salads that were completely eaten and the number of servings of vegetables that were completely eaten. More than 83 percent of the salads, but only 46 percent of the servings of vegetables, were eaten.

The statement "Most students in our school prefer salad to cooked vegetables at lunch" is a generalization that the reader can accept. The facts support the generalization.

Exercise **Generalizing**

Read each pair of statements below. Decide which of the two statements is better. Explain what is wrong with the other.

1. The average child between the ages of two and five spends more than thirty-one hours a week watching television.

   According to the 1980 *Information Please Almanac*, the average child between two and five in America spent more than thirty-one hours a week watching television during 1978.

2. We observed pedestrians on High Street between Summer and Court Streets for six hours last Friday. Ninety-seven people crossed High Street in that area during that time. Only thirty-nine crossed within the crosswalks. We concluded that most pedestrians do not use the crosswalks on High Street.

   Pedestrians do not use the crosswalks on High Street.

3. Americans are more concerned about inflation than any other problem.

   In yesterday's paper I read the result of a poll showing that most people think inflation is America's biggest problem.

4. The voters of South Hargrove want Connolly for Mayor. A majority of the voters of South Hargrove want Connolly for Mayor.

5. In last night's game, Jackson struck out three times. Jackson can't hit.

Review Exercises Putting Your Thinking Skills Together

A. Tell which of the following are statements of fact and which are opinions. Tell how you would check each fact.

1. Businesses spend too much money on advertising.
2. Television networks sell advertising time.
3. Advertising time on a popular show can be outrageously expensive.
4. More than forty-three billion dollars was spent on advertising in the United States during 1978.
5. Approximately twenty-eight billion dollars was spent on advertising in 1975.
6. The increase from 1975 to 1978 was huge.
7. About 27 percent of the money is spent on radio and television advertising.
8. Most of the rest is spent on newspapers and magazines.

B. Following are examples of faulty generalizing. Use a qualifying word or phrase to make each generalization accurate.

1. People are interested only in their own problems.
2. Old people do not drive well.
3. People in Maine love snowy winters.
4. Everybody loves a sunny day.
5. No one in this city wants to see taxes go up.
6. Left-handed people are generous.
7. Young people do not like hard work.
8. Commuters would rather ride in private cars than use public transportation.

Chapter 12

The Library and How To Use It

Each year that you are in school, the building, your teachers, and the courses you take may change, but the uses of a library and the organization of a library will not. Each year you will be expected to be able to work more independently in the library.

The books in every library are organized by the same basic system. Of course, not all libraries have exactly the same books. For that reason it is important for you to become familiar with all of the materials offered in the library that you use.

Just how well do you know the library that you use? This chapter will help you to review what you already know about the library. The chapter will also help you make better use of the library than ever before.

Part 1 The Classification and Arrangement of Books

Books are classified into two major groups: **fiction** and **nonfiction** books. Each group is classified in a different way.

Fiction

Fiction books contain stories that an author has imagined or invented. These books are arranged on the shelves alphabetically by the author's last name and are usually marked with an *F* for fiction on the spine.

Nonfiction

Nonfiction books are books that are true and factual. They can help you to learn about any subject. Nonfiction books are classified according to the Dewey Decimal System. This system was originated by the famed American librarian, Melvil Dewey. The Dewey Decimal System classifies all books by number in one of ten major categories:

	The Dewey Decimal System
000–099	**General Works** (encyclopedias, almanacs, etc.)
100–199	**Philosophy** (conduct, personality, psychology, etc.)
200–299	**Religion** (the Bible, mythology, theology)
300–399	**Social Science** (economics, law, education, government)
400–499	**Language** (languages, grammars, dictionaries)
500–599	**Science** (mathematics, chemistry, physics, biology, etc.)
600–699	**Useful Arts** (farming, cooking, sewing, nursing, radio, television, business, gardening)
700–799	**Fine Arts** (music, painting, acting, photography, sports)
800–899	**Literature** (poetry, plays, essays)—not fiction
900–999	**History** (biography, travel, geography)

The Dewey Decimal System is a highly organized system for classifying books. Each major section is divided into smaller categories. By looking at the list on the left below, you can see how the 900–999 History section is further divided. Each of the divisions within the 900 History category is then subdivided to become even more detailed, as in the list on the right.

900	History		970	North America
910	Geography, travel, description		971	Canada
			972	Middle America
920	Biography		973	United States
930	Ancient history		974	Northeastern states
940	Europe		975	Southeastern states
950	Asia		976	South central states
960	Africa		977	North central states
970	North America		978	Western states
980	South America		979	States of the Great
990	Other places			Basin and Pacific Slope

These divisions and subdivisions of the Dewey Decimal System make it possible for all of the books on one subject to be put on the library shelves together so that you can find them easily.

Call Numbers

The **call number** is an organized sequence of numbers and letters printed on the spine of a book. The call number helps you to identify a book. Books are arranged on the shelves according to the details included in their call numbers. This arrangement makes it easier for you to find the book you need. The following example identifies the parts of a call number.

Book: *Bicycling*
Author: Nancy Neiman Baranet

Call number: **796.6**
B 225 b

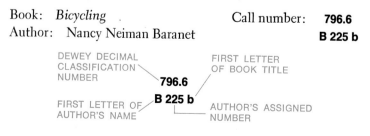

DEWEY DECIMAL CLASSIFICATION NUMBER

FIRST LETTER OF BOOK TITLE

796.6
B 225 b

FIRST LETTER OF AUTHOR'S NAME

AUTHOR'S ASSIGNED NUMBER

Books are first arranged by the Dewey Decimal number on the top line of the call number. Then, within each classification number, the books are arranged by the first letter of the author's last name.

Both the Dewey Decimal number and the call number identify books as precisely as possible in order to make it easier for you to find them. Within this system, there are three sections that deserve special mention:

Biography. Biographies and autobiographies are nonfiction books classified together and shelved in a special section of the library. The class numbers reserved for biography are 920 and 921.

> **920** This class number is reserved for collective biographies. These are books that contain the life stories of more than one person. The call number for a collective biography is 920, plus the initial of the author's or editor's last name.

For example: *Five Artists of the Old West* by Clide Hollmann

Call number: 920
H

> **921** This class number is used for individual biographies and autobiographies. These books are arranged differently on the shelves. They are arranged alphabetically by the last name of the *person written about*. For this reason, the call number is composed of 921 and the initial of the last name of the person the book is about. For example, the call number for a biography about Benjamin Franklin would be: 921
> F

Reference Books. Reference books of particular types or on specific subjects are also shelved together, with the letter R above the classification number: R
423.1
D56

Fiction. Fiction books are arranged on the shelves alphabetically by the author's last name. For this reason, fiction books are labeled with an *F* on the top line and the first initial of the author's last name on the second line along with the author number and the initial of the first word of the title. This is especially important when the author has written more than one book.

The Outsiders   F
by S. E. Hinton   H666O

Short Story Collections. Most libraries keep the fiction books that contain several short stories in a separate section. They are usually marked with *SC*, which stands for "Story Collection." The initial of the author's or editor's last name is placed below the SC. The books are arranged alphabetically by the author's or editor's name. Here is an example:

SC   *Journey to Another Star and Other Stories*
E   by Roger Elwood

Exercises The Classification and Arrangement of Books

A. Using the Dewey Decimal System on page 184, assign the correct classification number to each of the following.

1. *Skylab, Pioneer Space Station*, Wm. G. Helder
2. *You and Your Feelings*, Eda J. LeShan
3. *Inside Jazz*, James Lincoln Collier
4. *The Right To Remain Silent*, Milton Meltzer
5. *Understanding Photography*, George Sullivan
6. *Plays for Great Occasions*, Graham DuBois
7. *Hieroglyphs for Fun*, Joseph and Lenore Scott
8. *Insects as Pets*, Paul Villiard
9. *Dictionary of Mis-information*, Tom Beunaur
10. *We, the Chinese*, Deirdre Hunter

B. Each of these books belongs in one of the special categories of *biography, collective biography,* or *short story collection.* After reading each title, assign it the proper call number code.

1. *Record-Breakers of the Major Leagues,* Lou Sabin
2. *Carly Simon,* Charles and Ann Morse
3. *Masters of Modern Music,* Melvin Berger
4. *The Phantom Cyclist and Other Short Stories,* Ruth Ainsworth
5. *Driven to Win: A. J. Foyt,* Mike Kupper
6. *Americans in Space,* Ross Olney
7. *Annie Sullivan, A Portrait,* Terry Dunnahoo
8. *Men and Machines; Ten Stories of Science Fiction,* Robert Silverberg

C. Go to your school library. List these headings on your paper: *Fiction, Nonfiction, Biography, Reference,* and *Magazines.* Under each heading, list three titles and authors of books and materials that you would be interested in using.

Part 2 Using the Card Catalog

The **card catalog** is a cabinet of small drawers in which a card for each book is filed alphabetically in the library. In the card catalog, there are usually three cards for each book in the library: the *author card,* the *title card,* and the *subject card.* Each of these cards has the same information. However, each would be found in a different section of the card catalog. Look carefully at the following examples for the book *A Special Kind of Courage* by Geraldo Rivera.

The Author Card

If you happen to know only the name of the author and not the title of the book, you should use the card catalog to look up the name of the author. The author card will tell you the call number of the book you want to read. Also, the titles of all of the other books that the author has written and that are in that library will be listed on a separate card and filed alphabetically by the first word in each title. Cards for books *about* the author are filed *behind* his or her author cards. Here is an example of an author card for the book *A Special Kind of Courage*:

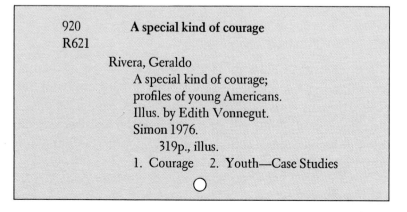

```
920      Rivera, Geraldo
R621

         A special kind of courage; profiles
         of young Americans.
         Illus. by Edith Vonnegut.
         Simon 1976.
             319p., illus.
         1. Courage    2. Youth—Case Studies
                       ○
```

The Title Card

When looking up the title of a book in the card catalog, remember that *A*, *An* and *The* do not count as first words in a title. Here is the title card for *A Special Kind of Courage*:

```
920           A special kind of courage
R621

         Rivera, Geraldo
             A special kind of courage;
             profiles of young Americans.
             Illus. by Edith Vonnegut.
             Simon 1976.
                 319p., illus.
             1. Courage    2. Youth—Case Studies
                           ○
```

The Subject Card

When you want to find resources on a particular subject, the best approach is to look up the subject in the card catalog. A subject card for the book A *Special Kind of Courage* will be found under the heading *Courage*, as in the following example:

920   **COURAGE**
R621

       Rivera, Geraldo
         A special kind of courage;
       profiles of young Americans.
       Illus. by Edith Vonnegut.
       Simon 1976.
         319p., illus.
       1. Courage   2. Youth—Case Studies

Notice that all three types of catalog cards (author, title, subject) give the same information. This information includes the following:

1. The call number.

2. The title, author, publisher, and date of publication.

3. The number of pages and a listing of special features, such as illustrations, index, maps, etc.

Often the card will also provide a brief description of the material in the book and a listing of other catalog cards for the book. Pay particular attention to the use of capitalization on the catalog cards. Only proper names and the first word of the title are capitalized. To find the title, look at the entry immediately following the author's name.

Cross-Reference Cards

When you look up a subject you will sometimes find a card that reads *See* or *See also*. The "See" card refers you to another subject heading in the catalog that has the information you want. For example, this "See" card tells you that the library catalogs all books on cars under the subject heading of *transportation*.

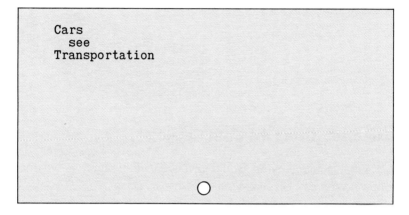

```
Cars
   see
Transportation




                    O
```

The "See also" card refers you to other subjects closely related to the one you are interested in. This card will help you to find a variety of information on the topic. A "See also" card will look like this:

```
        COOKING
           see also
     Appetizers
     Barbecue cookery
     Casserole cookery
     Food as gifts
     Frying
     Microwave cookery
     Salads
     Sandwiches
     Soups
     also names of individual foods, e.g., Rice
                    O
```

Guide Cards

Guide cards are placed in the card catalog to help guide you to the correct place in the alphabet for the word you are looking for. These cards extend above the other cards, and they have letters or general headings on them. For example, if you were looking up *housing* in the catalog drawer, you would look between the guide cards *Hob* and *How*.

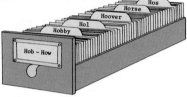

Exercises Using the Card Catalog

A. What subject cards would give you information about the following topics? Discuss your answers in class.

1. How to make a film
2. Backpacking in Maine
3. Records of the Super Bowl
4. Careers in medicine
5. How to play tennis
6. Designing stained glass
7. The early history of soccer
8. How to refinish furniture

B. Use the card catalog to find the title, author, call number, and publication date of each of the following books.

1. A book about rock music
2. A book of detective stories
3. A book about Pelé
4. A book about astronomy
5. A book on flags
6. A book of Christmas plays
7. A book about aquariums
8. A book about newspapers

C. Using the card catalog, list the title, author, call number, and publication date of all resources about two of the following:

1. Babe Didrikson
2. A career as a cartoonist
3. Hank Aaron
4. Franklin D. Roosevelt
5. Space exploration
6. A career as a dentist

Part 3   Using Reference Materials

Every library has either a reference room or a reference section. It is here that you will find a variety of reference materials, including dictionaries; encyclopedias; pamphlets, handbooks, and catalogs; almanacs and yearbooks; atlases; biographical reference books; and magazines. Each of these reference books is used for a certain purpose, and each has its own particular organization. Some offer you very general information about a topic while others are very specific and detailed.

Learning to use the many different reference books that are available will enable you to find the detailed, up-to-date information you need for a thorough report on any subject.

Dictionaries

General Dictionaries.   The dictionary is one of the best and most convenient general references you can use. A dictionary gives you the spelling, pronunciation, and meanings of a word, as well as brief information about such subjects as people, places, abbreviations, and foreign terms.

> **Unabridged Dictionaries.** These are the largest and most complete dictionaries. They contain well over 250,000 words, and give the complete history of each word and every definition and use for that word.

> **Abridged Dictionaries.** These dictionaries are often called "desk" or "collegiate" dictionaries. They contain about 130,000 to 150,000 words. They contain the information you would normally need about spellings, pronunciations, definitions, and matters of usage. In addition, they usually provide special sections that contain such information as biographical and geographical references.

> On the next page is a list of frequently used abridged dictionaries.

General Dictionaries

The American Heritage Dictionary of the English Language
The Random House Dictionary of the English Language
Thorndike-Barnhart Dictionary
Webster's New World Dictionary of the American Language

Pocket Dictionaries. These dictionaries are very limited in the number of words they contain. They should be used mainly to check the spelling of ordinary words or to give you a quick definition of an unfamiliar word.

Dictionaries About Your Language. Another group of dictionaries contains information about specific aspects of the English language, such as synonyms, antonyms, rhymes, and slang. These dictionaries have limited but specific uses.

Abbreviations Dictionary
Brewer's Dictionary of Phrase and Fable
A Dictionary of Slang and Unconventional English
A Dictionary of Word and Phrase Origins (3 volumes)
Mathew's Dictionary of Americanisms
The New Roget's Thesaurus in Dictionary Form
The Oxford Dictionary of English Etymology
Roget's International Thesaurus
Wood's Unabridged Rhyming Dictionary

The *thesauruses* that are included in the language dictionary list above serve a special purpose. A **thesaurus** is a dictionary of words that have similar meanings. It is sometimes called a dictionary of synonyms. By using a thesaurus when you write, you will be able to use words that convey the exact meaning you need, and you will avoid repeating already overused words.

Dictionaries on Specific Subjects. There are also many dictionaries that deal with specific subjects, such as music, geography, medicine, and science. The following list includes the names of many of these dictionaries. There are far too many to list here, so check to see what your library offers.

Specific-Subject Dictionaries

Compton's Illustrated Science Dictionary
Dictionary of American History (5 volumes)
Dictionary of Sports
Harvard Dictionary of Music
An Illustrated Dictionary of Art and Archaeology
Mathematical Dictionary
Webster's Biographical Dictionary

Encyclopedias

An encyclopedia contains general articles on nearly every known subject. This information is organized alphabetically into volumes. There are guide words at the top of each page to help you find information. Each set of encyclopedias also has an index, which you should check before looking for your information. The index is usually in the last volume of the encyclopedia. The following encyclopedias are used frequently by young people.

General Encyclopedias

Collier's Encyclopedia (24 volumes)
Compton's Encyclopedia (26 volumes)
Encyclopaedia Britannica (29 volumes)
Encyclopedia Americana (30 volumes)
World Book Encyclopedia (22 volumes)

The library also has many encyclopedias that contain information on specific subjects. Here are some of them:

Encyclopedias on Specific Subjects

The Baseball Encyclopedia
Better Homes and Gardens Encyclopedia of Cooking

The Encyclopedia of American Facts and Dates
Encyclopedia of Animal Care
Encyclopedia of Careers and Vocational Guidance
Encyclopedia of World Art (15 volumes)
Family Life and Health Encyclopedia (22 volumes)
The Illustrated Encyclopedia of Aviation and Space
The Mammals of America
Popular Mechanics Do-It-Yourself Encyclopedia
   (16 volumes)

This list is by no means complete. You should check your library to see the many kinds of encyclopedias that are available.

Exercises Using the Dictionary and the Encyclopedia

A. To answer the following questions, first determine whether you should use a dictionary or an encyclopedia. Then answer each question, and list the title of the reference book you used.

1. How many different kinds of rhinoceroses are there?
2. Where are these three colleges: *Monmouth, Hollins, Simpson*? Which is the oldest?
3. How many different methods of gold mining are there?
4. When was the French painter Henri Matisse born?
5. Where exactly is the Mason-Dixon line?
6. How are diamonds mined?
7. What are the chief events in the life of Neil Armstrong?
8. What are four synonyms for the word *meager*?
9. How do you draw the symbol for the Greek word *delta*?
10. Who discovered the Hawaiian Islands?

B. Using either your dictionary or thesaurus, answer the following questions. Write the name of the resource you used after each answer.

1. Would you use a *serigraph* to cook dinner, or would you hang it on your wall?

2. What are five synonyms for the word *serious?*

3. From what language is the word *aardvark* derived? What does the translation of the word mean?

4. What are four synonyms for the word *wet?* What is an appropriate noun for each synonym to describe?

5. Do you have a *palaestra* at your school?

6. What are five antonyms for the word *noisy?*

7. If you were a *plebe,* what would you be?

8. Does *quay* rhyme with *day, me,* or *buoy?*

9. What is the monetary value of a *krone?*

10. What words could replace the italicized words to make the following sentence more interesting?

He put on his *hat* and walked away *quickly.*

Almanacs and Yearbooks

Almanacs and yearbooks are published annually. They are most useful sources of information, facts, and statistics on current events and historical records of government, sports, entertainment, population, and many other subjects. The information in an almanac is not arranged in any particular order, so you will have to consult the index and the table of contents to find the location of the information you need. Here is a partial list of the most widely used almanacs and yearbooks:

Guinness Book of World Records
Information Please Almanac, Atlas, and Yearbook
World Almanac and Book of Facts
World Book Yearbook of Events

Atlases

An atlas is a reference book that contains many large, detailed maps of the world. It also contains other geographical information, such as statistics about population, temperatures, oceans, and rainfall. Some atlases publish other information, so it is a good idea to study the table of contents and any directions given to the reader before you try to use an atlas. The following is a list of reliable atlases:

Atlas of World History
The Britannica Atlas
Collier's World Atlas and Gazetteer
Goode's World Atlas
National Geographic Atlas of the World
Webster's Atlas with Zip Code Directory

Biographical References

Both a dictionary and an encyclopedia will give you information about people. However, the best references to use when you need detailed information about a person are biographical references. They are specific subject books that deal only with information about people. Here are a few.

Contemporary Authors
Current Biography
Dictionary of American Biography
The International Who's Who
Who's Who
Who's Who in America
Who's Who in the West
Who's Who of American Women

Exercises Using Almanacs, Atlases, and Biographical References

A. Use both an almanac and an atlas to answer the following questions. List the reference you used after your answer.

1. What is the largest lake in the world?
2. What were the first words sent over the telegraph?
3. Who wrote the Pledge of Allegiance to the flag?
4. What is the depth of the Dead Sea?

5. What are the three largest islands in the Mediterranean Sea?

6. What is the address for the League of Women Voters?

7. How long is a day on the planet Jupiter?

8. What are the world's highest and lowest elevations?

9. What is the most popular breed of dog in the United States?

10. What is the distance from the earth to the moon?

B. Using a biographical reference, answer the following questions. After each answer, list the title of the reference you used to answer the question.

1. For what two things was Philip K. Wrigley famous?

2. For what is Bruce Jenner famous? Where and when was he born?

3. What well known book did Harper Lee write? Who starred in the movie version?

4. For what newspaper does Bob Woodward write? In what historical event was he involved?

5. Jacques Cousteau is the co-inventor of what device?

6. What are the titles of three books written by Ray Bradbury?

7. How old was Dorothy Hamill when she won her Olympic Gold Medal?

8. Where and when was Bessie Smith born?

9. What is the name of a play written by Paul Zindel?

10. Who is Robyn Smith?

The Vertical File

Many libraries have a file cabinet in which they keep an alphabetical file of pamphlets, catalogs, handbooks, booklets, and clippings about a variety of subjects. Always check this vertical file when you are writing a report or looking for information, especially on careers.

Readers' Guide to Periodical Literature

The *Readers' Guide to Periodical Literature* is a monthly index of magazine articles listed alphabetically by subject and author. It is issued twice a month from September to June, and once a month in July and August. An entire year's issues are bound in one volume at the end of the year. There are two forms of the *Readers' Guide*. The unabridged edition indexes over 135 magazines and is used in high school and public libraries. The abridged edition of the *Readers' Guide* indexes 45 magazines and is generally used in junior high school libraries.

The *Readers' Guide* is a valuable source of information. It is important to read the abbreviation guide in the preface so that you will understand how to read each entry.

Exercises Using the *Readers' Guide*

A. Write the meanings of the following abbreviations used in the *Readers' Guide*:

Lib J	no	Je	Spr	bi-w	bibl	w
abr	m	cont	+	tr	il	supp

B. Use the excerpt from the *Readers' Guide* on page 201 to answer the following questions:

1. What magazines have articles on the subject of salt?
2. What issue of *Antiques* carried an article on the Boston Museum of Fine Arts? Was the article illustrated?
3. On what page of *Glamour* did the article "How to Ask for—and Get—a Raise" appear? In what issue did the article appear?
4. Who wrote an article on "How Not to Crumble under Criticism"? In what magazine did the article appear?
5. Give the complete magazine title for the following abbreviations:

   N Y Times Book R   *Field & S*   *Good H*

Excerpt from the *Readers' Guide*

SALARIES
How to ask for—and get—a raise [women's salaries] — *name of article*
S. S. Fader. il. Glamour 78:98 Jl '80
SALES promotion
See also
Trading stamps
SALESMEN and salesmanship — *"see also" cross-reference*
Boss as pitchman (chief executives appearing in commercials) A. M. Morrison. il. Fortune 102: 66-70+ — *volume number*
Ag 25 '80
New life of a salesman [L. J. Manara of American Cyanamid Company] H. D. Menzies. il por Fortune 102: 172-4+ Ag 11 '80 — *name of magazine*
On the road with a book salesman. N. R. Kleinfield. il N. Y. Times Bk R 86:3+ Ag 24 '80
SALESWOMEN
Cashing in on your spare time. G. L. Wohlner. McCalls 107:32+ Ag '80
SALINE, Carol — *author entry*
How not to crumble under criticism. il Redbook 155:19+ Ag '80
SALISBURY, Harrison E.
Code the Times can't crack [excerpt from Without fear or favor] Wash M 12:20-7 Jl/Ag '80 — *page reference*
SALMON, Larry
Textiles at the Museum of Fine Arts, Boston. bibl il Antiques 118:278-84 Ag '80
SALMON
Is capelin key to salmon problems? [Atlantic salmon] J. Gibbs. il Outdoor Life 166:38 Ag '80
SALMON fishing — *subject entry*
Coho caper [stocking New Hampshire's Great Bay] S. J. Bodio. il por Outdoor Life 166:54-7 Ag '80
Dreamer. G. Hill. il Field & S 85:20+ Ag '80
SALT
Food-lover's guide to salt. Good H 191:164+ Ag '80 — *date of magazine*
SALT in the body
Go easy on sugar and salt! E. Scott. Seventeen 39:26+ — *author of article*
Ag '80
Sodium-induced elevation of blood pressure in the anephric state. P. Hatzinikolaou and others. bibl f il — *illustrated article*
Science 209:935-6 Ag 22 '80
SALT water fishing
Salt water. L. Kreh. See issues of Outdoor life — *"see" cross-reference*

201

Chapter 13

Interviews and Group Discussion

Most of us enjoy talking with other people. You talk to your friends because you have something to tell them or because they have something to tell you. This kind of talking you call *conversation*. Conversation plays an important part in your daily social life. It helps you to know people better.

Conversations can also have more specific purposes. You may need to interview someone in order to obtain new information for a report you are writing. You and several others may need to have a group discussion to plan a project you are working on. Both interviewing and group discussion are forms of conversation with specific purposes.

This chapter will help you improve your interviewing skills and your group discussion skills.

Part 1 Interviewing Others

An interview is a special kind of conversation in which the purpose is either to *gather information* or to *supply information*. An interview gives people the opportunity to exchange questions and answers for a specific purpose. At times when you need to gather information for a report, interviewing a knowledgeable person will be very helpful. At other times, such as when you are applying for a job, you will be the one supplying most of the information.

Although an interview is basically conversational, it is more tightly organized than a casual conversation because it has a specific purpose. In order to make your interview a successful one, follow the guidelines on page 205.

Exercises Planning an Interview

A. List five purposes for which you might conduct interviews in connection with your classwork or extracurricular activities. Name an appropriate person to be interviewed for each purpose.

B. Choose one of the interviews you selected in the first exercise and make a list of ten questions as a guide for an interview.

Part 2 Group Discussion

Group discussion is an easy way to find an answer to a problem, to come up with a new idea, or simply to exchange information. This discussion can be either formal or informal, depending on the subject and purpose of the discussion.

There are two basic types of group discussion: **informal group discussion** and **formal group discussion.** It is important that you know which kind of discussion you are involved in because each has a specific purpose and a certain procedure to follow.

Guidelines for Conducting Interviews

1. **Plan the interview carefully.**

   a. Choose a person who has special knowledge or interesting opinions about the subject on which you are reporting.

   b. Make a definite appointment by arranging a time and date that is convenient for the person being interviewed. When you request an interview, be sure to identify yourself and explain why you want the interview.

   c. Do some basic research about the subject so you can ask intelligent questions.

   d. Prepare clear, specific questions in advance so that you are sure to get the information you need.

2. **Make a good impression.**

   a. Arrive for your interview on time.

   b. Introduce yourself and restate your purpose for the interview.

   c. Be ready to ask your questions, one at a time. If the person being interviewed wants to just talk about the subject, you may need to save your questions until the end, unless the person has already answered them.

   d. Be a good listener. Keep your attention on the speaker and what he or she is saying. The person may add some information that you hadn't thought of before.

   e. At the end of the interview, be sure to thank the person.

3. **Get the correct facts.**

   a. Take notes, especially on names and figures. Make the notes brief so that you are not writing continually while the person is talking.

   b. If you want to quote the person, be sure to ask permission.

   c. Go over your notes as soon as possible after the interview and write your report while the information is still fresh in your mind.

Informal Group Discussion

An informal group discussion usually takes place as soon as a problem or the need for a decision arises. Consider the following situations.

> What would you do if your family has decided to go on a vacation, but you all want to go to different places?
>
> What would you do if your intramural team has to decide on the best day and time to practice together?

The best solution to these problems is to have an informal discussion. Why? Because you need to exchange your ideas and talk about the pros and cons of each idea for the purpose of arriving at a decision or plan of action that satisfies the group.

Most discussions in which you participate are informal. They usually occur spontaneously, so you don't have to prepare for them. The subjects you discuss are usually those that members of the group know something about from their common knowledge or experience. This is why informal discussions are often organized by the people involved in them.

Sometimes a class or club will break into small informal groups so that everyone will have a chance to express his or her ideas in a shorter period of time. When this method is used, you may need to select a temporary leader to help keep the discussion organized so that your purpose is accomplished.

Even though informal discussion may seem like a friendly conversation, it is more organized and has a specific purpose.

Informal Discussion	
Subjects	General knowledge
Preparation	Not required
Organization	Small groups with no audience; a temporary leader may be selected.
Purpose	To exchange ideas in order to make a group decision or plan of action.

Formal Group Discussion

A formal discussion requires more preparation and organization than an informal discussion does. Consider these topics:

Should space exploration be continued?

Is a college education necessary to achieve success?

You may know something about each of the preceding topics, but how much of what you know is only opinion and how much is fact? If you were asked to discuss one of these topics, you would first have to do some research. A formal discussion requires preparation.

Another major difference between the informal and the formal discussion is the subject to be discussed. Generally, the subject of a formal discussion is either assigned to you or is selected by your group according to the needs or interests of the audience. It is important to be prepared.

The formal discussion is highly organized. First, one person is selected to be chairperson. The chairperson states the problem or subject, directs the discussion, makes sure that everyone has a chance to speak, and keeps the discussion moving.

Each member of the group must present his or her information. Use the many references that are available in your library. The members of your group should freely exchange ideas based on the information you have prepared. In this way, both the members of the group and the audience will learn more.

Formal Discussion

Subjects	Assigned or determined by the needs or interests of the audience.
Preparation	Very important; researched facts are needed.
Organization	A chairperson is selected; discussion is presented in front of an audience.
Purpose	To exchange ideas and information in order to inform the audience.

Exercises Informal and Formal Group Discussion

A. Look at the following list of subjects. Tell which you think should be discussed formally, and which should be discussed informally. Then explain the reasons for your decision.

> Which team will win the Super Bowl or World Series?
> Should schools be air-conditioned?
> Should people use seat belts?
> What is approximately the average time per day that teenagers spend watching TV?
> What should be the theme for the spring dance?
> What are some suggestions for a new school mascot?
> What are the best ways of conserving energy?
> How does Edgar Allan Poe create suspense in his short stories?

B. Try the following informal discussion. First, divide the class into three groups. Then follow these directions:

Calculate the average height in feet and inches of the members of your group. If you don't know your exact height, you may estimate. The group must agree on the answer and submit it to the teacher.

Once you have finished your calculations and the exercise, discuss the following questions about the exercise. This will help you to understand how a group is organized.

> Did anyone take over leadership?
> Was he or she elected by the group?
> Was a leader needed? Why or why not?
> What responsibility did each member have?
> Did anything slow down the group?
> How could the group solve the problem faster or better next time?

Part 3 Roles of Responsibility

From your own experience in different classes and organizations, you've probably noticed that when one person talks too much, nothing ever gets accomplished. Sometimes a simple discussion turns into an argument and still nothing gets accomplished. For a group discussion to be successful, everyone in the group must accept some responsibility.

When you are a member of either an informal discussion or a formal discussion, you will find that it will be much easier to achieve the purpose of the discussion if the following five roles of responsibility are accepted by members of the group. Each of these roles has a specific purpose.

The Chairperson or Temporary Leader

The role of chairperson or temporary leader carries a lot of responsibility. Each member of the group looks to the chairperson for guidance. The leader must know the subject well, be fair with all members, and see that the purpose of the discussion is accomplished. The chairperson:

1. Starts the discussion by defining the problem or by offering the first bit of information. For example:

"The purpose of our discussion is to decide the importance of using seat belts. There are many areas to consider in this issue, including safety, insurance benefits, government standards, and the results of manufacturers' tests. Barry, will you tell us what information you have found about this issue?"

"If we're going to discuss what gift the student council should buy the school, let's first make a list of things that are needed. I would like to suggest a new and larger trophy case."

2. Organizes the group into task forces if the subject involves a lot of material or if more than one decision is needed.

"Andrea will discuss the insurance benefits of using seat

belts, Paul will tell us about government standards that are required, and David and Sharon will discuss the results of the manufacturers' testing to provide safety precautions."

"Since we have enough money to buy two gifts and since our ideas fall into two main categories, let's divide into two groups to make our final decision."

3. Keeps the discussion on the subject so that time and ideas won't be wasted.

"I think we're talking too much about the performance of individual cars rather than the use of seat belts in those cars. Let's get back to the importance of using seat belts."

"Instead of complaining about what's wrong with the gym, how about some good suggestions for gifts to make it better?"

4. Makes sure that everyone has a chance to talk so that all information and ideas are exchanged.

"Andrea, I think now would be a good time for you to tell us about the insurance benefits people receive when they use seat belts."

"Ed, we haven't heard your ideas yet about what we should buy as a gift. What is your suggestion?"

The Initiator

In an active discussion, everyone should "initiate" new ideas and facts. However, some people will serve only as initiators, while others choose to serve in other roles. The initiator:

1. Offers new ideas for discussion.

"I think we should also consider the safety of a small child in a car seat that has a seat belt."

"My idea is that the student council should buy more typewriters for the library. Everyone could benefit from that gift."

2. Gives additional information to support someone else's idea.

"The *Newsweek* article I read agrees with your statement that it's just as important for people in the back seat to use seat belts as for those in the front seat."

"I agree with Ann. The library needs more typewriters. It seems they are always taken when my friends and I need to type a report."

The Clarifier

As the clarifier, you help other group members to support their information and to think of new ideas. The responsibility of the clarifier is to stimulate thought, help others to make their ideas and information clear, and to initiate new ideas. The clarifier:

1. Asks questions about other people's information.

"Sharon, how do we know that the test results for that manufacturer are true for all cars?"

"A new trophy case might be a good idea, but do you really think it's something the whole school would care about?"

2. Asks for additional information.

"Paul, do you have more current statistics to prove that the majority of people seriously hurt in car accidents were not wearing seat belts?"

"We have a lot of good ideas, but do we have to spend all of the money?"

The Summarizer

The summarizer keeps everyone in touch with what's happening during the discussion. It is important for you to listen carefully in order to keep track of the main points that have been made. Take notes during the discussion in order to keep the group informed of its progress. The summarizer:

1. States the main points that have been made so that the group is aware of its progress and what it still has to cover.

"So far we have discussed the government regulations for seat belts and the manufacturers' testing results showing why people should use seat belts. Who has some accident statistics that will bring us closer to our goal?"

"We know that we have enough money to buy more than one gift, and that we have several good ideas and the approximate price of each. Now we need to make a final decision about what to buy."

2. Points out areas of disagreement based on information from different sources or different group members. This helps to prevent arguments and helps the group to remember what is really important about the information.

"Government regulations state that there should be enough seat belts in every car for the number of people it can hold. But David's research shows us that several manufacturers put only two seat belts in the back seat."

"Joe says that a new trophy case is a good idea because the whole school is proud of its winning teams. But Ann says that the hall is always so crowded near the trophy case that most people don't ever bother to look at it."

The Evaluator

The evaluator states the conclusions of the group at the end of the discussion. During the discussion, the evaluator can choose another role and express his or her opinions.

The evaluator:

States the conclusions of the group at the end of the discussion.

"The information presented by this group shows that the government, car manufacturers, and insurance agencies are all interested in the safety that seat belts give. The information also proves that you are less likely to be hurt seriously in an accident and that your insurance is cheaper if you use seat belts. Therefore, it is important for you to use seat belts for your own safety."

"We have enough money to buy two gifts. Since most of the gifts were suggested for the gym and the library, our final decision is to buy six new gymnastic mats for the gym and two new typewriters for the library."

The more group discussion you participate in, the easier it will be to see the importance of the five roles of responsibility. You may find that you are especially good at one role, or you may want to change roles in different discussions. The five different roles help the group to achieve the purpose of the discussion.

Exercises Roles of Responsibility

A. Read each of the following statements and identify who is speaking: the chairperson or temporary leader, the initiator, the clarifier, the summarizer, or the evaluator.

1. "What we need to do is to divide into groups to get each part of this problem solved."
2. "Do you have more facts to prove that point?"
3. "Our final decision is to hold the Christmas dance on Friday, December 18, from 7:30 to 10:00 in the gym."
4. "I would recommend any of Jack London's books for good reading, especially *Call of the Wild*."
5. "So far we have three books that we all agree to recommend, but we still need two more titles."

B. With four or five other people, plan a formal discussion to present to your class. Choose a topic that interests all of you and that can be easily researched in your school library. Elect a chairperson and decide what information each person will be responsible for. Do your research carefully and keep accurate records of your sources. Present your discussion to the class.

Grammar and Usage

The Mechanics of Writing

A detailed Table of Contents of Sections 1–14 appears in the front of this book.

Section 1

The Simple Sentence

In conversation, you do not always have to use complete sentences. For example, you can answer a question with a word or two:

> Yes.   No.   My sister.

You can even ask a question without using what are usually considered complete sentences:

> Whose car?   Which girl?   What building?

In writing, you must use complete sentences to make your meaning clear, because the reader is not at hand to ask you to repeat, to explain, or to fill in words you have left out.

Sentences are clear when all the parts are properly put together. In this section you will study the different parts of sentences. You will also learn how to put these parts together most effectively.

Part 1 Sentences and Sentence Fragments

The surest way to get your meaning across is to use complete sentences.

A sentence is a group of words that expresses a complete thought.

By "complete thought" we mean the clear and entire expression of whatever you want to say. Which of the following groups of words expresses a complete thought?

1. Karen
2. Found a kitten
3. Karen found a kitten.

The third group of words expresses a complete thought. It is a complete sentence.

Sentence fragments do not express a complete thought. They are usually the result of carelessness. The writer's thoughts come faster than he or she can write them. The writer goes on to a new sentence without finishing the sentence he or she has started. The effect is something like this:

1. Last night a funny thing   2. We were sitting around the dinner table   3. Suddenly, a loud bang

The first and third groups of words above are sentence fragments.

Other fragments are the result of incorrect punctuation. Parts of sentences are written as if they were whole sentences:

1. About 3,300 feet down   2. In one of the world's deepest mines in Idaho   3. In the warmth and dampness
4. The miners have grown a lemon tree   5. About seven feet tall   6. Under light bulbs

Which of these six groups of words are sentences and which are fragments?

You can usually understand sentence fragments if they fit in with what a speaker has already said. You often use fragments in spoken conversation. You also use them in written conversation. In other writing, however, you should avoid sentence fragments.

Exercises Recognize sentences and fragments.

A. Number your paper from 1–10. For each group of words that is a sentence, write **S.** For each sentence fragment, write **F.** In class be ready to add words to change the fragments into sentences.

1. I saw a TV show last Sunday afternoon
2. The show was about dolphins
3. Actually a kind of small whale
4. Dolphins are very intelligent
5. Playful animals
6. Under the water in the big tank
7. It is very entertaining to watch the dolphins
8. Just for fun
9. Dolphins can hear very well
10. Because dolphins breathe air

B. Follow the directions for Exercise A.

1. During the relay race
2. A very high wind and then some flashes of lightning
3. Tracy Austin is one of several good young tennis players
4. A report about car fumes in an underground parking lot
5. Mr. Troy, owner of Troy and Brown Sports Shop
6. Whose work on the blackboard
7. Ella T. Grasso, the first woman governor of Connecticut
8. Martha Jane Canary was better known as "Calamity Jane"
9. The fire engines rushed down the street
10. No one else gave a report on solar energy

Part 2 Subjects and Predicates

Every sentence has two basic parts: the subject and the predicate. The **subject** tells whom or what the sentence is about. The **predicate** tells something about the subject.

| SUBJECT | PREDICATE |
(Who or what)	*(What is said about the subject)*
Hungry dogs	bark constantly.
A cold rain	fell all through the night.
My brother	laughed at his own mistake.

Each of these sentences expresses a complete thought. Each of them tells something (**predicate**) about a person, place, or thing (**subject**).

An easy way to understand the parts of a sentence is to think of the sentence as telling who did something, or what happened. The subject tells *who* or *what*. The predicate tells *did* or *happened*. You can divide sentences, then, in this way:

WHO OR WHAT	DID OR HAPPENED
The runner	crossed the finish line.
My parents	planted a garden.
The car	skidded on the wet pavement.
The bike	needs air in its tires.

The subject of the sentence names someone or something about which a statement is to be made.

The predicate of the sentence tells what is done or what happens.

Exercises Find the subjects and predicates.

A. Label two columns on your paper *Subject* and *Predicate.*
Write the proper words from each sentence in the columns.

EXAMPLE: My sister is fixing her bicycle.

SUBJECT   PREDICATE
My sister   is fixing her bicycle.

1. Gayle made limeade.
2. The Packers will play the Bears on Sunday.
3. Beth went bowling with Jenny.
4. My parents were fishing in Maine.
5. Heavy white smoke came out of the chimney.
6. Calligraphy is the art of fine handwriting.
7. I like short stories.
8. Rebecca learned to sail last summer.
9. Rugby/is a very rugged sport.
10. Rugby is a British sport similar to our football.

B. Follow the directions for Exercise A.

1. Monarch butterflies migrate every year.
2. Sugar cane is the chief product of Hawaii.
3. North Dakota produces barley, wheat, and flaxseed.
4. Kathy ate all the brownies.
5. The bike-a-thon raised money for muscular dystrophy.
6. Our homeroom will play intramural hockey tomorrow.
7. *Gone with the Wind* is the best movie I have ever seen on television.
8. Tim built a rock garden.
9. Photography is Elizabeth's main interest.
10. Our 4-H Club showed Black Angus cattle at the Ohio State Fair.

Part 3 Simple Subjects and Predicates

In every sentence there are a few words that are more important than the rest. These key words make the basic framework of the sentence. Study these examples.

> Hungry **dogs**   **bark** constantly.
> A cold **rain**   **fell** throughout the night.
> My **brother**   **laughed** at his own mistake.

The subject of the first sentence is *Hungry dogs*. The key word in this subject is *dogs*. You can say *dogs bark constantly*. You cannot say *hungry bark constantly*.

The predicate in the first sentence is *bark constantly*. The key word is *bark*. Without this word you would not have a sentence.

The key word in the subject of a sentence is called the simple subject. It is the subject of the verb.

The key word in the predicate is called the simple predicate. The simple predicate is the **verb.** Hereafter we will use the word *verb* rather than the phrase *simple predicate*.

Finding the Verb and Its Subject

The verb and its subject are the basic framework of every sentence. All the rest of the sentence is built around them. To find this framework, first find the verb. Then ask *who* or *what* before the verb. This will give you the subject of the verb.

> My brother's cookies melt in your mouth.
>
> *Verb:* melt
> *What melts?* cookies
> *Simple subject:* cookies

You will be able to tell a fragment from a sentence easily if you keep your eye on subjects and verbs.

A group of words without a subject makes you ask *Who did? What did? Who was? What was?* A group of words without a verb makes you ask *What about it? What happened?*

Fragment   Ran down the street (Who ran down the street?)
Sentence   *The child* ran down the street.

Fragment   A cold rain (What about it? What happened?)
Sentence   A cold rain *fell all day.*

Looking at the Sentence as a Whole

The **complete subject** is the simple subject plus any words that modify or describe it.

EXAMPLE: Hungry dogs bark constantly.

Hungry dogs is the complete subject. What is the simple subject?

The **complete predicate** is the verb plus any words that modify or complete its meaning. What is the complete predicate in the sentence above?

Diagraming Subjects and Predicates

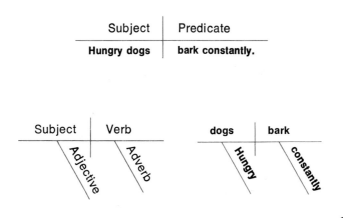

Subject	Predicate
Hungry dogs	**bark constantly.**

You will remember that adverbs may modify adjectives or other adverbs. Here is how they appear in a diagram.

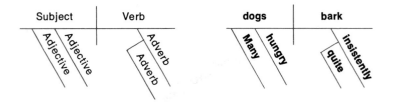

Exercises Find the verb and its subject.

A. Label two columns *Verb* and *Simple Subject.* Number your paper from 1–10. For each sentence, write the verb and its simple subject.

1. A crate of oranges arrived from Florida.
2. The new IBM computer printed our class schedules.
3. A tiny, gray kitten perched itself on our windowsill.
4. The bike in the garage has a flat tire.
5. The jubilant, cheering crowd rose to its feet.
6. The tall, wiry center sank the winning basket.
7. The locker next to the library belongs to Miki and me.
8. My sister Laura won an award at the art fair.
9. The woman in the pin-striped suit is my math teacher.
10. The aluminum cans in those plastic bags go to the recycling center.

B. Follow the directions for Exercise A.

1. The chestnut-brown thoroughbred trotted victoriously around the track.
2. An abandoned nest in the old oak tree became home for three little sparrows.
3. The corridor outside the cafeteria leads to the music room.

4. A shaggy white puppy wandered aimlessly into the gym.

5. The new booklet on bicycle rules explains the need for safety in cycling.

6. A tiny, tiger-striped kitten chased playfully after the huge ball of yarn.

7. The sound-slide show on energy conservation explained the importance of natural resources.

8. The friendly driver assisted the passenger off the bus.

9. A continuous, heavy snow delighted the skiers.

10. The drought reduced the waterfall to a trickle.

Part 4 The Parts of a Verb

A verb may consist of one word or of several words. It may be made up of a **main verb** and **helping verbs.** In naming the verb of any sentence, be sure to name all the words that it is made of.

HELPING VERBS	+	MAIN VERB	=	VERB
might have		gone		might have gone
will		see		will see
are		driving		are driving
could		go		could go

Sometimes the parts of a verb are separated from each other by words that are not part of the verb. In each of the following sentences, the verb is printed in red. The words in between are not part of the verb.

I **have** never **been** to Disney World.
We **did** not **see** the accident.
The bus **has** often **been** late.

Some verbs are joined with other words to make contractions. In naming verbs that appear in contractions, name only the verb. The word *not* is an adverb. It is never part of a verb.

	CONTRACTION	VERB
	hasn't (*has not*)	*has*
	weren't (*were not*)	*were*
	I've (*I have*)	*have*
we'd (*we had* or *would*)		*had* or *would*

Exercises Find the verb.

A. Number your paper from 1–10. List the verbs in the following sentences.

1. We have not gone to the lake once this summer.
2. This report has not been completed.
3. The buses often arrive late.
4. I have never been to Martha's Vineyard in Massachusetts.
5. Cheryl did not see *Rocky* or *Star Wars*.
6. The 747 will arrive at midnight.
7. The hockey team is practicing on the ice until 6 P.M.
8. Our class is going on a field trip next week.
9. The package may have been delivered to the wrong house.
10. I am going to a ski lodge next weekend.

B. Follow the directions for Exercise A.

1. We aren't giving our panel discussion today.
2. I don't really like Barry Manilow or Linda Ronstadt.
3. The ambulance had cautiously approached every intersection.
4. Jim and I will finish this job later.
5. It hasn't rained for a month.
6. Our play rehearsal wasn't very successful.
7. Raul was carefully walking around the fountain.
8. We haven't planted a flower garden this year.
9. My sister and I made a rock garden, however.
10. The counselors had quickly collected the test booklets.

Part 5 Subjects in Unusual Positions

Sentences Beginning with *There*

Many sentences begin with the word *there*. Sometimes *there* is used as an adverb modifying the verb to tell *where* something is or happens.

> There stood the boy. (The boy stood *there*.)
> There is our bus. (Our bus is *there*.)

In other sentences, *there* is only an introductory word to help get the sentence started.

> There is no candy in the machine. (No candy is in the machine.)
> There are some mistakes here. (Some mistakes are here.)

In diagraming sentences that begin with *there*, it is necessary to decide whether *there* is used as an adverb or whether it is simply an introductory word. When *there* modifies the verb, it is placed on a slant line below the verb. When *there* is an introductory word, it is placed on a straight line above the sentence line.

In most sentences beginning with *there*, the subject comes after the verb. To find the subject, first find the verb. Then ask *who* or *what*.

Exercises Find the verb and its subject.

A. Write down the simple subject and the verb in each sentence. Tell whether *There* is used as an adverb or as an introductory word.

1. There he goes.
2. There stood the trophy.
3. There they are.
4. There will be basketball practice tomorrow.
5. There go the runners.
6. There I sat.
7. There I waited in line for over an hour.
8. There will be a picnic tomorrow.
9. There was a sudden pause.
10. There will be pony races.

B. Follow the directions for Exercise A.

1. There goes the runner.
2. There is cheesecake for dessert.
3. There will be no school on Monday.
4. There is the lock for your bicycle.
5. There are plenty of napkins.
6. There might be a thunderstorm later tonight.
7. There is a swimming meet on Friday.
8. There came a chilly wind.
9. There will be an assembly at noon.
10. There are several students in line.

Other Sentences with Unusual Word Order

The usual order of words in a sentence is *subject–verb*. In many sentences, however, the subject comes after the verb or between parts of the verb. You have seen one example of this arrangement in sentences beginning with *there*. Here are some others.

1. Sentences beginning with *here*

Here is your hat. (Your hat is here.)
Here are the keys. (The keys are here.)

Unlike *there,* the word *here* is always an adverb telling *where* about the verb.

2. Questions

Are you leaving? (You are leaving?)
Has the mail come? (The mail has come?)

3. Sentences beginning with phrases or adverbs

Onto the field dashed the team. (The team dashed onto the field.)
Finally came the signal. (The signal finally came.)

To find the subject in a sentence with unusual word order, first find the verb. Then ask *who* or *what.*

> EXAMPLE: Here comes the parade.
>
> > *Verb:* comes
> > *Who* or *what comes?* the parade
> > *Subject:* parade

To diagram sentences with unusual word order, find the verb and its subject. Place them in their proper positions. Then place the modifiers where they belong.

Imperative Sentences

In imperative sentences, which state commands or requests, the subject is usually not given. Since commands and requests are always given to the person spoken to, the subject is *you.* Since the *you* is not given, we say that it is *understood.*

(*You*) Bring me the newspaper.
(*You*) Wipe your feet.

In the diagram of an imperative sentence, the subject is written in parentheses.

(You)	Have	patience

Exercises Find the verb and its subject.

A. Label two columns *Subject* and *Verb*. Number your paper from 1–10 and write down the subject and verb for each sentence.

1. Hang on!
2. Are there two minutes left?
3. Did you read the article about bicycles?
4. Economy is one advantage of the bicycle.
5. Down the slopes raced the skiers.
6. Down came the rain.
7. Is our team in the play-offs?
8. There comes the bus.
9. On the porch hung several plants.
10. Have you seen that movie?

B. Follow the directions for Exercise A.

1. Are these books due today?
2. Out came the sun.
3. Here are the T-shirts for the Pep Club.
4. Have you heard the new Fleetwood Mac album?
5. All along the shoreline swimmers basked in the sun.
6. After the storm a beautiful rainbow appeared.
7. Over the phone came the reply.
8. Don't just stand there.
9. Here comes the mail.
10. Do you like frozen yogurt?

Part 6 Objects of Verbs

Some verbs complete the meaning of a sentence without the help of other words. The action that they describe is complete.

The boys *came.*   We *are going.*

Some verbs, however, do not express a complete meaning by themselves. They need other words to complete the meaning of a sentence.

Sue hit _____. (Hit what? Sue hit the *ball.*)
Jane raised _____. (Raised what? Jane raised the *window.*)

Direct Objects

The word that receives the action of a verb is called the **direct object** of the verb. In the sentences above, *ball* receives the action of *hit.* *Window* receives the action of *raised.*
Sometimes the direct object tells the *result* of an action.

We dug a *hole.*
Edison invented electric *lights.*

To find the direct object, first find the verb. Then ask *whom* or *what* after it.

Carlos saw the President.   Anne painted a picture.
  Verb: saw   *Verb:* painted
  Saw whom? President   *Painted what?* picture
  Direct object: President   *Direct object:* picture

A verb that has a direct object is called a **transitive verb.** A verb that does not have an object is called an **intransitive verb.** A verb may be intransitive in one sentence and transitive in another.

Intransitive   We were watching.
Transitive   We were watching the race.

Direct Object or Adverb?

Many verbs used without objects are followed by adverbs that tell *how, where, when,* or *to what extent.* These words are adverbs that go with or modify the verb. Do not confuse them with direct objects. The direct object tells *what* or *whom.*

To decide whether a word is a direct object or a modifier of the verb, decide first what it tells about the verb. If it tells *how, where, when* or *to what extent,* it is an adverb. If it tells *what* or *whom,* it is a direct object.

> Don worked *quickly.* (*quickly* is an adverb telling *how.*)
> Sue worked the *problem.* (*problem* is a direct object.)

Exercise Recognize direct objects and adverbs.

Number your paper from 1–10. Decide what the italicized word is in each sentence. Write *Adverb* or *Direct Object.*

1. Several guests left *early.*
2. Someone left a red *sweater.*
3. The band plays *often.*
4. The band plays *well.*
5. The band plays good *music.*
6. I liked that delicious *pie.*
7. Please return *soon.*
8. Please return my *camera.*
9. Michele tried *again.*
10. Mark tried the *door* again.

Indirect Objects

Some words tell *to whom* or *for whom* something is done. Other words tell *to what* or *for what* something is done. These words are called the **indirect objects** of the verb.

> We gave **Mary** some *money.* (gave *to* Mary)
> Anne knitted **Kim** a *sweater.* (knitted *for* Kim)
> We gave the **boat** a *coat* of paint. (gave *to* the boat)

In these sentences, the words in red type are the indirect objects. The words in italics are the direct objects.

The words *to* and *for* are never used with the indirect object. The words *to* and *for* are prepositions. Any noun or pronoun following *to* or *for* is its object.

> They baked *me* a cake. (*me* is the indirect object of *baked*.)
> They baked a cake for *me*. (*me* is the object of the preposition *for*.)

In a diagram, the direct object is placed on the main line after the verb. Notice that the line between verb and object does not go below the main line.

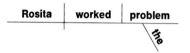

The indirect object is placed below the main line.

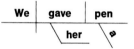

Exercises Find the sentence parts.

A. Number your paper from 1–10. Label three columns *Verb*, *Indirect Object*, and *Direct Object*. Fill in the parts that you find for each sentence. After each verb write *Transitive* or *Intransitive*.

> EXAMPLE: Todd drew us a very rough map.

VERB	INDIRECT OBJECT	DIRECT OBJECT
drew (transitive)	us	map

1. I brought Cindy her scarf.
2. We gave our dog a good bath.
3. Maria made us a Mexican dinner.
4. Paul gave the beans a stir.

233

5. I hooked Mom a rug for her birthday.
6. The principal gave the co-captains the trophy.
7. Will you bring me some ice?
8. The sun sparkled on the waves.
9. Brenda must have hoed the garden.
10. Pat got a digital watch for Christmas.

B. Follow the directions for Exercise A.

1. Our class cleaned the courtyard.
2. Jill loaned me her thesaurus.
3. Steve gave Paula the tickets.
4. Judy was whistling an old Beatles' song.
5. Uncle Don gave the cactus to me.
6. Did you buy me some more film?
7. Liz shouted down the stairs.
8. Did you adjust the thermostat?
9. Please get me some stamps.
10. We fixed the antenna for my CB.

C. Look at the verbs in the following sentences. If the verb has no object, write another sentence using the same verb and an object. If the verb already has an object, write a sentence with the same verb but no object.

EXAMPLE: An old highway looped around the mining town.

Verb: *looped* (no object)
Bob looped the rope twice.

1. Dad had already packed.
2. We reached the airport about 2 o'clock.
3. I ran a mile without stopping.
4. The plane climbed another 2000 feet.
5. Elizabeth painted the garage door.

Part 7 Predicate Words and Linking Verbs

Some verbs do not express action. They tell of a state of being. These verbs link the subject of a sentence with a word or group of words in the predicate. Because they link the subject with some other word or words, they are often called **linking verbs.**

> He *is* a doctor.
> They *are* good swimmers.

The most common linking verb is the verb *to be*. The verb can have many forms. Study these forms of *to be* to make sure you recognize them:

be	been	is	was
being	am	are	were

The verbs *be, being,* and *been* can also be used with helping verbs. Here are some examples:

might be	is being	have been
could be	are being	might have been
will be	was being	would have been

The words linked to the subject by a linking verb like *be* are called **predicate words.** There are **predicate nouns, predicate pronouns,** and **predicate adjectives.**

Renée is *president.* (predicate noun)

This is *she.* (predicate pronoun)

Bill was *happy.* (predicate adjective)

Notice how the subjects and the predicate words in the above sentences are linked by *is* or *was.*

Here are some other common linking verbs:

seem   feel   become   look
appear   taste   grow   sound

Like *be*, these verbs can have various forms (*seems, appears, felt*), or they can be used with helping verbs (*will appear, could feel, might have become*).

The *music* sounded *beautiful*. (predicate adjective)

The *plants* grew *taller*. (predicate adjective)

I have become an *expert*. (predicate noun)

In diagrams, the predicate words appear on the main line with subjects and verbs. Note that the line between the verb and the predicate word slants back toward the subject.

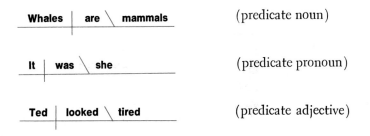

Whales | are \ mammals	(predicate noun)
It | was \ she	(predicate pronoun)
Ted | looked \ tired	(predicate adjective)

Exercises Find predicate words and linking verbs.

A. As your teacher directs, point out the subject, linking verb, and predicate word in each sentence.

1. Snakes are reptiles.
2. The singing sounded good.
3. This is he.
4. The flowers looked wilted.
5. Has Kathy been sick?

6. The driver was angry.
7. The house seemed empty.
8. Karen felt lonesome.
9. Was it she?
10. Sue became chairperson.

B. Make four columns on your paper. Number from 1–12 down the columns. Label the columns *Subject, Verb, Direct Object,* and *Predicate Word.* Find these parts in the sentences below and place them in the right columns.

1. Our new puppy has behaved badly.
2. We left him in his pen today.
3. We left him some water.
4. He looked miserable.
5. On returning we were angry.
6. The puppy had spilled the water.
7. He had escaped from the pen.
8. He had chewed the sofa pillow.
9. Feathers covered the floor.
10. The puppy looked very happy.
11. He had taught us a lesson.
12. We will never leave him inside alone again.

Part 8   Compound Sentence Parts

The word *compound* means "having two or more parts."

Every part of the sentences we have studied in this chapter can be compound—subjects, verbs, direct objects, indirect objects, and predicate words.

If the compound form has only two parts, there is usually a conjunction (*and, or, but*) between them. If there are three or more parts, the conjunction usually comes between the last two.

Compound Subjects

The *dog* and the *cat* are good friends.
Soap, *butter*, and *potatoes* spilled from the bag.

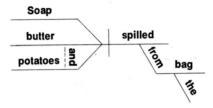

Compound Verbs

The skier *swerved*, *dodged*, and *careened* down the icy slope.
Dr. Rosen *called* and *asked* for you.

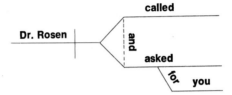

Compound Objects of Verbs

We saw the *President* and his *family*. (direct objects)
The boss showed *Nancy* and *me* the shop. (indirect objects)

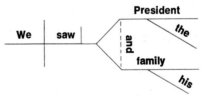

Compound Predicate Words

The backpackers were *tired* and *hungry*. (predicate adjectives)
The winners were *Rebecca* and *Sherry*. (predicate nouns)

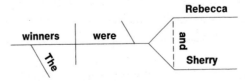

Exercises Find the compound sentence parts.

A. As your teacher directs, show the compound parts in the following sentences. Tell whether they are compound subjects, verbs, objects, or predicate words.

1. The water was cool and refreshing.
2. Last weekend we skated and skied.
3. The engine hesitated and then purred.
4. Tara and Charlene painted the scenery.
5. Jeff and I washed and waxed the car.
6. We brought Fritos and popcorn to the picnic.
7. Did you give Cindy the posters and the flyers?
8. Marla and Robin made hanging planters in shop class.
9. We suspended the balloons and the prizes from the ceiling.
10. The gymnasts showed discipline and control.

B. In each of the following sentences, make a compound of the part noted in parentheses.

EXAMPLE: We unpacked the crates. (*direct object*)
We unpacked the crates and the cartons.

1. Jon carried the groceries into the house. (*direct object*)
2. The pizza was spicy! (*predicate word*)
3. Did you remember the Kleenex? (*direct object*)
4. There are pickles over here. (*subject*)
5. The hypnotist's performance was fascinating. (*predicate word*)
6. Mrs. Lopez gave Janelle a bracelet. (*direct object*)
7. Next came the President's car. (*subject*)
8. Linda fixed the handlebars. (*direct object*)
9. Mr. and Mrs. Karnatz gave Meredith a job at the store. (*indirect object*)
10. There are ten divers competing. (*subject*)

Part 9 Avoiding Run-on Sentences

A **run-on sentence** is two or more sentences written incorrectly as one. These are examples:

> Incorrect *(run-on)* Tony made deep-dish pizza it tasted great.
>
> Correct Tony made deep-dish pizza. It tasted great.
>
> Incorrect *(run-on)* Danielle went to the museum, her sister did not go.
>
> Correct Danielle went to the museum. Her sister did not go.

As you can see, a run-on confuses readers. It doesn't show clearly where one idea ends and another one begins. You can avoid run-ons by using a period or other end mark to show the reader where each complete thought ends.

Exercise Correct the run-on sentences.

Rewrite the following run-on sentences correctly.

1. Laurie sings with the chorus, she is an alto.
2. Britt rides horses she entered a show.
3. I answered the phone somebody laughed and hung up.
4. Did you see that TV program, wasn't it good?
5. Marissa plays the violin Carlos plays the cello.
6. I like science fiction movies, *Alien* was my favorite.
7. The helicopter landed, four men stepped onto the field.
8. Loggers cut down trees then the logs are shipped to the mill.
9. Marcus races on his ten-speed he works out every day.
10. Jenny joined the hockey team, she is a good forward.
11. The Bombers have two outs, Beth is at bat.
12. The sailors saw stormy skies, they turned back.
13. Sit in the balcony you'll see best there.
14. Our class studied pollution, we cleaned up the pond.
15. Look for a green Chevy, that's my mom's car.

Additional Exercises — Review

The Simple Sentence

A. Recognize sentences and sentence fragments.

Number your paper from 1–10. For each group of words that is a sentence, write **S.** For each sentence fragment, write **F.** In class, be ready to add words to change the fragments into sentences.

1. Because of the driving snow
2. A special track was designed and built for the skateboard races
3. A big wave broke over the side of the boat
4. Thousands of people along the parade route
5. Bill's new yellow car out in the driveway
6. A heavy gray sky over the lake
7. The coach explained the basic rules
8. A cheer from the grandstand
9. A helicopter over the traffic jam
10. Brownies and Dutch chocolate ice cream for dessert

B. Find complete subjects and complete predicates.

Number your paper from 1–10. Label two columns *Complete Subject* and *Complete Predicate*. Write the proper words in each column.

1. Rick caught the ball easily.
2. The atomic submarine surfaced before dawn.
3. A red-tailed hawk circled the field.
4. My uncle uses mulch on his tomato plants.
5. Our janitor was cleaning the basement.

6. A new apartment building was constructed near the shopping center.

7. They unloaded the elephants in the pouring rain.

8. My sister and I went canoeing on Sunday.

9. The tall brunette in the front row spiked the ball over the net.

10. You could hear the crickets outside the cabin.

C. Find the verb and its simple subject.

Number your paper from 1–10. Write the simple subject and the verb in each sentence. Tell whether *there* is used as an adverb or as an introductory word.

1. There is the library.
2. There will be band practice in the morning.
3. There is an MGB parked in the driveway.
4. There wasn't a cloud in the sky.
5. There was no play rehearsal today.
6. There was no more room in the stadium.
7. There will be a dance next Friday.
8. There sat the box by the bus stop.
9. There were only two commercials during the show.
10. There will be a slight delay before take-off.

D. Find the verb and its subject in unusual kinds of sentences.

Number your paper from 1–10. Label two columns *Subject* and *Verb*. Write down the subject and verb for each sentence.

1. Through the back door Jim and his dog scampered.
2. Over the hill the motorcyclists raced.
3. Did the rocket misfire?
4. Find the villain.
5. Here is the newspaper.
6. Out swarmed the bees.
7. Here are the results of the test.

8. Onto the field the marching band paraded.
9. Fire this ceramic vase in the kiln.
10. Did you read the editorial in the newspaper?

E. Recognize direct objects and adverbs.

Number your paper from 1–10. Decide what the italicized word is in each sentence. Write *Adverb* or *Direct Object* beside each number.

1. The telephone rang *loudly*.
2. The lightning flashed *overhead*.
3. Pelé scored the winning *goal*.
4. The crowd cheered *wildly*.
5. Paula lost her *wallet*.
6. The laundromat charges 50 *cents*.
7. My horse won *again*.
8. The newscaster smothered a *yawn*.
9. Mrs. Brock checked the *meter*.
10. Steve rose *quickly* from his chair.

F. Find the sentence parts.

Number your paper from 1–10. Label three columns *Verb*, *Indirect Object*, and *Direct Object*. For each sentence below fill in those parts that you find. After each verb write *Transitive* or *Intransitive*.

1. Two tugboats were pulling the barge through the canal.
2. The crowd gave the coach a big hand.
3. That cub scooped a fish out of the water.
4. Something is making a noise on the top shelf.
5. Write us a letter.
6. Sonia made Dad a lamp in shop class.
7. Mary threw the dog the Frisbee.
8. The center knocked the puck into the net.
9. I brought Chris her assignments from school.
10. I developed the film in the photo lab.

G. Find predicate words, linking verbs, and objects.

Number your paper from 1–10. Label four columns *Subject,
Verb, Direct Object,* and *Predicate Word.* Fill in the parts that
you find for each sentence. You will find either a direct object or
a predicate word in each sentence.

1. Nine men moved the piano.
2. The sky to the west looks strange.
3. The muffins in the oven smell delicious.
4. My mother canned peaches all morning.
5. The gulls on the beach faced the wind.
6. We picked apples from the orchard trees.
7. Their fishing boat weathered the storm.
8. From the airplane the toll road appeared empty.
9. The center snapped the ball to the quarterback.
10. The boughs on the mantle look lopsided.

H. Find the compound parts in a sentence.

As your teacher directs, show the compound parts in the
following sentences. Tell whether they are compound subjects,
verbs, objects, or predicate words.

1. Your backstroke is better and stronger.
2. Three monkeys and their trainers were juggling oranges.
3. Emily and Ken can walk on stilts.
4. The photography club furnished the doughnuts and cider.
5. A marathon runner must have experience and determination.
6. A landslide uprooted those trees and rocks.
7. The roadrunner looked fierce and determined.
8. The December wind was cold and biting.
9. The Ford Fiesta and the Chevy Chevette are American economy cars.
10. Laplanders and Finns traditionally hunt reindeer.

I. Avoid run-on sentences.

Pick out the run-on sentences in the following group and rewrite them correctly. If a sentence does not need to be rewritten, write *Correct*.

1. The train left early we missed it by five minutes.
2. The group of girls had a picnic in the park by the fountain.
3. We saw the magic show, the magician did terrific tricks.
4. Josh lives in a high-rise, his apartment is on the sixty-fifth floor.
5. The wind lifted my kite it stayed high for hours.
6. Lisa hung posters of Leif Garrett in her room.
7. Barry rode with Judith on a tandem bike.
8. This is the art museum it has a special exhibit of teenagers' art.
9. Call me tomorrow I'll be home all day.
10. Meredith took the bus to Yorkville with the other girls on the field hockey team.

Section 2

Using Nouns

Geologists, seeking oil or uranium, study samples of rock or soil. They can recognize different kinds of rock or soil at once, because most rocks and soils have been carefully analyzed and put into different classes.

Scholars have analyzed and classified the various elements of language. They have found that all the words used in sentences fall into certain groups or classes.

People can use words without knowing very much about these groups or classes. Skillful writers and speakers, however, have a good understanding of the groups or classes into which words fall.

In this section you will study in detail one very important group of words: **nouns.**

Part 1   What Are Nouns?

One important use of language is to name the people, places, and things around us. Words used to name are called **nouns.**

A noun is a word used to name a person, place, or thing.

The classes into which words are grouped are called **parts of speech.** Nouns are one of the most important parts of speech.

Nouns name all sorts of things. They name things you can see, such as horses, boats, and footballs. They name things you cannot see, such as feelings, beliefs, and ideas.

PERSONS	PLACES	THINGS
doctor	Spain	book
Kimberly	home	building
Michelle	Chicago	loyalty

Exercise Find the nouns.

Make three columns on a sheet of paper. Use these headings: (1) *Names of Persons,* (2) *Names of Places,* (3) *Names of Things.* Under the proper heading, list each noun in the following paragraph:

> An unusually strong earthquake occurred in China in 1976. Tremors from the quake were felt hundreds of miles away. In the severely damaged city of Tientsin, thousands of Chinese evacuated collapsing buildings. The industrial city of Tangshan was devastated, and its nearby mines were also damaged. An estimated 655,000 people lost their lives.

Proper Nouns and Common Nouns

Look at the drawings of dogs. How do the nouns differ from each other? How does *dog* differ from *Lucky?*

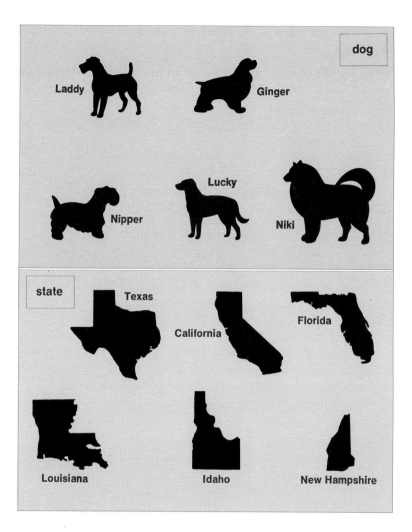

There are two kinds of nouns. A **common noun** is a name common to a whole group of things. *Dog* is a common noun. But the names *Laddy, Nipper,* and *Ginger* are names of individual dogs. They are **proper nouns.**

1. A common noun is the name of a whole group of persons, places, or things. It is a name that is common to the whole group.

2. A proper noun is the name of a particular person, place, or thing.

Look at the drawings of states on page 249. Which nouns are proper nouns? Why do you think so? Are there any common nouns in the picture?

Look at the drawings again. Read the nouns that are capitalized. Notice that the common nouns *dog* and *state* are not capitalized. Remember this rule:

A proper noun always begins with a capital letter.

Exercises Find common and proper nouns.

A. Make two columns on your paper. Label one column *Common Nouns* and the other *Proper Nouns*. Decide whether the nouns below are common or proper. Place each in the right column. Capitalize the proper nouns.

1. salt lake city, las vegas, town, atlanta, city
2. dancer, maria tallchief, martha graham, opera, beverly sills, luciano pavarotti
3. pamphlet, reader's digest, magazine, sports illustrated, seventeen
4. montana, kansas, state, indiana, region
5. crater lake, lagoon, gulf of mexico, white's pond, lake champlain
6. continent, africa, europe, peninsula, korea, italy
7. track meet, XXII olympic games, cincinnati reds, hockey, world series
8. mountain, andes, old smoky, mount popocatepetl, hills
9. artist, georgia o'keeffe, sculptor, alexander calder, louise nevelson
10. monument, mount rushmore, statue of liberty, building, empire state building

B. Write five sentences of your own, using at least one proper noun in each sentence.

Part 2 | Forming the Singular and Plural of Nouns

The noun *shoe* is singular. It stands for only one shoe. The noun *shoes* is plural. It stands for more than one shoe.

When a noun stands for one person, place, or thing, it is **singular**. When it stands for more than one person, place or thing, it is **plural**.

Forming Plurals

The first two rules below cover most English nouns. The other five rules deal with words that you use frequently.

1. To most singular nouns, add *s* to form the plural:

ropes   boots   books   desks

2. When the singular form ends in *s*, *sh*, *ch*, *x*, or *z*, add *es*:

glasses   bushes   coaches   boxes   buzzes

3. When a singular noun ends in *o*, add *s* to make it plural:

rodeos   studios   photos   Eskimos   solos   pianos

For a few words ending in *o*, preceded by a consonant, add *es*:

potatoes   heroes   cargoes   echoes   tomatoes

4. When the singular noun ends in *y* with a consonant before it, change the *y* to *i* and add *es*:

city—cities   lady—ladies   country—countries

If the *y* is preceded by a vowel (*a, e, i, o, u*), do not change the *y* to *i*. Simply add *s*:

toy—toys   play—plays   day—days

5. Some nouns ending in *f* simply add *s*:

beliefs   chiefs   dwarfs   handkerchiefs

Many words ending in *f* or *fe* change the *f* to *v* and add *es* or *s*. Since there is no rule to follow, these words have to be memorized. Here are some examples of such words:

thief—thieves	leaf—leaves	life—lives
shelf—shelves	half—halves	calf—calves
loaf—loaves	wife—wives	knife—knives

6. Some nouns have the same form for both the singular and plural. Memorize these:

deer	salmon	trout	sheep	moose
tuna	cod	pike	bass	elk

7. Some nouns form their plurals in special ways:

child—children	goose—geese	man—men
mouse—mice	ox—oxen	woman—women

Here is a dictionary entry for the word *knife*. Notice that the entry shows the plural, *knives*. Most dictionaries show the plurals of nouns if the plurals are formed in an irregular way.

---

plural
knife (nif) **n.,** *pl.* **knives** [O.E. *cnif:* for IE. base see KNEAD] **1.** a cutting or stabbing instrument with a sharp blade, single-edged or double-edged, set in a handle **2.** a cutting blade, as in a machine—**vt. knifed, knif'ing 1.** to cut or stab with a knife ☆**2.** [Colloq.] to use underhanded methods in order to hurt, defeat, or betray—☆**vi.** to pass into or through something quickly, like a sharp knife—☆**under the knife** [Colloq.] undergoing surgery —**knife'like' adj.**

When you are in doubt about plurals, consult a dictionary.

Exercises Form the plurals of nouns.

A. Write the plural of each of these nouns. Then use your dictionary to see if you are right.

1. church	6. dish	11. company	16. baby
2. brush	7. elk	12. watch	17. city
3. elf	8. sheep	13. bookshelf	18. mouse
4. wish	9. fox	14. chimney	19. witch
5. potato	10. tooth	15. lady	20. radio

B. All but one of the following sentences have at least one error in the spelling of the plural. Write the sentences correctly.

1. We placed all of the dishs on the benchs in the hallway.
2. Several different companys make CB radioes.
3. The thieves took several loaves of bread.
4. The babys were getting new tooths.
5. Several companys sell frozen mashed potatos.
6. First, cut the loafs in halves.
7. The deers were eating the green shoots on the bushs.
8. Use these brushs to paint the bookshelfs.
9. The larger boxes had scratchs on them.
10. My blue jeans are covered with patchs.

C. Follow the directions for Exercise B.

1. Both of those churchs will have rummage sales.
2. The kitchen shelfs were filled with dishs and glasses.
3. We sliced the tomatos in halfs.
4. Bunchs of grapes were heaped on the carts.
5. Echos of the music could be heard in all the rooms.
6. These are photos of horses, cows, oxes, and sheeps.
7. The leafs on the trees were turning brown.
8. Those dictionarys are found in most librarys.
9. What qualities must heroes have?
10. The fire chieves met to discuss means of fire prevention in our citys.

Part 3 The Possessive of Nouns

Most people own or possess something. We say:

> Carol's coat   the doctor's bag   a lawyer's case

To show that something belongs to or is part of a person, we use the same form:

> Jill's face   Ann's tooth   Bill's worries

We usually speak of ownership, belonging, or possession for people and animals. Occasionally, however, things are also used in the possessive. We speak of a *city's problems, the day's end,* or *a stone's throw.*

Forming Possessives

There are two rules for making the possessive of nouns:

1. If the noun is singular, add an apostrophe and s:

> Bess's slicker   Mother's briefcase   Charles's bike

2. If the noun is plural and ends in s, add just the apostrophe:

> the Hoffmans' car   students' projects   babies' toys

If the noun is plural but does not end in s, add both the apostrophe and s.

> children's books   men's sweaters   women's jewelry

Exercises Form the possessive of nouns.

A. Write the possessive form of these nouns:

1. bee
2. Mary
3. carpenter
4. child
5. Marsha
6. princess

7. mouse	12. Les	17. Tracy
8. Andrea	13. mirror	18. singer
9. watchman	14. conductor	19. lake
10. waitress	15. Tricia	20. Vince
11. Thomas	16. winner	

B. Write the possessive form of these nouns:

1. watchmen	8. schools	15. dresses
2. teachers	9. boys	16. stereos
3. women	10. ladies	17. foxes
4. children	11. countries	18. ducks
5. people	12. dogs	19. engineers
6. birds	13. socks	20. statues
7. sheep	14. churches	

C. Write the possessive form for each italicized word:

1. Our *class* assignment sheets were sitting on the *teacher* desk.

2. The Student *Council* decision to have a walk-a-thon was supported by the *teachers* committee and the *principal* office.

3. Mrs. *Thomas* car was parked in the driveway.

4. My *brother* short story won first prize in the Young Writers Contest.

5. *Maurita* and *Amy* paintings were on display in the art room.

6. The *farmer* newly planted field was washed out by the heavy rain.

7. The *painter* ladders were on our front porch.

8. *Jonathan* bicycle needs new brakes.

9. Our *neighbor* treehouse is one of the best I've ever seen.

10. *Janine* time broke the school record for the 100-yard dash.

Additional Exercises — Review

Using Nouns

A. Find the common and proper nouns.

Label two columns *Common Nouns* and *Proper Nouns*. Decide whether the following nouns are common or proper. Place each in the right column. Capitalize the proper nouns.

1. sun valley, ravine, grand canyon, death valley, pike's peak
2. golden gate bridge, overpass, st. louis arch, brooklyn bridge
3. executive, doctor, senator rosenstein, judge, cardinal bonzano
4. musician, barry manilow, judy collins, guitar, andrés segovia
5. stream, des plaines river, niagara falls, rapids, colorado river
6. intersection, holland tunnel, haggar's corners, highway
7. nation, france, country, united states, scotland, india
8. queen, princess grace, prince charles, queen elizabeth
9. forest, yellowstone national park, westbrook park, lincoln
10. language, swahili, finnish, travel, spanish, greek

B. Form the plurals of nouns.

Write the plural of each of these nouns.

1. tomato	6. wolf	11. radio	16. toy
2. donkey	7. shelf	12. studio	17. perch
3. auto	8. party	13. scratch	18. switch
4. track	9. peach	14. cry	19. leaf
5. ditch	10. foot	15. play	20. deer

C. Form the possessive of nouns.

Write the possessive form in the singular or plural as indicated.

1. the horse (plural) mouths
2. Lisa (singular) equipment
3. the child (plural) beds
4. the cat (plural) paws
5. a doctor (singular) appointment
6. the bird (plural) beaks
7. one weather forecaster (singular) prediction
8. the water (singular) edge
9. Ms. Marsh (singular) business
10. the caddy (plural) hours
11. the gull (plural) cries
12. America (singular) resources
13. the bungalow (singular) owners
14. a bride (singular) bouquet
15. some duck (plural) backs
16. Sara (singular) singing
17. the President (singular) power
18. the moose (plural) antlers
19. the ship (singular) captain
20. Max (singular) shoes

Section 3

Using Pronouns

Our speech and writing would be very awkward if we had only nouns to refer to persons, places, or things. We would have to talk like this:

> David found David's music in David's locker.
> David took David's music to the rehearsal.

Fortunately, we have words that can be used in place of nouns. These are called **pronouns.** With pronouns we can talk like this:

> David found *his* music in *his* locker. *He* took *it* to the rehearsal.

The words *his* and *he* are pronouns that stand for the noun *David* and are used in place of it. The word *it* is a pronoun that stands for the word *music* and is used in its place.

Part 1　Personal Pronouns

Personal pronouns are used to take the place of nouns that name persons.

Personal pronouns refer to persons in three ways:

1. When the pronoun refers to the person speaking, it is in the **first person:** *I, me, we, our,* and *us,* for example.

2. When the pronoun refers to the person spoken to, it is in the **second person:** *you, your, yours.*

3. When the pronoun refers to some other person or thing that is being spoken of, it is in the **third person:** *he, his, him, she, her, it, they, their, them,* for example.

> EXAMPLES:　The letter was addressed to *me.*
> 　　　　　　(speaker—first person)
>
> 　　　　　　The phone call is for *you.*
> 　　　　　　(person spoken to—second person)
>
> 　　　　　　The boys are looking for *him.*
> 　　　　　　(person spoken of—third person)

The word *it* is also called a personal pronoun, even though it is never used in place of a person's name.

Pronouns in the third person that refer to male persons are said to be in the **masculine gender.** Pronouns that refer to female persons are said to be in the **feminine gender.** Pronouns that refer to things are said to be in the **neuter gender.**

> EXAMPLES:　Bob bought *his* ticket yesterday.
> 　　　　　　(*His* is masculine in gender.)
>
> 　　　　　　Marie says that book is *hers.*
> 　　　　　　(*Hers* is feminine in gender.)
>
> 　　　　　　Jill reached for the paddle, but *it* floated out of reach.
> 　　　　　　(*It* is neuter in gender.)

Animals are often referred to by *it* or *its.* They may also be referred to by *he, his, she, her,* or *hers.*

Exercises Find the pronouns.

A. Number your paper from 1–10. Write the pronouns you find in the following sentences. After each pronoun, write the noun or nouns it stands for (except for first-person pronouns).

1. Sue left her math book in her locker.
2. Snow was all over the ball park this morning, but it melted.
3. John and Ginny visited their cousins in Texas.
4. Ken came by and picked up his soccer ball before supper.
5. The store owners said that they would sponsor our team.
6. The Sierra Nevadas are mountains in California. They include Mount Whitney.
7. Dorinda lost her gloves.
8. The cat cared for its new baby kittens.
9. Linda and her best friend are going to New York, and they will compete in a speech contest there.
10. Jay opened the envelope, but he found nothing in it.

B. Follow the directions for Exercise A.

1. Jeff, would you like to play tennis with Carol and Sue?
2. A seismograph records earthquakes. It indicates their intensity.
3. Last summer, the neighbors painted their house, and Dad built a patio.
4. Joel and Jim Hertz raised tomatoes. They sold them to the neighbors and made money.
5. The Owens parked their cars in the driveway while the workers repaired their garage roof.
6. Mom and Dad have their tickets for the school concert.
7. Mary, have you found your umbrella?
8. Bill looked for his books but couldn't find them.
9. The sun had sundogs, circles of bright rainbow spots, around it. They are formed from ice particles.
10. Did Pam and Mary find the packages they had wrapped?

Part 2 Compound Personal Pronouns

A **compound personal pronoun** is formed by adding *-self* or *-selves* to certain personal pronouns:

First Person	myself	ourselves
Second Person	yourself	yourselves
Third Person	himself herself itself	themselves

Exercises Use compound personal pronouns.

A.   Number your paper from 1–10. Beside each number write the correct compound personal pronoun for each of these sentences. Then write the noun or pronoun to which it refers.

> EXAMPLE: He made (pronoun) a T-shirt in sewing class.
> himself, He

1. Cut (pronoun) a bigger piece of pie.
2. We made the loom (pronoun).
3. Bret let (pronoun) down by the rope.
4. The fans shouted (pronoun) hoarse.
5. Dan could not find the answer by (pronoun).
6. I will finish washing the car by (pronoun).
7. Mrs. Adel suggested we do the painting (pronoun).
8. Nancy, Carrie, and Sue made the movie (pronoun).
9. We don't weigh (pronoun) very often.
10. I built and stained these bookcases by (pronoun).

B.   Follow the directions for Exercise A.

1. The door just locked (pronoun).
2. Diane forgot to include (pronoun) when she counted.
3. Jamie, don't rush (pronoun).

4. We always can the peaches (pronoun).
5. Will you two be able to finish the job (pronoun)?
6. Bridget organized the presentation by (pronoun).
7. Read the article (pronoun); I think you'll find it fun.
8. They just bought (pronoun) a pumpkin.
9. The store more than pays for (pronoun).
10. He wasn't sure of (pronoun) on a high ladder.

Part 3   Indefinite Pronouns

Pronouns like *anyone* and *nobody* do not refer to any definite person or thing. They are called **indefinite pronouns.**

Most indefinite pronouns are singular in number. They refer to only one person or thing. Here they are:

Singular Indefinite Pronouns

another	each	everything	one
anybody	either	neither	somebody
anyone	everybody	nobody	someone
anything	everyone	no one	

EXAMPLES: Everyone has *his* invitation.
(*Not:* Everyone has *their* invitation.)

Everyone has *his or her* invitation.
(When the indefinite pronoun refers to both males and females, *his or her* is acceptable.)

A few indefinite pronouns are plural. They refer to more than one person or thing:

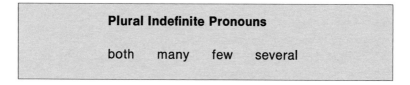

Plural Indefinite Pronouns

both   many   few   several

The pronouns *all, some,* and *none* may be singular or plural, depending upon their meaning in the sentence.

EXAMPLES: All of the pie *is* gone.
All of the members *are* here.

Some of the milk *is* sour.
Some of the apples *are* ripe.

None of the time *was* wasted.
None of the flowers *were* left.

Exercises Find the indefinite pronouns.

A. Number your paper from 1–10. For each sentence write down the indefinite pronoun or pronouns.

1. Is anything the matter?
2. Both of the games were postponed because of rain.
3. All of the photographs for the yearbook were too dark.
4. Somebody has left his or her jacket on the bus.
5. Either of the counselors will help you with your schedule.
6. In the spring, almost everyone rides his or her bike to school.
7. During the noon hour, anyone can go home to eat lunch.
8. All of the eighth-grade students went to the high school for orientation.
9. Each of the students filled out his or her registration cards.
10. Everyone took the high school placement test today.

B. Number your paper from 1–10. For each sentence write down the indefinite pronoun and pick the verb in the parentheses that agrees with it.

1. Neither of the keys (fits, fit) the lock.
2. Just a few of my relatives (is, are) coming.
3. Some of the band members (is, are) competing in the music contest.

4. Each of the countries (send, sends) two representatives.
5. Neither of the encyclopedias (explain, explains) the subject very well.
6. All of the runners (was, were) lined up for the race.
7. All of the bookcases (have, has) assembling instructions.
8. Several of those days last week (was, were) scorchers.
9. Neither of my shoes (is, are) wet.
10. Both of my brothers (works, work) at the ice cream parlor.

Part 4   Demonstrative Pronouns

The pronouns *this, that, these,* and *those* are used to point out which persons or things are referred to. They are called **demonstrative pronouns.**

This and *these* point to persons or things that are near. *That* and *those* point to persons or things farther away.

This is the right road.   **These** belong to Jim.
That is my camera.   **Those** are my boots.

Exercise   Use demonstrative pronouns.

Number your paper from 1–10. Write the correct demonstrative pronoun for the blank space in each sentence.

1. _____ are my boots over there.
2. _____ was Kate on the telephone.
3. _____ were the books I was telling you about.
4. _____ is the metric table we have to learn.
5. _____ are the tools you wanted to borrow.
6. _____ was my brother who read the announcements.
7. _____ are the chapters I read last night.
8. _____ are probably better than those.
9. _____ is my bike parked over there.
10. _____ was Ryan in the doorway.

Part 5   Interrogative Pronouns

The pronouns *who, whose, whom, which,* and *what* are used to ask questions.

EXAMPLES: *Who* rang the bell?   *Which* is your paper?
            Whose are those shoes?   *What* did you say?
            Whom do you mean?

Exercise Find and use different kinds of pronouns.

Number your paper from 1–10. Write all the pronouns in these sentences. After each pronoun, write *Indefinite, Demonstrative,* or *Interrogative* to show what kind it is.

1. Those are the best skates to buy.
2. Which of the new TV shows does Rhoda enjoy?
3. This is Jay's cassette player.
4. No one knew the answer to either of the questions.
5. What is everybody waiting for?
6. Which is the one Ann chose?
7. Nobody can solve the problems.
8. To whom did the caller wish to speak?
9. Which of the shelves does Ernest want painted?
10. These are the ones to be painted.

Part 6   The Forms of Pronouns

English personal pronouns have three special forms. Like nouns, they have a possessive form. In addition, they have two other forms: the subject form and the object form.

I own the ball. (subject form)
The owner of the ball is I. (subject form after linking verb)
The ball belongs to me. (object form)
It is my ball. (possessive form modifying a noun)
It is mine. (possessive form used as predicate)

The Subject Form of Pronouns

Personal pronouns are used in the subject form (1) when they are subjects and (2) when they follow linking verbs. Here are the subject forms of each of the personal pronouns:

Subject Forms of Pronouns		
I	you	he, she, it
we	you	they

Personal pronoun used *as subject*
$\begin{cases} \textit{I agree with you.} \\ \textit{She is not going.} \\ \textit{We understand.} \end{cases}$

Personal pronoun used *after linking verb*
$\begin{cases} \text{This is } \textit{he.} \\ \text{It was } \textit{I.} \\ \text{It is } \textit{they.} \end{cases}$

The Object Form of Pronouns

Personal pronouns are used in the object form (1) when they are direct or indirect objects of verbs and (2) when they are objects of prepositions. Here are the object forms of the personal pronouns:

Object Forms of Pronouns		
me	you	him, her, it
us	you	them

Direct Object
$\begin{cases} \text{The dog bit } \textit{him.} \\ \text{Jack helped } \textit{them} \text{ with the work.} \end{cases}$

Indirect Object   I gave *her* a gift.

Object of Preposition
$\begin{cases} \text{The candy is for } \textit{me.} \\ \text{Write a letter to } \textit{them.} \\ \text{The money came from } \textit{her.} \end{cases}$

267

The Possessive Form of Pronouns

Personal pronouns are used in the possessive form to show ownership or possession. Personal pronouns in the possessive form consist of two groups: (1) Pronouns used, like adjectives, to modify nouns; (2) Pronouns used, like nouns, as subjects of verbs, as predicate words, or as objects of verbs or prepositions.

Possessive Forms of Pronouns Used To Modify Nouns		
my	your	his, her, its
our	your	their

EXAMPLES: *my* sister   *our* car
           his book   *its* wheels
           her mother   *their* money

Possessive Forms of Pronouns Used Alone		
mine	yours	his, hers, its
ours	yours	theirs

EXAMPLES: This book is *mine*. (predicate word)
           Y*ours* is on the desk. (subject of verb)
           I don't see *hers*. (object of verb)
           Look at the pictures in *ours*. (object of preposition)

Exercises Choose the right pronoun.

A. Choose the right pronoun from those given in parentheses. Be ready to explain how it is used in the sentence.

1. Does this copy belong to (he, him)?
2. That was (her, she).

3. Mrs. Walsh gave the job to (I, me).
4. Donna and I helped (they, them) with the yard work.
5. Hasn't anybody seen (he, him)?
6. It was (her, she) who answered the call.
7. Was it (they, them) who called?
8. Is there anything of (your, yours) to go home?
9. This is (he, him).
10. Will you give these books to (she, her)?

B. Follow the directions for Exercise A.

1. The principal wanted to talk to Kelly and (I, me).
2. Could it have been (they, them)?
3. I have both of (theirs, their).
4. That looks more like (me, I).
5. Mother asked (me, I) for the key.
6. The award was given to (she, her) for outstanding achievement.
7. Each of (us, we) had a look at it.
8. I'm sure it was (he, him) on the telephone.
9. The test results were given by (they, them) at a special meeting.
10. (Me, I) am going to the museum.

C. The personal pronouns in these sentences are in italics. Write each one. After it, write *Subject Form* or *Object Form*.

1. The puck just missed *him*.
2. Ms. Anderson gave *us* several problems for homework.
3. *I* gave *you* the schedule.
4. *They* were taking *her* to dinner.
5. *He* gave the gifts to *them*.
6. *We* have been waiting for *him*.
7. The manager sold *us* the T-shirts at a discount.
8. Carl couldn't hear *me*.
9. Did Aunt Ellen get a good picture of *us*?
10. The third one in the front row is *she*.

Part 7   Pronouns in Compound Sentence Parts

You seldom make mistakes when you use one personal pronoun by itself. You would never say "Give *I* the pencil."

Trouble arises when two pronouns or a pronoun and a noun are used together in compound sentence parts. Would you say "Brian and me built a radio" or "Brian and I built a radio"?

Have you heard people say "between you and I"? Does this sound right? Should it be "between you and me"? How can you tell? Let's look at some sentences with pronouns correctly used in compound parts.

Compound Subject	*Terry and she* went to the rink.
Compound Direct Object	We visited the *Browns and them.*
Compound Indirect Object	Mrs. Hill gave *Sue and me* a job.
Compound Object of Preposition	The package was for *Jack and me.*

Now read the sentences above a second time. This time drop out the noun in each compound part. For example, read "*She* went to the rink." Each sentence will sound right and sensible to you.

Whenever you are in doubt about which form of the pronoun to use in a compound sentence part, drop out the noun. Read the sentence with just the pronoun, and you will usually choose the right one.

If there are two pronouns in the compound part, read the sentence for each pronoun separately.

Mrs. Huber will call for you and (she? her?).
Mrs. Huber will call for you.
Mrs. Huber will call for *her.*

Caution: After forms of the verb *be*, use only *I, we, he, she,* or *they* as predicate pronouns.

Exercises Choose the correct pronoun in compound sentence parts.

A. Choose the correct pronoun from those given in parentheses in each sentence.

1. Dawn and (her, she) will bring the peanuts.
2. Can you give Sandy and (we, us) a ride?
3. Gayle and (her, she) are trying out for cheerleading.
4. The doorman gave Al and (I, me) a pass.
5. There is no difference in weight between (he, him) and (me, I).
6. Wait for Lori and (I, me) after school.
7. Jeff lives between (them, they) and (I, me).
8. (Her, She) and I are the newspaper editors.
9. The ushers were Marla and (her, she).
10. Just between you and (me, I), that speaker wasn't very good.

B. All but one of the following sentences contain a pronoun error. Write the sentences, correcting the errors.

1. My parents and me are going to the ice show tonight.
2. Larry and them have gone to Detroit.
3. The telephone must be for either you or she.
4. Everyone had enough except Janet and she.
5. The packages were divided evenly between Tanya and I.
6. Judy and her just went out the back door.
7. Mrs. McGowan made Meg and I a sandwich.
8. The gas station attendant gave Mary Beth and I directions.
9. Peggy and Linda sat next to Lauri and I at the concert.
10. The helicopter kept circling around Pam and me.

Part 8 *Who* and *Whom*

The words *who, whose,* and *whom* are used to ask questions. When used in this way, they are called **interrogative pronouns.**

> *Who* told you that story? (*Who* is subject of *told.*)
> *Whose* is the yellow sweater? (*Whose* is subject of *is.*)
> *Whom* did you meet? (*Whom* is object of *did meet.*)
> To *whom* did you go? (*Whom* is object of preposition *to.*)

Who is the subject form. It is used as the subject of a verb.

Whom is the object form. It is used as the direct object of a verb or as the object of a preposition.

Whose is the possessive form. Like other possessives, it can be used with a noun to modify the noun: *Whose bike* is missing? When it is used without a noun, it may be the subject or object of a verb.

> *Whose* house is that? (*Whose* modifies *house.*)
> *Whose* were you using? (*Whose* is object of *were using.*)
> *Whose* are those boots? (*Whose* is subject of *are.*)

Exercises Choose the correct interrogative pronoun.

A. Choose the correct interrogative pronoun.

1. (Who, Whose) move is it?
2. (Whose, Who) are these binoculars?
3. (Who, Whom) are these people?
4. (Whom, Who) were you thinking of?
5. (Whom, Who) do these Adidas belong to?
6. (Who, Whom) swam ten lengths?
7. (Whom, Whose) speech did you like the best?
8. (Whose, Whom) is this?
9. (Whom, Whose) country has that flag?
10. For (who, whom) does the bell toll?

B. Follow the directions for Exercise A.

1. To (whom, who) did you give the library books?
2. (Who, Whom) is this letter from?
3. (Whom, Who) painted this picture?
4. (Who, Whom) do you know in Alaska?
5. (Who, Whom) is Randy talking to?
6. (Whose, Who) are these initials?
7. To (who, whom) should I give these letters?
8. For (who, whom) shall I ask?
9. (Whom, Who) did you ask for?
10. (Who, Whom) will get the MVP award in hockey?

Part 9 Possessive Pronouns and Contractions

Some contractions are formed by joining a pronoun and a verb and omitting one or more letters. The apostrophe is used to show where letters are left out.

it + is = it's	they + are = they're
you + are = you're	who + is = who's

The possessive forms of the pronouns *its, your, their,* and *whose* sound the same as these contractions: *it's, you're, they're,* and *who's.* Because they sound alike, the contractions and possessives are sometimes confused.

Wrong The groundhog saw it's shadow.
Right The groundhog saw its shadow.

Right You're (You are) late for your appointment.
Right They're (They are) planning to show their slides.
Right Who's (who is) the boy whose coat you are wearing?

There are two simple rules to follow to make sure that you use possessive pronouns and contractions correctly.

1. When you use one of these words that sound alike, ask yourself whether it stands for one word or two. If it stands for two words, it is a contraction and needs an apostrophe.

2. Never use an apostrophe in a possessive pronoun.

Exercises Possessive pronouns and contractions.

A. Choose the correct word from the two given in parentheses.

1. The amusement park gave free passes to (it's its) first 500 entrants.
2. (Whose, Who's) bike is chained to the tree?
3. (You're, Your) idea might work.
4. Are you sure that (they're, their) coming?
5. (Whose, Who's) going to the Ridgetown Fair?
6. (They're, Their) glad (its, it's) Friday.
7. (Whose, Who's) going to mow the lawn?
8. (Their, They're) going to pick up (their, they're) uniforms at noon.
9. Have you made up (you're, your) mind?
10. (Who's, Whose) got a dime that I can borrow?

B. Write the words each contraction below stands for.

1. It's twenty miles from this town to Omaha.
2. Who's next?
3. We've walked the whole way.
4. Who'd have thought it would snow in April?
5. They've come to repair the water main.
6. Who's been in my locker?
7. You've got a good sense of humor.
8. It's your turn now.
9. The book is called *Who's Who*.
10. When's the pizza being delivered?

Part 10   Special Pronoun Problems

Compound Personal Pronouns

The compound personal pronouns (*myself, yourself,* etc.) must not be used in place of personal pronouns. They are used *in addition* to personal pronouns. It is a good rule to use a compound personal pronoun only when the word it refers to has been used in the same sentence.

> I saw the weather balloon *myself.* (*myself* refers to *I.*)
> You can judge for *yourself.* (*yourself* refers to *you.*)
> She *herself* knows what to do. (*herself* refers to *she.*)

We Boys—Us Boys; We Girls—Us Girls

When you use phrases like *we girls* and *us boys,* you must be sure that you are using the right form of the pronoun. You can tell which pronoun to use by dropping the noun and saying the sentence without it.

> Problem   (We, Us) girls will be at Jan's house.
> Correct   We will be at Jan's house.
> Correct   We girls will be at Jan's house.
>
> Problem   Will you call for (us, we) boys?
> Correct   Will you call for us?
> Correct   Will you call for us boys?

Them and *Those*

The word *them* is always a pronoun. It is always used as an object of a verb or preposition.

Those is sometimes a pronoun and sometimes an adjective. If a noun appears right after it, *those* is probably an adjective. Used without a noun, it is a pronoun.

> We found *them* here. (object of verb)
> We have heard from *them.* (object of preposition *from*)

We like *those* best. (object of verb)
Those birds are cardinals. (adjective modifying *birds*)
We will order *those* cakes. (adjective modifying *cakes*)

Exercises Use the correct form.

A. Copy these sentences. Fill in the blank with the correct com-pound personal pronoun.

1. I finished building the end table _____.
2. You can both see for _____ that the experiment worked.
3. We went to the movies by _____.
4. If you jog, you compete only with _____.
5. Janelle planted the flower bed by _____.
6. They can read for _____ that the track meet was cancelled.
7. I went by _____ to the art exhibit.
8. We treated _____ to hot fudge sundaes.
9. Will you take the train to St. Louis by _____?
10. David directed the play _____.

B. Choose the correct word from the two words given.

1. Will you go to the beach with Diana and (me, myself)?
2. (We, Us) Scouts would like to sponsor a canoe trip.
3. (Them, Those) portraits look very old.
4. (We, Us) players are going to the Knicks-Bulls basket-ball game.
5. Will you call for (we, us) boys on the way to the stadium?
6. Who piled all (them, those) boards up?
7. Would you like to sit with (us, we) girls at the play?
8. Most of (us, we) boys will help paint the bleachers.
9. You won't need all of (them, those) pencils.
10. (We, Us) students held a pep rally yesterday.

Part 11 Pronouns and Antecedents

A personal pronoun, you remember, is used in place of a noun. This noun is the word to which it refers. The noun usually comes first, either in the same sentence or in the preceding sentence. The noun for which a pronoun stands is called its **antecedent.**

> We waited for Kay. *She* was making a phone call.
> (*She* stands for *Kay*. *Kay* is the antecedent.)
>
> The men had taken off *their* coats.
> (*Their* stands for *men*. *Men* is the antecedent.)

Pronouns themselves may be the antecedents of other pronouns:

> Does everyone have *his* books?
> (*Everyone* is the antecedent of *his*.)
>
> Do you have *your* music lesson today?
> (*You* is the antecedent of *your*.)

A pronoun must agree with its antecedent in number.

Here the word *agree* means that the pronoun must be the *same in number* as its antecedent. The word *number* here means *singular* or *plural*. The pronoun must be singular if the word it stands for is singular. It must be plural if the word it stands for is plural.

> The runners took *their* places.
> (*Runners* is plural; *their* is plural.)
>
> The scientist told of *her* early experiences.
> (*Scientist* is singular; *her* is singular.)
>
> Everybody brought *his* own records.
> (*Everybody* is singular; *his* is singular.)
>
> One of the girls left *her* project in the shop.
> (*One* is singular; *her* is singular.)

Exercises Pronouns and antecedents.

A. The personal pronouns in these sentences are italicized. Find the antecedent of each pronoun. Write it.

1. One of the boys had a cast on *his* arm.
2. You usually bring *your* own towel to the pool.
3. The box isn't pretty, but the paper around *it* is.
4. Everyone on the team had tears in *his* eyes.
5. Both of the owls had *their* eyes half shut.
6. Everyone thinks *you* can do the job, Sarah.
7. One of the glasses had a crack in *it*.
8. Brenda bought *her* own materials.
9. The members of the cast took *their* places.
10. One of the storm shelters had *its* entrance boarded up.

B. Choose the correct pronoun from those given in the parentheses.

1. Has everyone taken (his, their) turn?
2. If anyone wants to go, tell (him or her, them) to see Paul.
3. Few were able to finish (his, their) work.
4. Most of the cans had lost (its, their) labels.
5. Somebody has left (his, their) wallet on my desk.
6. Everyone had an opportunity to state (their, her) opinion.
7. None of the bottles had (its, their) label removed.
8. Nobody expected to hear (his, their) own name over the loudspeaker.
9. Neither of the actors could remember (his, their) lines at the first rehearsal.
10. Each of the students explained (his or her, their) collage to the class.

Additional Exercises — Review

Using Pronouns

A. Find the pronouns.

Number your paper from 1–10. Write the pronouns you find in each of the following sentences. After each pronoun, write the noun or nouns it stands for.

1. Mike said he would set the dinner table.
2. There's no stamp on the envelope. It must have come off.
3. One rancher drove his jeep ten miles out on the range.
4. There's the box. Its lid has a picture of a cornfield.
5. Brad and Joe said Scott could use their tent.
6. Claire and Joy put the camping equipment in their car.
7. Mr. Hernandez attached his trailer to the back of his van.
8. Two archaeologists told how they had discovered the ruins.
9. Sue and Wendy missed the bus, and then they got caught in the rain.
10. There's the tree where Megan snagged her kite.

B. Use compound personal pronouns.

Number your paper from 1–10. Beside each number write a correct compound personal pronoun for each of the following sentences. After it, write the noun or pronoun to which it refers.

1. The boys decorated the gym by (pronoun).
2. Julie cleaned the fish (pronoun).
3. I moved the plants (pronoun) so that they wouldn't get damaged.
4. Girls, please help (pronoun) to more dessert.

5. The drum majorette usually led the parade (pronoun).
6. Rob made the fudge (pronoun).
7. Why doesn't Janet try out for the team (pronoun)?
8. We watched (pronoun) on the TV screen.
9. Ken, Rachel, and Jill painted the scenery (pronoun).
10. A lion cub sunned (pronoun) on a rock.

C. Find the indefinite pronouns.

Number your paper from 1–10. For each sentence write down the indefinite pronoun. Write the verb that agrees with it from those given in parentheses.

1. Some of the candies (taste, tastes) like strawberry.
2. Several of the foreign exchange students (come, comes) from South America.
3. Everything in the boxes (is, are) wet.
4. None of those stars to the west (set, sets) before 10 P.M.
5. Each of the divers (perform, performs) twice.
6. One of those tires (has, have) a slow leak.
7. Somebody in the prop room always (forget, forgets) the king's cushion.
8. (Are, Is) anybody coming?
9. No one in the caves (wander, wanders) away from the guide.
10. Both of us (know, knows) the way around the swamp.

D. Find different kinds of pronouns.

Number your paper from 1–10. Write all the pronouns in each sentence. After each pronoun, write *Indefinite, Demonstrative,* or *Interrogative* to show what kind it is.

1. How did Kirk get these out of the water?
2. No one admitted leaving the phone off the hook.
3. Several of the girls carried these from the station.
4. Why would anyone bring these to a picnic?

5. Everybody heckled the pitcher.
6. Who let the cat out of the bag?
7. Nobody knew the right answer.
8. Pete is buying this as a present.
9. What's that by the rock pile?
10. Both of the teams had practiced vigorously.

E. Choose the correct pronoun.

Choose the correct pronoun from the two given in parentheses. Be ready to explain how it is used in the sentence.

1. Was it (he, him) who won the trophy?
2. It was (she, her) who painted that picture.
3. The workers demanded (their, theirs) pay immediately.
4. (We, Us) organized the pep assembly.
5. Strong winds blew the shack over on (it, its) side.
6. We thought it was (he, him) who made the announcements.
7. The manager gave Ann and (me, I) tickets to the movie.
8. Caryl and (me, I) are going to the shopping mall.
9. Jack wanted you to bring (your, yours) along.
10. Please give these music books to Darla and (she, her).

F. Use the correct pronoun in compound sentence parts.

Choose the correct pronoun from the two given in parentheses.

1. (He, Him) and Sally set up the ping pong table.
2. Did you meet John and (they, them) at the exhibit?
3. A waiter showed Mrs. Ryan and (she, her) to a table.
4. (She, Her) and (me, I) were digging for clams.
5. They gave Ted and (we, us) just ten minutes to get ready.
6. My father packed Ken and (me, I) a lunch.

7. Barb waited fifteen minutes for Mr. Kopp and (they, them).

8. Bob and (us, we) had to mow and rake the lawn.

9. The setter came to Greg and (he, him) right away.

10. The lifeguard warned Patty and (we, us) about the undercurrent.

G. Choose the correct interrogative pronoun.

Choose the correct interrogative pronoun from the two given in parentheses.

1. (Whom, Who) came in second?
2. (Who, Whose) was the best answer?
3. (Who, Whom) left her sunglasses on the counter?
4. To (whom, who) are you giving the macramé hanger?
5. (Who, Whom) did Scott give the folder to?
6. (Whom, Who) knows how to get to the airport?
7. (Whose, Whom) phone number is that?
8. (Who, Whom) did the coach choose for the starting line-up?
9. (Whom, Who) let the cats out of the house?
10. (Whose, Whom) are these cookies for?

H. Choose possessive pronouns or contractions.

Choose the right word from the two given in parentheses.

1. (It's, Its) too early.
2. The panther boxed (its, it's) cub's ears.
3. (Who's Whose) team do we play next week?
4. (Your, You're) appointment with the orthodontist is tomorrow.
5. Christie and Tom said (they're, their) report was on bicycle safety.
6. (Whose, Who's) got the relish?
7. (It's, Its) Monday and it's (you're, your) turn to cook.

8. (Their, They're) ready for take-off.
9. (It's, Its) (your, you're) turn.
10. (They're, Their) always late starting the meeting.

I. Use the correct form with special pronoun problems.

Choose the correct word from the two given in parentheses.

1. The coach handed the trophy to (me, myself).
2. (Them, Those) are too big.
3. The principal presented (we, us) students with diplomas.
4. Please put (them, those) boxes in the trash can.
5. (Us, We) girls got special recognition for our efforts.
6. (Them, Those) posters are to be hung in the cafeteria.
7. (Them, Those) shops on Central Street are open until 9 P.M. on Thursday evening.
8. Would you like to go to the show with (us, we) girls?

J. Find the antecedent of the pronoun.

The personal pronouns in these sentences are italicized. Write the antecedent of each pronoun.

1. The paramedics entered the fiery building carrying all of *their* equipment.
2. Chris's coat had a tear in *it*.
3. Phil fixed *his* back tire.
4. Vicki's yard has a fence all around *it*.
5. Mrs. Kohl was knitting a sweater for *her* granddaughter.
6. Bring *your* gym clothes for the intramural game tomorrow.
7. Bandit looked at *his* dog dish and walked away from *it*.
8. Lara and Pete told *their* parents about the band concert.
9. Susie brought *her* tape recorder.
10. The swallows always make *their* nests in the barn.

Section 4

Using Verbs

Of all the parts of speech, the **verb** is the most important. It is the moving power, the motor, of a sentence.

Verbs are important because you need them for sentence building. They are important, too, because they, more than any other part of speech, help you to say exactly what you mean. See the variety of ways in which *go* can be used:

I go.	I went.
I am going.	I have gone.
I am going to go.	I had gone.
She goes.	She should have gone.

In Section 1 you studied some of the forms and uses of verbs. In this chapter you will study verbs in greater detail.

Part 1 What Are Verbs?

A verb is a word that tells of an action or state of being.

Action Verbs

Some verbs tell of an action:

Sam *clung* to the rope.   The rain *drenched* us.

Sometimes the action is one you cannot see:

Carlos *needed* help.   Kate *had* a good idea.

Whether you can see the action or not, an action verb tells that something is happening, has happened, or will happen.

Linking Verbs

A few verbs do not tell of an action. They merely tell that something is. They express a state of being:

The clock *is* slow.   The sky *looks* gloomy.
The house *seems* empty.   The gloves *feel* soft.

These verbs are called **linking verbs** because they connect the subject with some other word or words in the sentence.
Here are the most common linking verbs:

be (am, are, is, was,	look	smell
were, been, being)	appear	taste
become	feel	grow
seem	sound	

Many linking verbs can also be used as action verbs.

LINKING VERB	ACTION VERB
The melon *looked* ripe.	Ann *looked* at the melon.
The melon *felt* ripe.	Ann *felt* the melon.
The night *grew* cold.	Tom *grew* tomatoes.

Exercises **Find the verbs.**

A. Find the verb in each sentence. Write it. After the verb write *Action* or *Linking* to show what kind it is.

1. That Dutch apple pie smells delicious.
2. These candy sticks taste sour.
3. The florist appeared at the door with flowers for my sister.
4. Sherry looked in the attic.
5. Many visitors waited in line for tickets.
6. The horses raced toward the finish line.
7. Those bananas look overripe.
8. The sun broke through the smog at noon.
9. The sky looks ominous.
10. The record sounds scratchy.

B. Follow the directions for Exercise A.

1. The air smells clean and fresh after that storm.
2. The first wrestler pinned his opponent in ten seconds.
3. A beautiful rainbow appeared across the meadow.
4. Our dog is a German shepherd.
5. I finished my social studies assignment in class.
6. After dinner, Erica and I cycled to the park.
7. The yearbook staff sold hot dogs and soft drinks at the football games.
8. The speaker for the assembly sounds interesting.
9. The weekend at Six Flags was fun.
10. Mrs. Bauer grows cantaloupe and watermelon in her garden.

C. Write two sentences using each of the following words. In one sentence, use the word as an action verb. In the other sentence, use the word as a linking verb.

1. tasted   2. smell   3. feel   4. looked

Part 2 Helping Verbs and Main Verbs

You will also remember that a great many verbs consist of more than one word. Verbs can be made up of a **main verb** and one or more **helping verbs.**

Verb	Helping Verbs	Main Verb
had gone	had	gone
was seen	was	seen
can go	can	go
might have gone	might have	gone
must have been caught	must have been	caught

There are three verbs that can be used either as main verbs or as helping verbs. Here are their forms:

do	has	is	was	be
does	have	am	were	been
did	had	are		

Used as Main Verb	Used as Helping Verb
Can you *do* this job?	I *do know* your sister.
Who *has* my key?	Sue *has gone* home.
Where *were* you?	The boys *were working*.

Here is a list of words frequently used as helping verbs.

can	shall	will	may	must
could	should	would	might	

Sometimes parts of a verb are separated from each other by words that are not part of the verb.

I *did* not *ask* the right question.
Mac *was* certainly *trying* hard.

Exercises Find the verbs.

A. Find the parts of the verb in each sentence. Write them in two columns labeled *Helping Verb* and *Main Verb.*

> EXAMPLE: They will deliver the packages tomorrow.
>
> HELPING VERB   MAIN VERB
>
> will   deliver

1. We are going to the circus tomorrow.
2. We have completed our study of the U. S. Constitution.
3. Everyone has gone home.
4. Can Manny and Liz go to the baseball game with us?
5. It must have snowed all night.
6. After the concert, we are going to the pizzeria.
7. I was writing my composition during study hall.
8. My sister is running in the marathon race.
9. Colleen and I have skated at the new roller rink.
10. The hot air balloons had landed in the stadium.

B. Follow the directions for Exercise A.

1. Mopeds have been designed for economical transportation.
2. A moped can go up to 30 miles per hour.
3. It is considered a motorized bicycle.
4. No licenses are required for moped drivers in many states.
5. Consumers are concerned about the price of fuel.
6. Energy conservation has become everyone's responsibility.
7. Car pools and public transportation can help our energy resources.
8. Each of us must make individual efforts to save energy.
9. Solar energy can help us in the years ahead.
10. Some day we will probably heat our homes, schools, and offices with solar energy.

Part 3 Progressive Forms

Sometimes we tell the time of an action like this:

> I *am* talking. (instead of *I talk*)
> I *was* talking. (instead of *I talked*)

We use a form of the verb *be* with the form of the main verb that ends in *-ing*. We call these the **progressive forms** of the verb. Here are the **progressive forms** of *talk* that are used with *I*:

I am talking.	I have been talking.
I was talking.	I had been talking.
I shall (will) be talking.	I shall (will) have been talking.

Exercises Identify progressive forms.

A. Number your paper from 1–10. Write down the verb in each sentence.

1. The Allens are raising Dalmatians.
2. I will be going to Florida in April.
3. Julia was talking to Ms. O'Shea about the Science Fair.
4. I will be running for vice-president of the French Club.
5. We will be keeping in touch.
6. I was watching the "Movie of the Week" last night.
7. Bill, Tom, and Maria have been managing the pool.
8. We will be playing more soccer next year.
9. I was listening to the radio.
10. Raul and Marlene will be working at Indian Lake next July and August.

B. Copy these sentences, changing each verb to its progressive form.

1. This machine filters our drinking water.
2. From now on, the sun will set later and later.
3. The dishwater, as usual, had gotten cold.

4. Kurt practiced his diving.
5. Peggy has collected information on Japan.
6. I talked to my counselor about next year's class schedule.
7. We telephoned my sister at college.
8. Ray talked to Mrs. Pampel about his assignments.
9. The audience laughed at the entertainer.
10. We waited for the bus.

Part 4   The Tenses of Verbs

Verbs are time-telling words. They not only tell of an action or a state of being. They also tell when the action takes place. They tell whether the action or state of being is past, present, or future.

Verbs tell time in two ways:

1. By changing their spelling:

   walk—walked   sleep—slept

2. By using helping verbs:

   will creep   has crept   had crept

Verbs can express six different times. Each verb has a form to express each of these six different times. The forms of a verb used to indicate time are called the **tenses** of a verb.

The Simple Tenses

The **present tense** of the verb is the same as the name of the verb:

   run   go   walk

The **past tense** of regular verbs is formed by adding -*d* or -*ed* to the present tense:

   walked   placed

The past tense of irregular verbs is usually shown by a change of spelling:

shine—shone   swing—swung

The **future tense** is formed by using *shall* or *will* with the present tense:

shall go   will run

The three tenses described above are called the **simple tenses.** They describe:

1. What is happening now: *present tense*
2. What happened before: *past tense*
3. What will happen later: *future tense*

The Perfect Tenses

Sometimes we have to speak of two different times, one earlier than the other. To make these times clear, we can use the **perfect tenses.** The perfect tenses are formed by using *has, have,* or *had* with the past participle.

The perfect tenses are formed as follows:

Present Perfect	has run, have run
Past Perfect	had run
Future Perfect	will have run, shall have run

Exercises **Recognize verb tenses.**

A. Find each verb in the following sentences. Tell the tense of each.

1. What have you done with the scissors?
2. We have always enjoyed these travelogs.
3. My brother and I walk to school.
4. Will you come to the party tonight?
5. Have you ever gone to a volleyball game?

6. The new ice cream parlor will open in June.
7. My parents and I have traveled to Mexico.
8. We will have eaten the cake by tomorrow.
9. When will the fair open?
10. Lynn hasn't seen the ice show.

B. Write a sentence for each of the verbs below. Use the verb in the tense indicated.

1. fill (past tense)
2. drop (past perfect tense)
3. stay (future tense)
4. glisten (past tense)
5. close (future perfect tense)
6. splash (present tense)
7. flash (present progressive tense)
8. cause (present tense)
9. attach (past perfect tense)
10. touch (future tense)

Part 5   The Principal Parts of Verbs

Every verb has certain forms on which nearly all other forms of the verb are based. These essential forms of a verb are called the **principal parts** of the verb.

The principal parts of a verb are the **present tense,** the **past tense,** and the **past participle.**

PRESENT	PAST	PAST PARTICIPLE
talk	talked	talked
knit	knitted	knitted
add	added	added
divide	divided	divided

The present tense and the past tense are **simple tenses** of the verb. The past participle is used for all **perfect tenses** of the verb.

As you can see, the past and the past participle forms of *talk, knit, add,* and *divide* are the same. These are **regular verbs.** In all regular verbs the past and past participle are formed by adding *-d* (*divided*) or *-ed* (*talked*) to the present form.

Many regular verbs change their spelling when *-d* or *-ed* is added to them. These changes are made in accord with regular spelling rules.

knit + -ed = knitted   hurry + -ed = hurried
fit + -ed = fitted   try + -ed = tried
pat + -ed = patted   pity + -ed = pitied

Some verbs change their spelling this way:

say + -d = said   pay + -d = paid   lay + -d = laid

Exercise Principal parts of verbs.

The verbs below are regular verbs. Make three columns on your paper. Label them *Present, Past,* and *Past Participle.* Write the principal parts of each verb in the right column.

1. worry
2. sob
3. pay
4. carry
5. grab
6. help
7. pass
8. end
9. slip
10. use
11. rob
12. like
13. rap
14. hurry
15. rub
16. try
17. flip
18. push
19. vary
20. glow

Part 6   Irregular Verbs

There are hundreds of verbs in our language that follow the regular pattern of adding -d or -ed to the present to form the past and past participle.

Those verbs that do not follow this pattern are called **irregular verbs.** There are only about sixty irregular verbs that are frequently used. Many of these have only one change. They present few problems.

buy	bought	bought
make	made	made
feel	felt	felt

A few irregular verbs do not change at all from one principal part to another. They offer no problems in usage.

hit   let   set   shut

Most verb problems come from the irregular verbs that have three different forms:

throw	threw	thrown
ring	rang	rung

If you are not sure about a verb form, look it up in a dictionary. If the verb is regular, only one form will be listed.

If the verb is irregular, the dictionary will give the irregular forms. It will give two forms if the past and past participle are the same: *say, said.* It will give all three principal parts if they are all different: *sing, sang, sung.*

Dictionary Entry for *Begin*

present

be-gin (bi gin′), **v.** to start being, doing, acting, etc.; get under way [Work *begins* at 8:00 A.M. His cold *began* with a sore throat.] —**be-gan′,** *p.*; **be-gun′,** *p.p.*

past participle

past

Common Irregular Verbs

Present	Past	Past Participle	Present	Past	Past Participle
begin	began	begun	lay	laid	laid
break	broke	broken	lie	lay	lain
bring	brought	brought	ride	rode	ridden
choose	chose	chosen	ring	rang	rung
come	came	come	rise	rose	risen
do	did	done	run	ran	run
drink	drank	drunk	see	saw	seen
eat	ate	eaten	sing	sang	sung
fall	fell	fallen	speak	spoke	spoken
freeze	froze	frozen	steal	stole	stolen
give	gave	given	swim	swam	swum
go	went	gone	take	took	taken
grow	grew	grown	throw	threw	thrown
know	knew	known	write	wrote	written

Practice Pages on Irregular Verbs

Irregular verbs can cause problems in writing as well as in speaking. Pages 298–309 provide practice in the correct use of some irregular verbs.

How well do you use these verbs? The exercise on the next page will tell you.

If the exercise shows that you need more practice with certain verbs, your teacher may ask you to turn to those verbs on the following pages. For each verb there are many sentences that will help you to "say it right," "hear it right," and "write it right."

Exercise   Use irregular verbs correctly.

Number your paper from 1–30. For each sentence, write the correct word from the two given in parentheses.

1. The party (began, begun) at about seven o'clock.
2. The gate had been (broke, broken) long ago.
3. Who (bring, brought) these posters to class?
4. Has everyone (chosen, chose) a topic for his or her report?
5. Jack (came, come) home after the debate.
6. Rob has never (did, done) such a good job.
7. At camp, we (drunk, drank) a quart of milk every day.
8. Someone had (ate, eaten) all the brownies.
9. We had never (saw, seen) such a sight.
10. The plumber (did, done) the work well.
11. Lauren has (given, gave) a good report about Presidential elections.
12. Everyone had (went, gone) home by then.
13. That tree has (grew, grown) several feet this year.
14. I wouldn't have (known, knew) what to do.
15. Our science class has (grew, grown) different plants for an experiment.
16. The team (known, knew) all of the defensive plays.
17. The alarm had (rung, rang) too soon for me.
18. The church bells (rung, rang) at seven.
19. The sun had (rose, risen) early.
20. We (run, ran) the relay races on the indoor track.
21. Bill (seen, saw) two deer.
22. The audience (sang, sung) the chorus of the song.
23. The President has (spoke, spoken) to the reporters.
24. The thief had (stole, stolen) several appliances from the shop.
25. We had never (swum, swam) as far as that.
26. We have (went, gone) skiing every winter.
27. Terry (threw, thrown) the Frisbee to Darcy.
28. Eric has (write, written) a good short story.
29. The pitcher had (threw, thrown) a curve to strike out the batter.
30. Have you (wrote, written) your report for consumer ed?

Say It Right   Hear It Right

Begin
Began
Begun

A. Say these sentences over until the correct use of *began* and *begun* sounds natural to you.

1. Have you begun yet?
2. Jill hasn't begun.
3. Bill began his job.
4. He began yesterday.
5. Mary began thinking.
6. I began to daydream.
7. I haven't begun the book.
8. Have they begun reading?

Bring
Brought
Brought

B. Say these sentences over until the correct use of *bring* and *brought* sounds natural to you.

1. Did you bring the map?
2. Sam brought an atlas.
3. Did Mike bring the radio?
4. Yes, he brought it.
5. What did Suzi bring?
6. She has brought the food.
7. Claire had brought the soda.
8. I wish I'd brought some too.

Write It Right

Write the correct word from the two words given.

1. Has the movie (began, begun) yet?
2. Yes, it (began, begun) ten minutes ago.
3. I haven't missed that series since it (began, begun).
4. Have you (began, begun) your new book yet?
5. We (began, begun) our day playing tennis.
6. The people (began, begun) to leave the scene of the accident.
7. Jory has (began, begun) to mow the lawn.
8. Patti (bring, brought) me a present for my birthday.
9. The messenger (bring, brought) good news.
10. The jury (bring, brought) in the verdict.
11. Did you (bring, brought) the book I wanted to read?
12. I have (bring, brought) candy for everyone in the class.
13. Did you (bring, brought) sleeping bags for our weekend?
14. We have (bring, brought) plenty of food, too.
15. Have you (bring, brought) all the equipment for your new experiment?

298

Say It Right   Hear It Right

A. Say these sentences over until the correct use of *broke* and *broken* sounds natural to you.

Break
Broke
Broken

1. Pam broke the school record.
2. No one else has broken it.
3. The car broke down in Ohio.
4. Dennis broke the window.
5. Dan had broken the mug.
6. Steve broke his ankle.
7. The mirror was broken.
8. I have broken my watch.

B. Say these sentences over until the correct use of *came* and *come* sounds natural to you.

Come
Came
Come

1. Nathan came yesterday.
2. Your friends have come.
3. They all came together.
4. Janelle should have come.
5. No one came late.
6. Joe came early.
7. He has come early before.
8. Hasn't Heather come yet?

Write It Right

Write the correct word from the two words given.

1. I have (broke, broken) the can opener.
2. Now that it's (broke, broken), we'll need to replace it.
3. The clock is (broke, broken) beyond repair.
4. The VW had (broke, broken) down on the road to the beach.
5. Someone has (broke, broken) into the storeroom.
6. The heat wave (broke, broken) all records for July.
7. Sara (broke, broken) the record for the 100-yard dash.
8. Peter has (came, come) to the game with us.
9. He had (came, come) with us before.
10. My parents (came, come) to our play.
11. Summer has finally (came, come).
12. The coach (came, come) to see me in the hospital.
13. The sailboat (came, come) toward us.
14. We have (came, come) to the parade every Fourth of July.
15. The time has (came, come) for action.

Say It Right   Hear It Right

Choose
Chose
Chosen

A. Say these sentences over until the correct use of *chose* and *chosen* sounds natural to you.

1. Have you chosen a book?
2. No, I haven't chosen one.
3. Bill chose his.
4. What has he chosen?

5. He chose a biography.
6. Renée had chosen a novel.
7. Ginny chose a book of poems.
8. Trina chose a book on sports.

Do
Did
Done

B. Say these sentences over until the correct use of *did* and *done* sounds natural to you.

1. I did my work early.
2. Sue has not done hers yet.
3. Amy has done two sketches.
4. Did you do this diorama?

5. Doug has done his job well.
6. Tom did the dishes tonight.
7. Have you done any hiking?
8. Sue did nothing to help.

Write It Right

Write the correct word from the two words given.

1. Our club has (chose, chosen) a new treasurer.
2. Who was (chose, chosen)?
3. Have you already (chose, chosen) a new president?
4. Yes, we have (chose, chosen) our president.
5. The students have (chose, chosen) good officers.
6. Which rucksack have you (chose, chosen)?
7. I have (chose, chosen) this one and a down sleeping bag.
8. Jonathan has (did, done) a beautiful painting.
9. Do you know how he (did, done) it?
10. He (did, done) it with oil paints.
11. Have you (did, done) your essay?
12. I (did, done) it last night.
13. We (did, done) our work and went skating.
14. Pablo had (did, done) the organizing for the program.
15. He (did, done) a better job than anyone else had ever (did, done).

Say It Right   Hear It Right

A. Say these sentences over until the correct use of *drank* and *drunk* sounds natural to you.

**Drink
Drank
Drunk**

1. Who drank the milk?
2. Liz must have drunk it.
3. We have drunk all the tea.
4. Tom drank Squirt.

5. Sue drank all the lemonade.
6. I have never drunk Coke.
7. Al drank orange juice.
8. Who drank the soda?

B. Say these sentences over until the correct use of *eat, ate,* and *eaten* sounds natural to you.

**Eat
Ate
Eaten**

1. Have you eaten yet?
2. Yes, I have eaten.
3. Jenny ate quite early.
4. Did you eat at noon?

5. When did you eat dinner?
6. We ate at 6 o'clock.
7. Last night we ate outside.
8. José had eaten with us.

Write It Right

Write the correct word from the two words given.

1. The kittens (drank, drunk) all the milk.
2. Have you ever (drank, drunk) a black cow?
3. No, I've never (drank, drunk) one.
4. We (drank, drunk) the lemonade and went back to work.
5. The patient (drank, drunk) the medicine.
6. Dad has not (drank, drunk) coffee for a month.
7. Jill (drank, drunk) all the chocolate milk.
8. The oranges have all been (ate, eaten).
9. Which one of you has (ate, eaten) all the ice cream?
10. Have you ever (ate, eaten) nectarines?
11. Yes, I have (ate, eaten) them.
12. We (ate, eaten) dinner at the Spaghetti Factory.
13. Carl and I had (ate, eaten) dinner with our grandparents.
14. Mary had (ate, eaten) before we got home.
15. Pam and Sal (ate, eaten) half the watermelon.

Say It Right   Hear It Right

Give
Gave
Given

A. Say these sentences over until the correct use of *give*, *gave*, and *given* sounds natural to you.

1. Who gave you that hat?
2. It was given to me by Amy.
3. Sue gave Al an aquarium.
4. I have given him a book.

5. Did he give his pen away?
6. I have given two pens away.
7. Dick gave me his puzzle.
8. I had given him a model.

Grow
Grew
Grown

B. Say these sentences over until the correct use of *grew* and *grown* sounds natural to you.

1. The fern grew quickly.
2. The tree hasn't grown.
3. Mr. Smyth grew apples.
4. He has also grown pears.

5. The weather grew colder.
6. It has now grown warmer.
7. The child had grown tired.
8. Have you ever grown herbs?

Write It Right

Write the correct word from the two words given.

1. Jerry has (gave, given) up playing baseball.
2. We have always (gave, given) toys to the orphanage.
3. Maria (give, gave) me a compliment.
4. Pete has (gave, given) two recitals this year.
5. Nancy (give, gave) her brother a sweater.
6. Have you (given, gave) that album away?
7. Our team (give, gave) our rivals a beating.
8. Les has (grew, grown) faster than his cousin has.
9. What have you (grew, grown) in your garden?
10. We've (grew, grown) lettuce and tomatoes.
11. We have also (grew, grown) beans and peppers.
12. The beans have (grew, grown) quite tall.
13. Jean (grew, grown) strawberries in her garden.
14. Alan has (grew, grown) too tall to wear his old uniform.
15. The sapling (grew, grown) into a beautiful tree.

Say It Right   Hear It Right

A. Say these sentences over until the correct use of *knew* and *known* sounds natural to you.

Know
Knew
Known

1. I knew the results.
2. I have known Jim for years.
3. Who knew the answers?
4. Bret knew the answers.

5. I knew the answers, too.
6. Have you known Josh long?
7. Who knew about the race?
8. Al had not known about it.

B. Say these sentences over until the correct use of *ran* and *run* sounds natural to you.

Run
Ran
Run

1. Bill ran a race.
2. He had never run faster.
3. He ran 20 kilometers.
4. The race was run in Chicago.

5. Ed ran the race in an hour.
6. Have you run the relay?
7. I have never run in a race.
8. Sue ran the raffle.

Write It Right

Write the correct word from the two words given.

1. How long have you (knew, known) the Bernsteins?
2. We have (knew, known) them for a long time.
3. Had you (knew, known) Christmas vacation was extended?
4. Some things are (knew, known) with certainty.
5. I (knew, known) about the airplane accident yesterday.
6. Very few others (knew, known) about it then.
7. Lou had never (knew, known) anyone from Israel before.
8. That calculator is (ran, run) by four batteries.
9. The Lions Club (ran, run) the carnival this year.
10. They had never (ran, run) it before.
11. They (ran, run) for shelter when the tornado alert sounded.
12. Have you ever (ran, run) in a relay race?
13. Our air conditioner (ran, run) for twenty-four hours.
14. Janice has (ran, run) in the Fourth of July race for two years.
15. The thieves (ran, run) when the burglar alarm went off.

Say It Right   Hear It Right

Ring
Rang
Rung

A. Say these sentences over until the correct use of *rang* and *rung* sounds natural to you.

1. Has the telephone rung?
2. I thought it rang.
3. It rang an hour ago.
4. It hasn't rung since.
5. The doorbell rang.
6. Who rang it?
7. I had rung it earlier.
8. The dinner bell rang.

Ride
Rode
Ridden

B. Say these sentences over until the correct use of *rode* and *ridden* sounds natural to you.

1. Who rode the horse?
2. The horse was ridden well.
3. Jim rode the horse.
4. I have ridden often.
5. Julie rode her bike.
6. She has ridden it often.
7. Anne rode in our new car.
8. Marla has ridden in it, too.

Write It Right

Write the correct word from the two words given.

1. Sleigh bells (rang, rung) out merrily.
2. All the church bells were (rang, rung) in celebration.
3. Christmas carols (rang, rung) out everywhere.
4. The telephone has (rang, rung) several times.
5. The cries of the hounds (rang, rung) in the air.
6. We have (rang, rung) many doorbells selling magazines.
7. Has the tardy bell (rang, rung) yet?
8. Have you ever (rode, ridden) a snowmobile?
9. I (rode, ridden) one several times last winter.
10. Tammy and Jill (rode, ridden) the bus to Atlanta.
11. Ron has (rode, ridden) in the Goodyear blimp.
12. Do you know anyone who has (rode, ridden) a camel?
13. We (rode, ridden) horseback in the mountains.
14. My family has (rode, ridden) on a DC-10 to Hawaii.
15. Have you (rode, ridden) on a roller coaster?

Say It Right   Hear It Right

A. Say these sentences over until the correct use of *rose* and *risen* sounds natural to you.

Rise
Rose
Risen

1. The sun has risen.
2. It rose at 6:15.
3. The river rose rapidly.
4. It has risen before.
5. The road rose sharply.
6. The moon rose over the hill.
7. The kite rose swiftly.
8. Jo had risen from her seat.

B. Say these sentences over until the correct use of *sang* and *sung* sounds natural to you.

Sing
Sang
Sung

1. Craig sang a solo.
2. He has sung before.
3. The tenor sang softly.
4. Lori also sang a solo.
5. She had sung last year.
6. Has she sung an aria?
7. The birds sang loudly.
8. The violin had sung sadly.

Write It Right

Write the correct word from the two words given.

1. The audience had (rose, risen) from their seats.
2. The official has (rose, risen) to a high rank.
3. The moon (rose, risen) over the mountain.
4. Why hasn't the dough (rose, risen)?
5. The crowd had (rose, risen) to cheer the players.
6. The divers had (rose, risen) to the surface.
7. The temperature has (rose, risen) to 35 degrees C.
8. Our chorus (sang, sung) in the assembly program.
9. We (sang, sung) a medley of show tunes.
10. We had (sang, sung) them before.
11. Our quartet (sang, sung) at the state competition.
12. They had (sang, sung) last year, too.
13. Has Phil ever (sang, sung) in the choir?
14. The choir has (sang, sung) in many cities.
15. Had Jean (sang, sung) the alto or soprano part?

Say It Right   Hear It Right

A. Say these sentences over until the correct use of *saw* and *seen* sounds natural to you.

1. Have you seen Dan?
2. Yes, I saw him.
3. Ted has seen him, too.
4. Maureen saw him Sunday.
5. I saw that movie.
6. Have you seen it?
7. We saw it Saturday.
8. Bret hasn't seen it yet.

B. Say these sentences over until the correct use of *spoke* and *spoken* sounds natural to you.

1. Jan spoke to us yesterday.
2. She had spoken to us before.
3. Manny spoke first.
4. Has Liz spoken yet?
5. No, she hasn't spoken.
6. Terri spoke at the meeting.
7. She hadn't spoken before.
8. She spoke rather well.

Write It Right

Write the correct word from the two words given.

1. Have you ever (saw, seen) this TV program?
2. It's the best show I've ever (saw, seen).
3. Judy (saw, seen) the President at the airport.
4. Penny (saw, seen) her friends at the library.
5. I have (saw, seen) parachute jumping many times.
6. In the mountains Art (saw, seen) wild horses.
7. Jack had (saw, seen) the Bolshoi Ballet.
8. Dr. Wagner has (spoke, spoken) to me about a job.
9. I have (spoke, spoken) to my parents about it.
10. Everyone in the class has (spoke, spoken) at least once.
11. Rita hasn't (spoke, spoken) to me about her plans yet.
12. Jean has not (spoke, spoken) a word.
13. Our group (spoke, spoken) on energy consumption.
14. Which person had (spoke, spoken) at the meeting?
15. Tracy Austin (spoke, spoken) at our sports banquet.

Say It Right   Hear It Right

A. Say these sentences over until the correct use of *stole* and *stolen* sounds natural to you.

Steal
Stole
Stolen

1. Who stole the money?
2. Two gangsters stole it.
3. Why have they stolen it?
4. Had they stolen before?
5. When was it stolen?
6. It was stolen yesterday.
7. They stole it at noon.
8. They stole it wearing masks.

B. Say these sentences over until the correct use of *swam* and *swum* sounds natural to you.

Swim
Swam
Swum

1. I swam in the pool.
2. Have you swum there?
3. Kelly swam all day.
4. We swam in the lake.
5. They had swum in the ocean.
6. Mark swam ten laps.
7. Linda had swum thirty.
8. I swam at the Y. W. C. A.

Write It Right

Write the correct word from the two words given.

1. Someone has (stole, stolen) our spare tire.
2. Why has someone (stole, stolen) it?
3. Lou Brock has (stole, stolen) more bases than anyone else.
4. He (stole, stolen) over 800 bases in his baseball career.
5. Ty Cobb had (stole, stolen) the most bases until Brock broke his record in '77.
6. The thief (stole, stolen) three oil paintings.
7. We know why he might have (stole, stolen) them.
8. Beth (swam, swum) at a very early age.
9. We haven't (swam, swum) much until now.
10. Our team (swam, swum) in the state meet.
11. During vacation, Sally (swam, swum) every day.
12. Have you (swam, swum) in the new pool?
13. Tanya has (swam, swum) there many times.
14. Chuck became ill when he (swam, swum) in the icy water.
15. Our team has often (swam, swum) in the medley relay.

Say It Right   Hear It Right

Throw
Threw
Thrown

A. Say these sentences over until the correct use of *threw* and *thrown* sounds natural to you.

1. Who threw the ball?
2. Carrie threw it.
3. Have you thrown it?
4. Bruce hasn't thrown it.

5. I threw the paper away.
6. Bill threw the door open.
7. Lee has thrown the list away.
8. Chris threw a fast pitch.

Take
Took
Taken

B. Say these sentences over until the correct use of *took* and *taken* sounds natural to you.

1. Paula took a walk.
2. Steve took one, too.
3. Lori has taken the book.
4. Craig took three cookies.

5. Who took these pictures?
6. Gene took them.
7. He has taken lots of them.
8. We took a helicopter ride.

Write It Right

Write the correct word from the two words given.

1. The captain had (threw, thrown) the cargo overboard.
2. The runner was (threw, thrown) out at home plate.
3. The quarterback (threw, thrown) a touchdown pass.
4. I had (threw, thrown) cold water over my face.
5. The athlete (threw, thrown) the discus expertly.
6. I have (threw, thrown) those magazines away by mistake.
7. Have you ever (threw, thrown) a horseshoe?
8. Gabe has (took, taken) the wrong route.
9. I have never (took, taken) the expressway.
10. It (took, taken) us an hour to drive downtown.
11. The troops had (took, taken) the enemy by surprise.
12. We (took, taken) our sleeping bags with us.
13. Ms. Miller has (took, taken) our guest speaker to the airport.
14. It has (took, taken) a long time to save money for the party.
15. I have never (took, taken) that kind of medicine before.

Say It Right   Hear It Right

A. Say these sentences over until the correct use of *went* and *gone* sounds natural to you.

**Go
Went
Gone**

1. Who went skating?
2. Pete has gone home.
3. Julie went to the park.
4. Have they gone swimming?
5. Janice went downstairs.
6. Have they gone yet?
7. They went an hour ago.
8. Everyone has gone.

B. Say these sentences over until the correct use of *wrote* and *written* sounds natural to you.

**Write
Wrote
Written**

1. I've written my paper.
2. Have you written one?
3. I wrote a letter.
4. Sue hasn't written yet.
5. Who has written to you?
6. Paul wrote to me.
7. Donna has written a speech.
8. They wrote the script.

Write It Right

Write the correct word from the two words given.

1. The spacecraft (went, gone) around the earth many times.
2. Another one has (went, gone) into orbit around the moon.
3. We (went, gone) to Disneyland last summer.
4. The Petersons have (went, gone) to New York for a week.
5. My sister has (went, gone) to France to study French.
6. Have you ever (went, gone) skiing?
7. Judy has (went, gone) to Florida for spring vacation.
8. That novel was (wrote, written) by Mark Twain.
9. Jim has (wrote, written) several humorous poems.
10. Melinda (wrote, written) to her friend.
11. Have you (wrote, written) your composition?
12. I've (wrote, written) the first draft.
13. Our class has (wrote, written) letters to the governor.
14. Last year we (wrote, written) to the mayor.
15. Why haven't you (wrote, written) that letter yet?

Part 7 Active and Passive Verbs

One of the interesting things about our language is the great variety of ways in which it expresses ideas. You have seen how many different times can be shown by the tenses of verbs. Now you will see another way in which verbs help you say exactly what you have in mind.

Suppose that a window has been broken. If you know who broke it, you can say something like this:

My little brother broke the window yesterday.

But suppose you don't know who broke it, or suppose you don't want to say who broke it. You might then say:

The window was broken yesterday.

In the first sentence, the subject tells who performed the action. When the subject performs the action, the verb is said to be **active.**

In the second sentence, the subject tells what received the action. When the subject tells the receiver or the result of the action, the verb is said to be **passive.** (The word *passive* means "acted upon.")

Forming the Passive

The passive form of the verb is made by using a form of *be* with the past participle.

ACTIVE

Megan has finished the project.
Chris has shown the slides.
The store will add the tax.

PASSIVE

The project has been finished by Megan.
The slides have been shown by Chris.
The tax will be added by the store.

Find the direct objects in the sentences labeled **Active**. What has happened to them in the sentences labeled **Passive?** Only verbs that have objects (transitive verbs) can be changed from active to passive.

A verb is active when its subject performs the action stated by the verb.

A verb is passive when its subject names the receiver or result of the action stated by the verb.

Exercises Use active and passive forms.

A. Change the verbs in the following sentences from active to passive. Rewrite the sentences.

1. Mr. Harvey cleaned the rug.
2. The digital scoreboard shows the scores and time.
3. Those children fed the ducks.
4. The Art Club decorated the gym.
5. Our team had already won the trophy once before.
6. The fire destroyed five buildings.
7. Almost everybody knows Mr. Walters.
8. Our class had written letters to our Senators.
9. The lawyer will appeal the judge's decision.
10. Bret has found the error.

B. Rewrite each sentence, changing the verb. If the verb is active, make it passive. If it is passive, make it active.

1. One of the boys baked a cake.
2. His plans were affected by inflation.
3. The group discussed playground regulations.
4. The committee held a meeting at one o'clock.
5. Ms. O'Brien read the class an interesting article.
6. The tour had been planned by Aviation Travel Company.
7. Several alternatives were considered by the club.
8. The Potter's Wheel also sells ceramic supplies.

Part 8 Troublesome Pairs of Verbs

There are certain pairs of verbs that cause trouble because they are alike in meaning. They are *alike*, but they are not the same. We cannot substitute one of the pair for the other. Learn the differences so that you can use these words correctly.

Sit and Set

Sit means "to occupy a seat." The principal parts are *sit, sat, sat*.

Set means "to place." The principal parts are *set, set, set*.

Present	*Sit* in the car. *Set* the box down.
Past	We *sat* in the car. Beth *set* the box down.
Present Perfect	We *have sat* for an hour. We *have set* the box down on the ground.

Lie and Lay

Lie means "to rest in a flat position" or "to be situated." The principal parts are *lie, lay, lain*.

Lay means "to place." The principal parts are *lay, laid, laid*.

Present	*Lie* down, Fido. *Lay* the blankets here.
Past	Fido *lay* down. We *laid* the blankets here.
Present Perfect	Fido *has lain* down. We *have laid* the blankets on the grass.

Let and Leave

Let means "to allow or permit." The principal parts are *let, let, let*.

Leave means "to go away from" or "to allow something to remain where it is." The principal parts are *leave, left, left*.

Present	*Let* us help you. *Leave* your coats here.
Past	Bill *let* us help. The girls *left* their coats.
Present Perfect	Bill *has let* us help on other projects. Sue *has left* her coat in the closet.

Rise and Raise

Rise means "to go upward." The principal parts are *rise, rose, risen.*

Raise means "to lift or to make something go up." The principal parts are *raise, raised, raised.*

Present	The balloon *rises* fast. Please *raise* the flag.
Past	The balloon *rose* quickly. Jeff *raised* the flag.
Present Perfect	The balloon *has risen* above the tree tops. Jeff *has raised* the flag every morning.

May and Can

May refers to permission or to something that is possible. *Might* is another form of the word. There are no principal parts. *May* and *might* are used only as helping verbs.

May we go swimming?   You *might* catch cold.

Can refers to ability. *Could* is another form of the verb. There are no principal parts. *Can* and *could* are used as helping verbs.

Janet *can* swim beautifully because she has practiced.
You *can* catch a cold if you are tired.

Learn and Teach

Learn means "to gain knowledge or skill." The principal parts are *learn, learned, learned.*

Teach means "to help someone learn." You must be taught by someone. The principal parts are *teach, taught, taught.*

Present	*Learn* to swim well. Please *teach* me the trick.
Past	Janet *learned* quickly. My mother *taught* me the trick.
Present Perfect	We *have learned* our lesson. Pam *has taught* us another trick.

Exercises Choose the correct verb from the pair.

A. Number your paper from 1–10. Choose the correct verb.

1. The geyser (rose, raised) at least 100 feet up in the air.
2. The sun (rises, raises) over those hills around 6 A.M.
3. (Let, Leave) your books in your locker.
4. (Let, Leave) your assignment on the desk.
5. The audience (rose, raised) and applauded the orchestra.
6. (Lie, Lay) still and listen.
7. You must have (laid, lain) your package down by the fountain.
8. A slow, cool mist had been (raising, rising) off the lagoon.
9. The dog won't (lie, lay) down.
10. They (lay, laid) wall-to-wall carpeting.

B. Follow the directions for Exercise A.

1. We usually (sit, set) on the porch steps and talk.
2. The moon (sat, set) well before midnight.
3. (May, Can) I use your telephone?
4. (Can, May) I go to the movie tonight?
5. I (set, sat) the box on the big chair.
6. (Teach, Learn) Ryan not to bellyflop, will you?
7. (Can, May) we borrow your tape recorder?
8. They were (sitting, setting) up waiting for Roger.
9. That's a snap. I (could, might) do that easily.
10. Marcia (learned, taught) the speech by heart.

Additional Exercises — Review

Using Verbs

A. Find the verbs.

Find the parts of the verb in each sentence. Write them in two columns labeled *Helping Verb* and *Main Verb*.

1. Where did you buy those socks?
2. Don't take it so hard.
3. Ken should have been the villain in the play.
4. Are Nancy and the others standing in line for hockey tickets?
5. You might have told me about the news report.
6. Can you read the sign?
7. He must have come down the chimney.
8. Our homeroom has decorated the school lobby for the holidays.
9. Do you think so?
10. Shall I make banana nut bread for Friday?

B. Use progressive forms.

Copy each sentence, changing each verb to its progressive form.

1. Paul ate the melon.
2. Have you watched the series?
3. We will call my grandparents tonight.
4. Mrs. Levy directs the junior high band.
5. Mandy and Jenny could help us with the gardening.
6. Several volunteers will collect aluminum cans for the recycling center.

7. Jay has worked here since May.

8. Nancy and Marla must have fished here yesterday afternoon.

9. The choir will sing tonight.

10. I had saved my money for a new ten-speed bike.

C. Recognize verb tenses.

Find each verb in the following sentences and tell the tense of each.

1. Have you subtracted correctly?

2. The tickets for the tournament will be available in the main office.

3. Will the new school have air-conditioning?

4. My sister and I flew to Alaska.

5. My sister's graduation will take place in June.

6. Rod Carew is an excellent baseball player.

7. Our music class attended an afternoon performance by the Chicago Symphony Orchestra.

8. Liza Minnelli and Barbra Steisand are exciting performers.

9. We had waited in line for over an hour.

10. With the help of McDonald's, we raised $1000 for the fight against muscular dystrophy.

D. Use passive verb forms.

Change the verbs in the following sentences from active to passive. Rewrite the sentences.

1. Tramco sponsored the program.

2. Everybody in grade nine takes consumer education.

3. Stacy threw the ball out-of-bounds.

4. About fifty people called the radio station.

5. A flat tire delayed the school bus.

6. My little sister designed and painted these covers.

7. This computer will record the sun-spot activity.
8. The Fisher Company is building a condominium on this site.
9. Snow covered the ice rink.
10. Juan developed the photographs.

E. Choose the correct verb from the pair.

Number your paper from 1–10. Choose the correct verb.

1. (Let, Leave) Craig work by himself.
2. (Raise, Rise) the shelf about another inch.
3. Dan (raised, rose) a skeptical eyebrow.
4. The tool box is (laying, lying) on the workbench.
5. I saw the shovel (lying, laying) out in the rain.
6. Cindy lost her balance and (set, sat) down hard.
7. (May, Can) I use your telephone?
8. Would you (sit, set) the groceries on the table?
9. No one (learned, taught) Laurie to roller skate.
10. How our coach can (sit, set) so calmly is beyond me!

Section 5

Using Modifiers

Nouns and pronouns help us name and identify things and people in the world about us. Verbs help us make statements and ask questions about things and people.

Modifiers—adjectives and adverbs—help us describe what we have seen and heard.

> She wore a *yellow* sweater.
> We heard the jet *faintly* in the distance.

In addition, modifiers help us state how we feel about things and people.

> The room was *messy*.
> Our new puppy was *extremely* energetic.

We have already studied nouns, pronouns, and verbs in detail. In this section we shall study modifiers closely.

Part 1　Adjectives

What is the difference between these sentences?

> Rain fell.
> A cold, hard rain fell.

The difference is in the descriptive words that tell what kind of rain fell. These words are **adjectives.** They are one of the parts of speech.

An adjective is a word that goes with, or modifies, a noun or pronoun.

Some adjectives tell *what kind* about the words they modify:

> Look at the *huge, white* balloon.

Some adjectives tell *how many* or *how much* about the words they modify:

> Jim found *twenty* dollars.
> We have had *little* rain.

Some adjectives tell *which one* or *which ones* about the words they modify:

> *That* door sticks.
> *These* pens work better.

Predicate Adjectives

Sometimes an adjective is separated from the word it modifies by a linking verb:

> Everyone was quiet.　　Phil seemed annoyed.

An adjective that follows a linking verb and that modifies the subject is called a **predicate adjective.**

Proper Adjectives

Proper adjectives are adjectives formed from proper nouns. They are always capitalized. Here are some examples of proper adjectives:

an American dollar	the Spanish language	the French flag
a Norwegian sardine	the English custom	an Oriental rug

Pronouns Used as Adjectives

The words *this, that, these,* and *those* can be used as demonstrative pronouns. When used alone, they are pronouns. When followed by a noun, they are adjectives.

These are my sunglasses. (pronoun)
These problems are easy. (adjective modifying *problems*)
That is the wrong answer. (pronoun)
That answer is wrong. (adjective modifying *answer*)

The words *my, your, his, her, its, our,* and *their* are possessive pronouns, but they can also be classed as adjectives. They are modifiers that make the meaning of the nouns they modify more definite. They tell *which one* or *which ones.*

My mother works at home; *your* mother commutes.
His sweater is blue; *her* sweater is red.
Our house is a ranch house; *their* house has two stories.

Exercises Find the adjectives.

A. Number your paper from 1–10. Write the adjectives you find in each sentence. After each adjective, write the word it modifies. Do not include *a, an,* or *the.*

1. The jockey in the blue satin shirt mounted the black racehorse.

2. Jubilant teammates carried the goalie off the muddy field.

3. Two sleek, silver Mercedes were parked in the circular driveway.

4. I feel comfortable in a plaid flannel shirt, corduroy jeans, and brown suede boots.

5. Colonial costumes and decorative furniture were on display at the huge, white Georgian mansion.

6. The red, orange, yellow, and brown leaves created a beautiful scene.

7. A tall, wiry player stood at the free-throw line and sank the winning basket.

8. Wicker baskets of white daisies and yellow roses decorated the table.

9. I have worn these old Adidas for two years.

10. The small, brown puppy nestled against me as I sat on the old, rickety bench.

B. Number your paper from 1–10. Find the predicate adjectives in these sentences. Write them down.

1. The morning sun was red.
2. Over the lake the mist looked steamy and strange.
3. Gradually the air grew warm.
4. Small birds around us were busy and noisy.
5. The woods seemed full of them.
6. The woods smelled fresh and good in the sunlight.
7. Everyone appeared happy.
8. Our packs felt light.
9. Ahead of us the path was smooth and easy.
10. Life seemed great.

C. Write ten sentences of your own, using many colorful adjectives. Try to use all the different kinds of adjectives discussed on pages 320 and 321. Underline the adjectives in your sentences.

Part 2 Adverbs

In order to make our meaning clear, vivid, and complete, we often have to tell *how, when, where,* or *to what extent* something is true. Adverbs are used for this purpose.

Adverbs Used with Verbs

Adverbs are used to go with, or modify, verbs to tell *how, when, where,* or *to what extent* an action happened.

Study the following list of adverbs:

HOW?	WHEN?	WHERE?	TO WHAT EXTENT?
secretly	then	nearby	often
quickly	later	underground	deep
sorrowfully	afterwards	here	seldom
hurriedly	finally	there	always

Now use some of the above adverbs in this sentence:

The pirates buried their gold.

You can see what a great difference adverbs make. They can make the meaning of the verb *buried* clearer, and add vividness and completeness to the whole sentence.

Adverbs Used with Adjectives or Other Adverbs

Besides being used to modify verbs, adverbs are also used to modify adjectives and other adverbs. Notice the italicized adverbs in the following sentences:

Niki was happy.　　　　　　　Rick spoke slowly.
Niki was *extremely* happy.　　Rick spoke *too* slowly.

On the next page are some more adverbs that are often used to modify adjectives or other adverbs:

very	nearly	so
just	somewhat	more
quite	rather	most

These adverbs all tell *to what extent* something is true. You can see how useful adverbs are in making clearer, more complete, or more vivid the adjectives or other adverbs that we use.

Adverbs are words that modify verbs, adjectives, and other adverbs.

Forming Adverbs

Many adverbs are made by adding *-ly* to an adjective:

secret + -ly = secretly
bright + -ly = brightly

Sometimes the addition of *-ly* involves a spelling change in the adjective:

easy + -ly = easily (*y* changed to *i*)
capable + -ly = capably (final *-le* dropped)
full + -ly = fully (*-ll* changed to *-l*)

Many words, like *quite* or *so,* can be used only as adverbs:

This footprint is *quite* recent.
Sue never looked *so* happy before.

Some other words, like *early* or *fast,* can be used either as adverbs or as adjectives:

Bill arrived *early.* (adverb)
He ate an *early* breakfast. (adjective)

Dana can run *fast.* (adverb)
She is a *fast* runner. (adjective)

Exercises Recognize adverbs.

A. Number your paper from 1–10. Write the adverb in each sentence. After each adverb write the word it modifies. Be ready to explain what the adverb tells about the word it modifies.

EXAMPLE: The actors usually stay here.

usually modifies *stay* (tells when)
here modifies *stay* (tells where)

1. The doctor has just left.
2. We have never studied about Greenland.
3. The runners raced vigorously around the track.
4. That movie was quite informative.
5. The newspaper was rather careful about its editorials.
6. The quarterback limped painfully off the field.
7. The runway lights shone brightly at the airport.
8. Our canoe drifted lazily down the river.
9. The summer rain fell heavily.
10. The pounding stopped immediately.

B. Follow the directions for Exercise A.

1. That pounding has started again.
2. It was nearly midnight before the train arrived.
3. The visiting football teams usually stay at the Hilton.
4. Those two cats wander aimlessly from yard to yard.
5. That pitcher seemed somewhat unsure of himself.
6. Alicia smiled weakly.
7. Because the train was ahead of schedule, we arrived early.
8. The play went smoothly until the last act.
9. Mexico City's climate is usually ideal.
10. It is extremely important that you relay the message.

C. Change the following adjectives into adverbs by adding -ly. Be careful of your spelling.

sure	cruel	terrible	grim
icy	heavy	impatient	careful
full	sad	peaceful	happy
loud	beautiful	dizzy	cool
rough	smooth	crazy	hopeful

An Adverb Tells	An Adjective Tells
When? Where? How? To What Extent?	Which One? What Kind? How Many?
About a Verb, Adjective, or Adverb	**About a Noun or Pronoun**

Part 3 Adjective or Adverb?

Study the following sentences. Which sentence sounds right?

Our team won *easy.*
Our team won *easily.*

The second sentence is the correct one. An adverb (*easily*) should be used, not an adjective (*easy*).

It is often difficult to decide whether an adjective or an adverb should be used in sentences like the two given above. When you are not sure which form to use, ask yourself these questions:

1. Which word does the modifier go with? If it goes with an action verb (like *won* in the sentences above), it is an adverb. It is also an adverb if it goes with an adjective or another adverb. If it goes with a noun or pronoun, it is an adjective.

2. What does the modifier tell about the word it goes with? If the modifier tells *when, where, how,* or *to what extent,* it is an adverb. If it tells *which one, what kind,* or *how many,* it is an adjective. In the sentences above, the modifier tells *how* our team won; it must therefore be an adverb: *easily.*

Exercises Find the adjectives and adverbs.

A. List each adjective and adverb, together with the word it modifies. (Do not list *a, an,* or *the.*)

EXAMPLE: The tall runner in the red shirt won easily.

tall runner   red shirt   easily won

1. Two white puppies walked carelessly through the flowers.
2. Red, white, and blue bunting was decoratively hung around the platform.
3. He paid the bill quite promptly.
4. The suspect answered the questions rather cautiously.
5. The young swimmers dived unhesitatingly into the large pool.
6. The small child cried loudly in the dentist's office.
7. The dancers moved gracefully across the tiny stage.
8. The American ambassador spoke openly and honestly about our foreign policy.
9. The commuters walked briskly toward the long, yellow train.
10. The new puppies are too big for the basket.

B. Choose the correct modifier from the two given in parentheses. Tell what word it modifies and whether it is an adjective or adverb.

1. These flowers smell (fresh, freshly).
2. My brother drives (careful, carefully).
3. Debbie's drawings were (real, really) good.
4. The leaves turned very (quick, quickly) this year.
5. Mrs. Watson explained the assignment (clear, clearly).
6. Our dog peered (cautious, cautiously) around the sofa.
7. Ted appeared at the door (prompt, promptly) at eight.
8. Everything fitted in place just (beautifully, beautiful).
9. Please work (quiet, quietly) during the test.
10. Renée and Marsha walked (slow, slowly) to town.

Adverbs and Predicate Adjectives

You will remember that a predicate adjective appears after a linking verb and modifies the subject.

The rose is red. (*red* modifies *rose*)

The sky became cloudy. (*cloudy* modifies *sky*)

The pizza tastes good. (*good* modifies *pizza*)

You also remember that in addition to the forms of *be*, the following can be used as linking verbs: *become, seem, appear, look, sound, feel, taste, grow,* and *smell.*

Sometimes these verbs are action verbs. When they are action verbs, they are followed by adverbs, not adjectives. The adverbs modify the verbs and tell *how, when, where,* or *to what extent.*

Look at the following sentences to see when adjectives are used and when adverbs are used:

ACTION VERBS WITH ADVERBS	LINKING VERBS WITH ADJECTIVES
Bob *felt* his way *slowly.*	The *cloth* felt *smooth.*
We *tasted* the fudge *eagerly.*	The *fudge* tasted *good.*
A stranger *appeared suddenly.*	The *dog* appears *sick.*
Erin *looked up.*	The *water* looks *green.*
The plant *grew fast.*	The *horse* grew *tired.*
We *smelled* smoke *suddenly.*	The *flower* smells *good.*

If you are uncertain about whether to use an adverb or adjective after verbs like *sound, smell,* and *look,* try these tests:

1. Does the modifier tell *how, when, where,* or *to what extent?* If it does, the modifier is probably an adverb.

2. Can you substitute *is* or *was* for the verb? If you can, the modifier is probably an adjective.

Exercise Choose the correct modifier.

Choose the correct modifier for the following sentences.

1. The ice looked (thick, thickly).
2. This water tastes (bitter, bitterly).
3. Mother spoke (calmly, calm).
4. At the start of the game we played (cautiously, cautious).
5. Those people were talking rather (loud, loudly) in the library.
6. Carol's idea sounded (reasonable, reasonably).
7. Press (firm, firmly) on the button.
8. The tape stopped (abruptly, abrupt).
9. The waiter served (quick, quickly). He was (quick, quickly).
10. The music sounded (strange, strangely).

Good and *Well*

The meanings of *good* and *well* are very much alike, but they are not exactly the same. You cannot substitute one for the other in all sentences. Study the following sentences. Can you see the difference between *good* and *well?*

I feel good.   This patient is well.
I feel well.   His health is good.
Betty plays well.

Good is always an adjective.

Well is sometimes an adjective and sometimes an adverb. In which of the previous sentences is *well* used as an adverb? In which sentences is it used as an adjective? You can see that when *well* refers to a person's health, it may be used as an adjective.

Exercise Use *good* and *well* correctly.

Number your paper from 1–10. Choose the correct word.

1. Shake the bottle (good, well).
2. That swim felt (good, well).
3. All of the gymnasts did quite (well, good).
4. That looks (well, good) enough to eat!
5. Both teams played (well, good) in the second half.
6. John was sick, but now he's (good, well) again.
7. The new manager has worked out quite (good, well).
8. The soup tasted (well, good).
9. Mr. Marks looks (well, good) in his new jacket.
10. Most of the performers did quite (well, good).

Part 4　Articles

The adjectives *a*, *an*, and *the* are called **articles.**
The is the **definite article.**

> Please buy me *the* book (*a particular* book).

A and *an* are **indefinite articles.**

> Please bring me *a* book (*any* book).
> Please give me *an* apple (*any* apple).

Note that we use *a* before a consonant sound (*a* book, *a* cap, *a* dog). We use *an* before a vowel sound (*an* apple, *an* egg, *an* olive).

The sound, not the spelling, makes the difference. Do we say *a honest man* or *an honest man? a house* or *an house?*

Exercise Use the correct article.

Choose the correct article in each of the following sentences.

1. (A, An) elephant supposedly has a good memory.
2. (A, The) best book on that shelf is *Treasure Island.*

3. That is (a, an) heavy chair.
4. I have (a, an) hunch you're right.
5. Joe was wearing (a, an) orange T-shirt.
6. We had (an, a) history test this week.
7. That was (a, the) best thing to do.
8. Don't use (a, an) onion in that recipe.
9. Each of us had to do a report on (a, an) event in history.
10. Tracy made (an, a) honest effort to meet the deadline for the newspaper.

Part 5 Adjectives in Comparisons

Comparing people and things is one way of learning about the world. We compare new things to those we already know. We say, "This new calculator is *like* a mini-computer. Of course, it is *smaller* and it is *less accurate*." Or we say, "The new girl is *taller* than I am."

Adjectives are very useful in comparing things and people. In comparisons, adjectives have special forms or spellings.

The Comparative

If we compare one thing or person with another, we use the **comparative** form of the adjective. It is made in two ways:

1. For short adjectives like *sweet* and *happy*, add *-er*.

   sweet + -er = sweeter   quick + -er = quicker
   happy + -er = happier   wise + -er = wiser

2. For longer adjectives like *beautiful*, use *more*.

   more beautiful   more capable

Most adjectives ending in *-ful* and *-ous* form the comparative with *more*.

   more healthful   more ambitious

The Superlative

When we compare a thing or a person with all others of its kind, we use the **superlative** form of the adjective. In fact, when we compare a thing or person with more than one other, we use the superlative.

> This is the *best* dinner I have ever tasted.
> Pat is the *smartest* person I know.
> This is the *most interesting* book I have ever read.

The superlative form of adjectives is made by adding *-est* or by using *most*. For adjectives that add *-er* to form the comparative, add *-est* for the superlative. For those that use *more* to form the comparative, use *most* for the superlative.

	COMPARATIVE	SUPERLATIVE
high	higher	highest
big	bigger	biggest
strong	stronger	strongest
agreeable	more agreeable	most agreeable
expensive	more expensive	most expensive
careful	more careful	most careful

There are three things to remember in using adjectives for comparison:

1. Use the comparative to compare two persons or things. Use the superlative to compare more than two.

> This car is *wider* than that one.
> This car is the *widest* one I have ever seen.

2. Do not leave out the word *other* when you are comparing something with everything else of its kind.

> Wrong   New York is larger than any American city.
>   (This sentence says that New York is not an
>   American city.)
> Right   New York is larger than any *other* American city.

Wrong	Claire runs faster than any girl in her class.
	(Is Claire a girl? Is she in her class?)
Right	Claire runs faster than any *other* girl in her class.

3. Do not use both -er and more or -est and most at the same time.

Wrong	Diamonds are more harder than jade.
Right	Diamonds are *harder* than jade.
Wrong	Diamonds are the most hardest of all materials.
Right	Diamonds are the *hardest* of all materials.

Irregular Comparisons

We form the comparative and superlative of some adjectives by changing the words:

	COMPARATIVE	SUPERLATIVE
good	better	best
well	better	best
bad	worse	worst
ill	worse	worst
little	less *or* lesser	least
much	more	most
many	more	most
far	farther	farthest

Exercises Use adjectives correctly in comparisons.

A. Number your paper from 1–10. Two of the comparisons in the following sentences are correct, but the others are wrong. If a sentence is correct, write *Correct*. If there is an error, write the sentence correctly.

1. These shelves are more high than those over there.
2. The VW Rabbit is the bigger of these three foreign cars.
3. The dictionary was more helpful than the almanac.
4. It was the worst storm I had ever seen.

5. Our new dog is much more friendlier than the old one.
6. Of the two plants, the fern is the healthier.
7. It was the most warmest day of the summer.
8. Math is harder than any subject in school.
9. What happened was even surprisinger.
10. The most funniest thing happened yesterday.

B. Follow the directions for Exercise A.

1. That was the worser of the two jokes.
2. His joke was the goodest of all.
3. Marcy felt worse than she had felt in a long time.
4. He chose the lesser of the two evils.
5. She had littler time than usual.
6. Mine was worse, but Janet's was the worstest.
7. This is the most best I can do.
8. That was a more better game than the one last week.
9. At the leastest noise Prince perked up an ear.
10. Between the ivy and the fern, the ivy is the healthiest.

Part 6 Adverbs in Comparisons

Adverbs are used to compare one action with another. We say, "This engine runs *smoothly*, but that one runs *more smoothly*."

Or we say, "Julie planned her exhibit *more carefully* than any other student in the class."

Adverbs have special forms or spellings for use in making comparisons, just as adjectives do.

The Comparative

When we compare one action with another, we use the

comparative form of the adverb. The comparative form is made in two ways:

1. For short adverbs like *soon* and *fast,* add *-er.*

> We arrived *sooner* than you did.
> Kim can run *faster* than Peg.

2. For most adverbs ending in *-ly,* use *more* to make the comparative.

> Bill acted *more quickly* than Jeff.
> The water flowed *more rapidly* than before.

The Superlative

When one action is compared with two or more others of the same kind, we use the **superlative** form of the adverb.

> Peg and Bill run fast, but Kim runs *fastest.*
> Of the three boys, Scott speaks Spanish the *most fluently.*

The superlative form of adverbs is formed by adding *-est* or by using *most.* Adverbs that form the comparative with *-er* form the superlative with *-est.* Those that use *more* for the comparative use *most* for the superlative.

	COMPARATIVE	SUPERLATIVE
hard	harder	hardest
long	longer	longest
rapidly	more rapidly	most rapidly
clearly	more clearly	most clearly

In using the comparative and superlative forms of adverbs, keep in mind the following three pointers:

1. Use the comparative to compare two actions and the superlative to compare more than two.

> It rained *harder* today than yesterday.
> Of all the players, Terry tries the *hardest.*

2. Do not leave out the word *other* when you are comparing one action with every other action of the same kind.

Wrong   Tara runs faster than any student in our school.
Right   Tara runs faster than any *other* student in our school.

3. Do not use both *-er* and *more* or *-est* and *most* at the same time.

Wrong   Tara runs more faster.
Right   Tara runs *faster*.

Exercises Use adverbs correctly in comparisons.

A. Write the comparative and superlative forms of these adverbs:

1. fast
2. wildly
3. hard
4. happily
5. closely
6. long
7. bravely
8. slowly
9. recently
10. naturally

B. Some of the following sentences are correct. Others contain errors in the comparative form of adverbs. Number your paper from 1–10. If the sentence is correct, write *Correct*. If there is an error, rewrite the sentence correctly.

1. We drove more carefully after seeing the collision.
2. Vacation ended more soon than we had expected.
3. Write the directions out more completer.
4. These photographs were trimmed more better than those.
5. That fish jumped more higher than any other.
6. This recipe is the more consistently successful of all.
7. Can't you walk more fast than that?
8. You could see the view more clearly from here.
9. He tried more harder than Wayne.
10. Will you read that paragraph again more slower, please?

Part 7   Special Problems with Modifiers

Them and *Those*

Them is always a pronoun. It is used only as the object of a verb or as the object of a preposition.

Those is an adjective if it is followed by a noun. It is a pronoun if it is used alone.

> We heard *them* in the night. (pronoun)
> *Those* bikes are too heavy. (adjective modifying *bikes*)
> *Those* are our gifts. (pronoun)

The Extra *Here* and *There*

How often have you heard someone say, "This here book" or "That there window"? The word *this* includes the meaning of *here*. The word *that* includes the meaning of *there*.

Saying *this here* is like saying, "This book is my mine," or like repeating your name every time you say *I* or *me:* "Please pass me John Jones the milk."

Kind and *Sort*

Kind and *sort* are singular. Use *this* or *that* with *kind* and *sort*. *Kinds* and *sorts* are plural. Use *these* or *those* with *kinds* and *sorts*.

> We like *this kind* of dessert.
> *Those kinds* of food give you energy.

The Double Negative

A **double negative** is the use of two negative words together when only one is needed. Good speakers and writers take care to avoid the double negative.

Wrong We haven't *no* more tape.
Right We haven't *any* more tape.

Wrong Jack didn't win *nothing* at the fair.
Right Jack didn't win *anything* at the fair.

Wrong She hasn't *never* gone there.
Right She hasn't *ever* gone there.

The most common negative words are *no, none, not, nothing,* and *never.*

In the sentences above, the first negative is a contraction for *not.* When you use contractions like *haven't* and *didn't,* do not use negative words after them. Instead, use words such as *any, anything,* and *ever.* Do not use *no, nothing, never,* or any other negative words after such contractions.

The club *hasn't any* new members.
We *couldn't* hear *anything.*
We *haven't ever* seen an eclipse.
The band *can't* play *any* popular songs.

Hardly, barely, and *scarcely* are often used as negative words. Do not use them after contractions like *haven't* and *didn't.*

Wrong We couldn't *hardly* breathe.
Right We could *hardly* breathe.

Wrong They can't *barely* talk.
Right They can *barely* talk.

Wrong The cars haven't *scarcely* moved.
Right The cars *have scarcely* moved.

Exercises Use modifiers correctly.

A. Choose the correct word in these sentences:

1. (Them, Those) are my favorite cookies.
2. Our dog won't eat (them, those) biscuits.
3. (Them, Those) gloves are too small.
4. We chose (those, those there) designs for our posters.
5. I always buy (that there, that) kind of bread.
6. (This, This here) watch needs to be fixed.
7. (Them, Those) are deer tracks.
8. These (kind, kinds) of dogs live a long time.
9. These (sort, sorts) of arguments are pointless.
10. Do you like (this, these) sort of design?

B. Number your paper from 1–10. Correct the double negatives in the following sentences. If a sentence does not contain a double negative, write *Correct* after the corresponding number.

1. The girls couldn't scarcely believe their ears.
2. Bryan hasn't had no piano lessons this year.
3. Rhoda hasn't never been sick.
4. The movers couldn't hardly lift the heavy box.
5. There isn't no time for games.
6. Marguerita couldn't find the stamps.
7. Ms. Ryan won't let nobody use the power tools.
8. We couldn't find the badminton net.
9. Nobody could have had more fun.
10. We had plenty of apples, but Ellen didn't want none.

Additional Exercises — Review

Using Modifiers

A. Find the adjectives.

Number your paper from 1–10. Write the adjectives you find in each sentence. After each adjective, write the word it modifies. Do not include *a, an,* or *the.*

1. A blue van was parked next to the large mobile home.
2. The library has a large display of old American flags.
3. A tiny gray kitten perched itself on our roof.
4. A rusty green truck clattered down the alley.
5. The narrow, rocky peninsula has a single road.
6. Tin cans and old shoes hung from the back of the black limousine.
7. Red and white geraniums filled the ceramic pots.
8. The new Japanese policy caused widespread concern.
9. Huge, white seagulls strutted across the sandy beach.
10. The automatic door was controlled by an electric eye.

B. Recognize adverbs.

Number your page from 1–10. Write the adverbs in the following sentences. After each adverb, write the word it modifies.

1. The students walked quickly through the corridors.
2. Gretchen cautiously opened the box.
3. The two Dalmatians barked loudly.
4. Nearly forty kegs of nails split open on the highway.
5. The paramedics moved quickly through the crowd.
6. Have you ever found your odometer?
7. The toast finally popped up.

8. We arrived precisely at 8:15 P.M.
9. The children anxiously awaited the clown's arrival.
10. Many tourists strolled casually through the town square.

C. Find the adjectives and adverbs.

Copy each sentence. Draw an arrow from the adjective or adverb to the word it modifies.

1. Enormous waves pounded unmercifully against the tiny boats.
2. The next lookout is the most spectacular.
3. A slight breeze danced lightly through the trees.
4. The weather was only moderately cold.
5. Gary has a very bad cold.
6. A gentle rain danced on the tin roof.
7. Four carolers in colorful costumes sang merrily in the lobby of the store.
8. A large yellow balloon drifted freely above the treetops.
9. A small cloud curled around the top of the mountain.
10. Large, white clouds were scattered across a brilliant blue sky.

D. Choose the correct modifier.

Choose the correct modifier for the sentences.

1. The afternoon passed (slow, slowly).
2. The guards moved (quick, quickly) up the basketball court.
3. The surface of the water glistened (bright, brightly).
4. Music was playing (quiet, quietly) in the doctor's office.
5. That tar smells (awful, awfully).
6. We felt (triumphant, triumphantly) about winning the game.
7. Please walk (careful, carefully) across the wet floor.

8. The desk top feels (smooth, smoothly).
9. The operator answered (angry, angrily).
10. Their change of plans seems (sudden, suddenly).

E. Use *good* and *well* correctly.

Choose the correct word from those given in parentheses.

1. Prospects for a sunny day were (well, good).
2. You play tennis very (good, well).
3. Her word is always (good, well).
4. The practice went (well, good).
5. Almost everyone dances pretty (good, well).
6. These scissors don't cut (well, good) any more.
7. They don't do it (good, well) enough.
8. This suit fits me (good, well).
9. Does that sewing machine work very (good, well)?
10. Clare and I did quite (good, well) on the history test.

F. Use comparisons correctly.

Number your paper from 1–10. Two of the comparisons in the following sentences are correct, but the others are wrong. If a sentence is correct, write *Correct*. If there is an error, write the sentence correctly.

1. This lemon is more sourer than others I've eaten.
2. This album is more better than those two.
3. My grandmother feels weller than usual.
4. Their kitchen is the most smallest room in the house.
5. These are the healthiest plants I've ever seen.
6. Always try your bestest.
7. New York is the largest American city.
8. This cake is more better than that one.
9. That was the worstest mistake I ever made.
10. This novel was more easier to read than the other one.

G. Use modifiers correctly in comparisons.

One of the following sentences is correct. The others contain errors in the comparative form. Number your paper from 1–10. If the sentence is correct, write *Correct*. If there is an error, write the sentence correctly.

1. Please hold the wheel more tightly.
2. John arrived more earlier than the others.
3. They weren't the carefulest house painters I've ever seen.
4. That was one of the bestest programs ever shown on TV.
5. Bill plays soccer better than any student in his class.
6. The old man looked at us more thoughtful.
7. Lara waited patienter than Jeff.
8. May is the most nice month of the year.
9. Katharine Hepburn is one of the very bestest actresses on stage or screen.
10. The crowd greeted his next announcement more enthusiastic.

H. Avoid special problems with modifiers.

Number your paper from 1–10. If the sentence is correct, write *Correct*. If there is an error, write the sentence correctly.

1. The coaches couldn't hardly believe the final score.
2. Them there rapids look dangerous.
3. I've eaten so much I can't eat no more.
4. Them bikes belong to Roberto and Denise.
5. Brian never catches no fish.
6. Them cattle haven't scarcely moved off the road.
7. That sort of behavior could get a player benched.
8. Meredith hasn't had no pizza.
9. Them Scouts couldn't barely finish the hike.
10. My bike doesn't need no repairs.

Section 6

Using Prepositions and Conjunctions

Often we can say what we mean by using short sentences:

> The grocer weighed the meat.
> Scott finished the painting.

Frequently, however, what we have to say is more complicated. Perhaps we want to say not merely that Scott finished the painting but also that he finished it at noon. We may want to tell someone that the grocer weighed not only the meat but also the pears and the potatoes. To express more complicated ideas like these, we use **connectives.**

Scott finished the painting *at* noon.
The grocer weighed the meat, the pears, *and* the potatoes.

This section will help you learn to use two important kinds of connectives: **prepositions** and **conjunctions.**

Part 1 Prepositions

Connectives are words that are used to join together two or more other words or groups of words. **Prepositions** are one important kind of connective.

Notice the prepositions in the following sentences:

The plane flew *into* the storm.
The plane flew *around* the storm.

In the first sentence, *into* connects *storm*, its object, with the verb *flew*. It points out the relationship between *flew* and *storm*.

In the second sentence, *around* connects *storm*, its object, with the verb *flew*. It points out the relationship between *flew* and *storm*.

You can see that *into* and *around* join parts of each sentence. Like all prepositions, they make clear a certain relationship between the words that they connect.

Now look at the prepositions in the following sentences:

My sister is the person *at* the counter.
My sister is the person *behind* the counter.

You can see that *at* and *behind* join parts of each sentence. They make clear the relationships between *person* and *counter*.

A preposition is a word used with a noun or pronoun, called its *object*, to show the relationship between the noun or pronoun and some other word in the sentence.

On the next page is a list of words often used as prepositions. Most of these prepositions tell *where*. Others show a relationship of *time*. Still others show such special relationships as *reference*, *separation,* and so on. Study these prepositions and see if you can tell the relationship that each of them shows between words.

Words Often Used as Prepositions

about	beneath	in	past
above	beside	inside	since
across	between	into	through
after	beyond	like	to
against	but (*except*)	near	toward
along	by	of	under
among	concerning	off	until
around	down	on	up
at	during	onto	upon
before	except	out	with
behind	for	outside	within
below	from	over	without

Exercises Find the prepositions.

A. Number your paper from 1–10. Label two columns *Preposition* and *Object.* Find the prepositions in the following sentences. Tell what the object of each preposition is.

EXAMPLE: On Saturday, Bret and Julie went to the beach.

PREPOSITION	OBJECT
On	Saturday
to	beach

1. The library will hold the book until tomorrow.
2. I hurried up the stairs and into the room.
3. A prop plane with several passengers made an emergency landing in a cornfield.

4. During the night we were awakened by thunder.

5. After the play, we're going to Mike's house.

6. The residents of Franklin Park are concerned about the pollution problem.

7. The football squad huddled around the coach for last-minute instructions.

8. Stack these cartons against that wall and put those books on the shelf.

9. The city was without power for several hours.

10. In the library there are several aquariums and plants on various bookshelves.

B. Follow the directions for Exercise A.

1. In July we are going to Florida for a visit to my grandparents.

2. Student Council will meet before school on Friday.

3. Two sky-writing planes flew over the stadium during the baseball game.

4. The bicycle shop is located on Green Bay Road.

5. On the Island of Oahu we visited the Polynesian Cultural Center.

6. The dog scampered down the stairs with my glove.

7. Tony Dorsett dazzled the crowd in the Coliseum with a 93-yard run.

8. We rode the elevator to the top of the John Hancock Building.

9. Cross-country skiing through forests and across open fields is fun.

10. The pancake house near the expressway is open around the clock.

Preposition or Adverb?

Many words used as prepositions may also be used as adverbs. A preposition never appears alone. It is always followed by its object, a noun or pronoun. If the word has a noun or pronoun following it, it is probably a preposition. If it is not followed by a noun or pronoun, it is probably an adverb.

I drew a line *across* the paper. (preposition)
He dared me to jump *across*. (adverb)

Ted put his books *down*. (adverb)
He ran *down* the street. (preposition)

Exercises Recognize adverbs and prepositions.

A. Decide whether the italicized words in these sentences are adverbs or prepositions. Write *Adverb* or *Preposition* for each sentence.

1. Janice turned *around*.
2. There is a new shopping center *near* our house.
3. The committee turned our request *down*.
4. The light bulb burned *out*.
5. The horses trotted *around* the track.
6. All local traffic was allowed *through*.
7. Pete threw his old track shoes *out*.
8. The Frisbee flew *across* the picnic table.
9. The doctor is *in*.
10. We all went *inside*.

B. Follow the directions for Exercise A.

1. Come *around* four o'clock.
2. We waited *outside* the theater.
3. The chain came *off*.
4. The chain came *off* the bicycle.
5. The lion cub rolled *over*.
6. Marsha and Jory went cycling *along* the lakeshore.
7. We heard a noise *below*.
8. John, Vince, and I sat *inside* the tent.
9. That dog always stays *within* the perimeter of his yard.
10. Lew and Niki talked *with* the assistant principal.

Part 2 Prepositional Phrases as Modifiers

A modifier may be a group of words as well as a single word. Frequently a prepositional phrase is a modifier. A **phrase** is a group of words that belong together but do not have a subject and verb.

Notice these phrases used as modifiers:

> The bears hibernated *during the long winter.*
> The player *in the blue jersey* sank the next basket.
> The principal's office is *on the first floor.*

The words in italics are **prepositional phrases.**

A prepositional phrase consists of a preposition, its object, and any modifiers of the object.

PREPOSITION	MODIFIERS	OBJECT
during	the long	winter
in	the blue	jersey
on	the first	floor

Nouns and pronouns are modified by adjectives.

Verbs are modified by adverbs.

Prepositional phrases may modify nouns, pronouns, or verbs. A phrase that modifies a noun or pronoun is an **adjective phrase.** A phrase that modifies a verb is an **adverb phrase.**

> Regina found a box *of marbles.* (adjective phrase modifying the noun *box*)
> Each *of us* needs a job. (adjective phrase modifying the pronoun *each*)
> Mandy came *into the room.* (adverb phrase modifying the verb *came*)

Adverbs tell *how, to what extent, when,* and *where* about verbs. Adverb phrases tell the same thing about verbs.

Often you will find two prepositional phrases in a row. Sometimes the second phrase is an adjective phrase modifying the object of the first phrase.

The cat was sitting *at the top* *of the stairs*.
(*at the top* is an adverb phrase telling where about the verb *was sitting*.)

(*of the stairs* is an adjective phrase modifying *top*. It tells which *top*.)

Cory put the powder *into the can* *of paint*.
(*into the can* tells where the powder was *put*.)
(*of paint* modifies *can*. It tells *which can*.)

Diagraming Prepositional Phrases

In diagrams a prepositional phrase is placed below the word it modifies.

The girl *with the red hair* plays *in the band*.

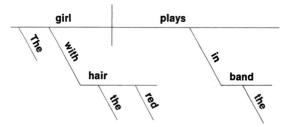

Sometimes two or more nouns or pronouns may be used as objects in a prepositional phrase.

Put butter *on the potatoes* and *squash*.

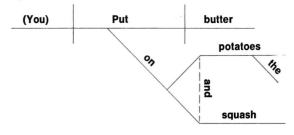

Exercises Use prepositional phrases as modifiers.

A. Copy these sentences. Circle each prepositional phrase. Draw an arrow from the phrase to the word it modifies. Tell whether the phrase is an adjective phrase or an adverb phrase.

> EXAMPLE: He took the book with the pictures of Ireland.
>
> *with the pictures*: adjective phrase modifying *book*
> *of Ireland*: adjective phrase modifying *pictures*

1. The man in the navy sport coat plays for the Celtics.
2. A brown terrier sat at the bottom of the staircase.
3. We peered through the windows of the deserted mansion.
4. Patti added some ice to the pitcher of iced tea.
5. That lady in the white suit is my social studies teacher.
6. The sign over the top of the door says "No Exit."
7. The window on the east side of the garage needs repair.
8. The dancer near the back of the stage is Rudolf Nureyev.
9. The sailboat in the water near the dock has a leak.
10. The electric sander is in the cabinet near the door.

B. Follow the directions for Exercise A.

1. The passengers on the jet were served a special dinner.
2. The trees in back of the house need pruning.
3. Are you going to the shopping center down the street?
4. Jane took these pictures with a wide-angle lens.
5. The sign on the door in the office said that school will end at 1 P.M. today.
6. The article about jogging was very informative.
7. The movie on television features Billy Dee Williams.
8. Jane Addams is well known for her contributions in social work.
9. I wrote a composition about my experiences at camp.
10. I enjoyed my work with small children last summer.

Part 3 Conjunctions

A second kind of word used to tie the parts of a sentence together is the **conjunction.**

A conjunction is a word that joins words or groups of words.

Notice the conjunctions in the following sentences:

Lucy *and* Linda look alike. (connects nouns)
Todd will call his father *or* mother. (connects nouns)
Mr. Morley hemmed *and* hawed. (connects verbs)
The cannister smelt spicy *but* damp. (connects adjectives)
The guide book is either in the closet *or* on the desk. (connects prepositional phrases)

Conjunctions are unlike prepositions in that they do not have objects. They are similar to prepositions in that they do show a certain relationship between the words they connect.

Coordinating Conjunctions

To connect single words or parts of a sentence that are of the same kind, we use **coordinating conjunctions.** The most common coordinating conjunctions are *and, but,* and *or.*

Maya *and* John are here. (*and* connects *Maya* and *John.*)
We can't see, *but* we can hear. (*but* connects *we can't see* and *we can hear.*)

Correlative Conjunctions

A few conjunctions are used in pairs:

both . . . and   not only . . . but (also)
either . . . or   whether . . . or
neither . . . nor

353

Such conjunctions are called **correlative conjunctions.**

Both the benches *and* the tables had been painted.
Either you *or* I have made an error.
Neither football *nor* baseball can be played on that field.
We need *not only* nails *but also* a hammer.
Shall I call *whether* it rains *or* snows?

Exercises **Recognize and use conjunctions.**

A. Find the conjunctions in the following sentences. Be prepared to tell what words or word groups are connected by the conjunction.

> EXAMPLE: The Rand Raiders and the Thomas Trojans were invited to play in the baseball tournament.
>
> *The Rand Raiders* and *the Thomas Trojans* are connected by the conjunction *and*.

1. The clowns and magicians entertained the children.
2. Freezing rain and poor visibility delayed most flights.
3. Either the yearbook staff or the newspaper staff will sell refreshments at the home football games.
4. Tom and I couldn't get tickets for the match.
5. The slight breeze, pleasant temperatures, and overcast skies were assets to the marathon runners.
6. At the school picnic, we had corn on the cob and barbecued chicken.
7. Are you going to the movies or to the roller rink?
8. Marcia and I are going either to the water polo game or to the indoor tennis meet.
9. We baked an apple pie and a bundt cake in home economics.
10. The San Diego Zoo and Disneyland were the highlights of my trip to California.

B. Follow the directions for Exercise A.

1. Neither the coaches nor the timekeepers knew the final score.
2. Canoeing and backpacking are my favorite outdoor activities.
3. Either Bob or Mike will be the starting quarterback for our team.
4. You can see an opera or the Grand Kabuki by the National Theatre of Japan.
5. Both my brother and my sister are studying medicine.
6. Racquetball, tennis, and squash require speed and endurance.
7. The roadblock and the detour have delayed our trip.
8. Skateboards, painter's pants, Bubble Yum, and Frisbees are fads that characterized the mid-1970's.
9. I like neither avocados nor asparagus.
10. We not only raised enough money for the orphanage, but we also made a donation to the children's hospital.

C. Write two sentences using *and,* two sentences using *or,* and two sentences using *but.* After each sentence write the words or groups of words that are joined by the conjunctions.

D. Write one sentence for each of the following pairs of correlative conjunctions:

both—and
either—or
neither—nor
not only—but (also)
whether—or

Part 4   Review of Parts of Speech

As you know, there are eight parts of speech.

The Eight Parts of Speech

nouns	adjectives	conjunctions
pronouns	adverbs	interjections
verbs	prepositions	

Interjections

Do you remember what interjections are?

An **interjection** is a word or short group of words used to express strong feeling. It may be a real word or merely a sound. It may express surprise, joy, longing, anger, or sorrow.

An interjection is often followed by a special punctuation mark called an **exclamation mark** (!).

> *Hooray!* We won the game.
> *No way!* I'm not riding that roller coaster.

Words Used as Different Parts of Speech

In Part 1 of this section, you learned that words may be used as prepositions or as adverbs. Other words in our language may also be used in different ways.

Since the same word can be used in different ways as a different part of speech, how can you tell what part of speech a word is? Usually you have to see how the word is used in a sentence.

What part of speech a word is depends on how it is used in a sentence.

Bruce moved the heavy *stone*. (*stone* is used as a noun.)

I sat on the *stone* wall. (*stone* is used as an adjective modifying *wall*.)

Don't *stand* in the doorway. (*stand* is used as a verb.)

Bob built a *stand* for his beer can collection. (*stand* is used as a noun.)

This book is exciting. (*This* is used as an adjective modifying *book*.)

This is an interesting book. (*This* is used as a demonstrative pronoun.)

Exercise Decide the part of speech.

Number your paper from 1–12. Write the italicized word in each sentence. After it, write the part of speech that it is in that sentence.

1. Two *fence* posts were wobbly.
2. Joan has gone around to the *back*.
3. We will *plant* a garden in the spring.
4. I have a couple of *stops* to make on Main Street.
5. The *garage* sale lasted until noon.
6. The harbor is patrolled by the *port* authorities.
7. Put these books *beside* the dictionaries.
8. Everyone *but* Nancy stayed for the entire game.
9. *Hurry!* Here's our train.
10. The *door* hinge creaked.
11. The *plant* shut down yesterday evening.
12. Tricia *backed* the car into the garage.

Additional Exercises — Review

Using Prepositions and Conjunctions

A. Find the prepositions.

Number your paper from 1–10. Write the prepositions in the following sentences. Write the object of each preposition.

1. An account of the race will be in the newspaper.
2. Trade-ins are usually accepted at Fernstone Motors.
3. On our doorstep was a lost puppy.
4. There is a new shopping mall near the school.
5. Manny and I went to the bakery for some doughnuts.
6. We rode the subway into the city.
7. In August you can't get in without reservations.
8. The list of winners will be announced in a few minutes.
9. The photographs in the display case were taken by Sue.
10. Rafferty High is beyond the municipal building.

B. Recognize adverbs and prepositions.

Decide whether the italicized words in these sentences are adverbs or prepositions. Write *Adverb* or *Preposition* for each sentence.

1. Dad drove twice *around* the block.
2. Think it *over*.
3. While we waited, it seemed as if days went *by*.
4. The talk show went *on* and *on*.
5. The Statue of Liberty was a gift *from* France.
6. Try their homemade cheesecake *after* dinner.
7. We followed the Freedom Trail *through* Boston.
8. Please turn the radio *off*.

C. Use prepositional phrases as modifiers.

Copy these sentences. Circle each prepositional phrase. Draw an arrow from the phrase to the word it modifies.

1. Look in the drawer with the brass handle.
2. Please give me a hamburger without mustard.
3. The plants in the greenhouse need watering.
4. Some of the books on the table are Kim's.
5. The aquarium in the den needs cleaning.
6. We visited Lincoln's home in Springfield, Illinois.
7. Many French laws originated with Napoleon.
8. The elevator ride to the top of the Sears Tower takes 54 seconds.
9. Carol's expression was too funny for words.
10. Last summer I was on the swimming team with my sister.

D. Recognize and use conjunctions.

Find the conjunctions in the following sentences. Tell what words are connected by the conjunctions.

1. Do you like Jackson Browne or Peter Frampton?
2. Last Saturday, Kathy and I went cycling and bowling.
3. Bob or Jeff can borrow this mitt.
4. "Checagou" or "land of stinking onions" is the Indian name originally given to the city of Chicago.
5. Every marathon race is 26 miles and 385 yards.
6. The origin of marathons and the Olympics can be traced back to ancient Greece.
7. Both Wisconsin and Mississippi were named by the Chippewa Indians.
8. "Ouisconsin" means "grassy place" and "mici zibi" means "great river."
9. We could go to the planetarium or to the zoo.
10. Neither the guitar nor the banjo is difficult to play.

Section 7

Sentence Patterns

In a sentence, one word follows another. The words are arranged in order. The order in which the words are arranged is very important. If the sentence is to make sense, the word order must follow a pattern. The words cannot simply be thrown together haphazardly.

In this section, you will learn several of the patterns for English sentences. You will also see how important word order is within these patterns. Word order is so important that changing the order of the words in a sentence can change its meaning.

Part 1   Word Order and Meaning

To make sense as a sentence, words must be put together in a certain logic. Read the groups of words below. Which group makes sense as a sentence?

> Katie trimmed the lawn.
> Lawn trimmed the Katie.

The first group makes sense. The words are in one of the patterns for an English sentence. The second group does not make sense. The words seem jumbled. Our experience tells us that the words are not in the right order for an English sentence.

Sometimes a group of words can be arranged in more than one order. Each arrangement will make sense and express a message. However, the message expressed by one arrangement is likely to be different from the message expressed by another. Read the following pair of sentences.

> Jon wrote to the President.
> The President wrote to Jon.

These sentences have very different meanings. What makes the meanings different? The words are the same in each sentence. The order of the words is the only thing that makes the sentences different. This difference in order makes an important difference in meaning.

Exercise   Change word order and meaning.

Read each sentence. Then change the order of the words to change the meaning. Write each new sentence on your paper.

1. Ann stopped the dog.
2. The pigeons saw the cat.
3. Water is in the boat.
4. Doug called the radio station.
5. The ball hit Jess.
6. The photograph is in the museum.
7. Tim stayed to help the teacher.
8. The balloon is in the air.

Part 2   The N V Pattern

Every sentence has a subject and a verb. The subject is usually a noun or a pronoun. The subject may have modifiers. It may be compound. The verb may also have modifiers, and it may also be compound. In this chart, N stands for the noun or pronoun in the complete subject. V stands for the verb in the complete predicate.

N	V
Christopher	cooked.
Christopher and Debbie	cooked and served.
The hungry campers	ate heartily.

The word order in these sentences follows a pattern. That pattern is noun-verb, or N V. This pattern is called the **N V pattern.**

Exercises   Use the N V pattern.

A.   Make a chart like the one above. Label one column *N* and the other *V*. Write these sentences on the chart.

1. Everyone shouted.
2. Our team won.
3. Stan and Meg whistled loudly.
4. I slept soundly.
5. The old stove works well.
6. My science book is in the desk.

B.   Copy this chart. Complete each sentence in the N V Pattern.

N	V
1. _____	howled.
2. The refrigerator	_____.
3. _____	exploded suddenly.
4. The people in the audience	_____.
5. _____	stood and sang.

C.   Make a chart of your own for the N V pattern. Write five sentences in the N V pattern.

Part 3   The N V N Pattern

The **N V N pattern** describes a sentence with three parts. The first N stands for the subject noun or pronoun. The V stands for the verb. The second N stands for the direct object noun or pronoun. Any of the parts may be compound. Each of the sentences in the following chart is in the N V N pattern.

N	V	N
Horses	like	apples.
Robin	will buy	that record.
Two of my classmates	write and illustrate	a comic strip.
My cousin and I	collect	bottle caps.

Exercises   Use the N V N Pattern.

A.   Make a chart like the one above. Label the three columns *N, V,* and *N.* Write these sentences on the chart.

1. Whales eat plankton.
2. The car hit the post.
3. Ellen fixed my old radio.
4. Every player scored points.
5. I ate two tacos.
6. Each one took one.
7. She buys and sells fruit.
8. Paul and I packed a bag.

B.   Copy this chart. Complete each sentence in the N V N pattern.

N	V	N
1. _____	fixed	my chipped tooth.
2. Captain Elliot	studied	_____.
3. _____	wrecked	_____.
4. Ann Redsky	_____	an umbrella.
5. _____	sells and services	tape recorders.

C.   Make a chart of your own for the N V N pattern. Write five sentences in the N V N pattern.

Part 4   The N V N N Pattern

The **N V N N pattern** describes a sentence with four parts. The first N stands for the subject noun or pronoun. The V stands for the verb. The second N stands for the indirect object, and the third N stands for the direct object. Any of the parts may be compound, but the verb rarely is. Each of the sentences in the following chart is in the N V N N pattern.

N	V	N	N
Tom	wrote	me	a letter.
Loud drums	give	Dad	a headache.
My mother	offered	Diane	a ride to school.
Phil and Jean	showed	Lola and me	slides and photos.

Exercises   Use the N V N N pattern.

A.   Make a chart like the one above. Label the four columns *N, V, N,* and *N.* Write these sentences on the chart.

1. Janet threw me a curve.
2. Mr. Ortiz gave John and Louisa the job.
3. The teacher asked me the trickiest question of all.
4. Every visitor sent us a thank-you note.
5. The Paines served us homemade bread and soup.

B.   Copy and complete each sentence in the N V N N pattern.

N	V	N	N
1. _____	sent	us	a bill.
2. The Senator	gave	the reporters	_____.
3. _____	offered	_____	a chance.
4. Television	_____	Phil and me	_____.
5. _____	left	_____	a message.

C.   Make a chart of your own for the N V N N pattern. Write five sentences in the N V N N pattern.

Part 5   The N LV N Pattern

The **N LV N pattern** describes a sentence with three parts. The first N stands for the complete subject noun or pronoun. LV stands for a linking verb. The second N stands for a predicate noun or pronoun. Any part may be compound, but the verb rarely is.

N	LV	N
Bees and ants	are	social insects.
The best movie	was	the last one.
English and art	are	my best subjects.
Alexis	will be	the director of the play.

Exercises   Use the N LV N pattern.

A.   Make a chart like the one above. Label the three columns *N*, *LV*, and *N*. Write these sentences on the chart.

1. A lizard is a reptile.
2. The painting was a fake.
3. The dodo is an extinct bird.
4. Eggrolls are a great snack.
5. Jeff and I are brother and sister.
6. My entry was my stamp collection.
7. Scotty may become the new mascot.
8. The prizes are a radio and a bicycle.

B.   Make a chart like the one below. Complete each sentence in the N LV N pattern.

N	LV	N
1. _____	is	my favorite snack.
2. The winner	was	_____.
3. _____	may become	superstars.
4. My father and sister	_____	the family cooks.
5. _____	will be	_____.

C.   Make a chart of your own. Label the columns *N*, *LV*, and *N*. Write five sentences in the N LV N pattern.

Part 6   The N LV Adj Pattern

There are three parts to sentences that have the N LV Adj pattern. The N stands for the subject noun or pronoun. LV stands for a linking verb. Adj stands for a predicate adjective. Any of the parts may be compound. Each of the sentences in the following chart is in the N LV Adj pattern.

N	LV	Adj
The surprise party	was	successful.
Bob's costume	is	weird.
Bert and I	were	lost.
Katy	looks and sounds	angry.
The audience	seemed	lively and enthusiastic.

Exercises Use the N LV Adj pattern.

A.   Make a chart like the one above. Label the three columns *N, LV,* and *Adj.* Write these sentences on the chart.

1. You look and act happy.
2. The crust was soggy.
3. Diana sounds impatient.
4. These socks feel scratchy.
5. The cat is cozy and warm.
6. My plants look healthy.
7. Nick and I felt seasick.
8. Nan's memory is accurate.

B.   Make a chart like the one below. Complete each sentence in the N LV Adj pattern.

N	LV	Adj
1. _____	was	hilarious.
2. Our town	looked	_____.
3. Velvet	feels	_____.
4. Jill	_____	talented and ambitious.
5. _____	will be	_____.

C.   Make a chart of your own. Label the columns *N, LV,* and *Adj.* Write five sentences in the N LV Adj pattern.

Additional Exercises — Review

Sentence Patterns

A. Put the words in order.

Arrange each group of words to form a sentence. Some groups may be arranged in more than one way.

1. tripped Peter
2. rang the once telephone
3. sat Elena the on cat
4. fun party the was
5. choice my first Lauren is

B. Find the N V pattern.

Each of the following sentences is in the N V pattern. Make a chart with two columns labeled *N* and *V*. Write each sentence on the chart.

1. Susan called.
2. The bus arrived on time.
3. Mr. Coe wrote quickly.
4. The faucet dripped constantly.
5. Ramon and his sisters were at work.
6. The paperclips spilled all over the floor.
7. My new sneakers fit perfectly.
8. Every store in town closed for the holiday.
9. The fifteen soccer players looked at the coach.
10. Two of the presents won't be delivered until Tuesday.

C. Find the N V N pattern.

Each of the following sentences is in the N V N pattern. Make a chart with three columns labeled *N, V,* and *N.* Write each sentence on the chart.

1. The bell startled everyone.
2. Kim and I made breakfast.
3. She can't find any good skates.
4. Someone has bought that old theater.
5. Greg ordered a pizza and some salad.
6. Terry and Paul use those machines.
7. We wanted one picture from each family.
8. Each animal follows a different diet.
9. The corner market sells a wide variety of magazines.
10. Everyone in the audience loved the songs and the music.

D. Find the N V N N pattern.

Each of the following sentences is in the N V N N pattern. Make a chart with four columns labeled *N, V, N,* and *N.* Write each sentence on the chart.

1. I offered him my seat.
2. The agency sent us a typist.
3. That company gives everyone a bonus.
4. Coach Allen handed me the stopwatch.
5. The Red Cross gave the victims food and clothing.
6. No one told me anything about it.
7. Doctor Wong gave the baby two vaccination shots.
8. The people in the street gave the musician money and applause.
9. The department store sent me an application form.
10. Some movie studios will send you autographed pictures of stars.

E. Find the N LV N pattern.

Each of the following sentences is in the N LV N pattern. Make a chart with three columns labeled *N*, *LV*, and *N*. Write each sentence on the chart.

1. Amelia Earhart is my idol.
2. Their vacation was a nightmare.
3. The rainbow is a symbol of good luck.
4. Sherry will be my new boss.
5. The best candidates are Frank and Elizabeth.
6. Bowling and basketball are good sports for the winter.
7. The manager of the team is Georgia.
8. The frog is one of the most common amphibians.
9. The best cure for hiccups is a spoonful of sugar.
10. The eruption of Mount St. Helens was front-page news.

F. Find the N LV Adj pattern.

Each of the following sentences is in the N LV Adj pattern. Make a chart with three columns labeled *N*, *LV*, and *Adj.* Write each sentence on the chart.

1. I am chilly.
2. That bus looks crowded.
3. Their costumes were flashy.
4. Grapefruit and lemons are sour.
5. My hands feel sticky.
6. Jim's fiddle is broken.
7. Those apartments look spacious and very modern.
8. Tony is becoming famous for his salads.
9. That application blank is awfully confusing.
10. The next scene will be frightening.

G. Find the patterns.

Write the pattern for each of the following sentences.

1. The dishes are dry.
2. Everyone ran outside.
3. Alan gave me an apple and half a sandwich.
4. That tree is a sugar maple.
5. Our television was new.
6. The lights in the auditorium flickered.
7. My sister Pam can fix anything.
8. Carlos offered me his new shinguards and face mask.
9. Jeff and his family visited the Statue of Liberty in New York.
10. The science fair will be fun.

Section 8

Using Compound and Complex Sentences

When you were studying Section 1, you noticed that the title was "The Simple Sentence." In that section you studied about subjects, predicates, objects, predicate words, and so on. You may have thought that all of this was far from simple.

The simple sentence has one kind of structure. There are also compound and complex sentences. They have other kinds of structure. The basis for these other kinds of sentences is the simple sentence. It is a good idea to begin your study of the more complicated kinds of sentences by reviewing the simple sentence.

Part 1 Review of the Simple Sentence

The **simple sentence** has two basic parts, subject and predicate.

SUBJECT	PREDICATE
Days	passed.
Time	flies.
People	asked.
Several people	asked questions.
Many people in the room	asked questions about the movie.

The **subject** of a sentence names the person or thing about which something is said. The **predicate** tells something about the subject.

The **simple predicate** is the verb. The subject of the verb is called the **simple subject.**

In the subject part of the sentence, you will find the simple subject and words that modify it. In the predicate part of the sentence, you will find verbs, objects, predicate words, and their modifiers.

Action Verbs and Linking Verbs

Some **action verbs** are complete in themselves.

Mike *was resting.*
A cold rain *fell.*

Some action verbs are followed by **direct objects,** which name the receiver of the action in the verb.

Bill *washed* the *car.*
Karen *raised* the *window.*

Some verbs do not tell of an action. They tell only that

something is or exists. They are called **linking verbs.** They link a predicate word to the subject.

> The horse *seems* tired.
> Dan *is* the director.

Compound Parts of the Simple Sentence

All of the parts of the simple sentence may be **compound.** That is, they may themselves have more than one part.

Compound Subject	*Bob* and *I* enjoyed the concert.
Compound Verb	The crowd *rose* and *cheered.*
Compound Object	I folded the *napkins* and the *tablecloth.*
Compound Predicate Word	The show was *long* but *interesting.* The leaders were *Ryan* and *Pam.*

Now we are ready for a definition of the simple sentence.

A simple sentence is a sentence that contains only one subject and one predicate. The subject and the predicate, or any part of the subject or predicate, may be compound.

Exercises Analyze simple sentences.

A. Copy each of the following sentences. Then draw a line between the subject and the predicate.

> EXAMPLE: Tom Mix and William S. Hart | were famous actors in old Western movies.

1. Movie-goers in the 1920's admired such greats as Greta Garbo, Rudolph Valentino, and Douglas Fairbanks, Sr.
2. Slapstick comedy was performed by Charlie Chaplin, Harold Lloyd, and Buster Keaton.

3. "Talkies," or movies with sound, became popular in the late 1920's.

4. The movies in the 1930's starred such people as Shirley Temple, Mae West, and Clark Gable.

5. The city of Hollywood was known as "the celluloid paradise."

6. One of the greatest movies was released in 1939.

7. This particular movie was discussed by hundreds of magazines and newspapers.

8. *Gone with the Wind* swept movie-goers off their feet.

9. The stars, Vivien Leigh and Clark Gable, were recognized by everyone.

10. Their movie became a film classic.

B. Number your paper from 1–10. Write the compound subjects, verbs, and objects you find in these sentences.

1. Yesterday's teens and today's youth have had a variety of interests.

2. Mini-skirts, long hair, and Beatlemania were accepted by most young people in the '60's.

3. Young people have danced and have listened to all different kinds of music.

4. Big bands and rock-and-roll music characterized the 1940's and 1950's.

5. Today's youth buys albums and tapes of lots of different musicians.

6. Some fads of the '70's included skateboards, platform shoes, Levis, Adidas, and T-shirts.

7. Popular music and fashion often dictate fads.

8. The Beatles and the Rolling Stones introduced a new kind of music.

9. Since then, radios and stereos have played the music of Elton John, Linda Ronstadt, Diana Ross, the Eagles, and many others.

10. In ten years, what will you and your friends be doing?

Part 2   Compound Sentences

Sometimes two sentences are so closely related in thought that we join them together. We can join them by using *and, but,* or *or.*

> We washed the car. Mom took us for a ride.
> We washed the car, *and* Mom took us for a ride.

> The book was long. It was very interesting.
> The book was long, *but* it was very interesting.

A compound sentence is made by joining two or more simple sentences together.

Compound sentences are useful, but they should be written with care. Two ideas should be put into one sentence only if they are closely related. If they are not closely related, the result may be confusing and hard to follow.

> Wrong   Jim painted the barn, and he is nineteen.
> Right   Jim painted the barn, and John repaired the roof.

Exercise   Make compound sentences.

Join each pair of sentences by using *and, but,* or *or.* Place a comma before *and, but,* or *or.* One of the pairs of sentences should not be joined because the ideas are not related.

1. I walked my bike to the garage. I filled my tires with air.
2. The car was full. They made room for one more.
3. Look closely at the map. You will see the river.
4. The trap was set. The fox was too crafty.
5. You must watch carefully. You will get lost.
6. It rained all night. The baseball game wasn't canceled.
7. The assembly was fun. Sit in this chair.
8. We like Jake. We will miss him.
9. Carl painted the picture. Suzi made the frame.
10. The girls bought Ray a sweater. He likes it very much.

Diagraming a Compound Sentence

The diagram of a compound sentence shows one simple sentence above the other. The two sentences are joined by a dotted line with a "step" for the coordinating conjunction. There are two main sentence lines. Each has a subject and a predicate.

The boys explored the cave, but they found nothing.

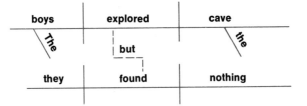

Exercise Recognize the parts of a compound sentence.

Show the two main parts of these compound sentences by diagraming, or as your teacher directs.

1. The football game was scheduled for TV, but the President's speech pre-empted all programming.

2. Lucinda and I cleaned the garage, and my brothers did the yardwork.

3. Babe Ruth was a leading contributor to the game of baseball, and Babe Didrikson contributed to women's participation in all sports.

4. Amelia Earhart was a school teacher, but she later became a famous pilot.

5. I enjoy reading the books of Laura Ingalls Wilder, but my favorite book is *The Good Earth* by Pearl S. Buck.

6. Do you like the modern dance of Martha Graham, or do you like the ballet of Maria Tallchief?

7. We are going to the planetarium tomorrow, and we will see a slide show there.

8. Betsy Ross may have made the first flag, but little evidence of this is available.

9. Harriet Tubman was a scout for the Union army, and she was also the most celebrated "conductor" of the Underground Railroad.

10. Tanya and I were playing checkers, but I prefer chess.

Punctuating Compound Sentences

In compound sentences, a comma should be used before the conjunction.

There is a very good reason for using the comma. The comma tells you where to pause. Without a comma, a sentence can be quite confusing:

Confusing I painted the chair and my sister   painted the table.

Better I painted the chair, and my sister painted the table.

Sometimes the parts of a compound sentence are joined by a **semicolon (;)** instead of by a conjunction and a comma.

It snowed heavily all night; classes were canceled the next day.

The whistle blew; the game was over.

Remember the two ways to join simple sentences:

1. Join them with a comma and one of the conjunctions *and, but,* or *or.* Place the comma before the conjunction.

2. Join them with a semicolon when there is no conjunction. Place the semicolon at the end of the first sentence.

Simple sentences should not be joined by placing a comma, alone, between them. A comma is not powerful enough to hold the sentences together.

Wrong The symphony was over, we went home.
Right The symphony was over; we went home.
Right The symphony was over, **and** we went home.

Exercise Punctuate compound sentences.

Number your paper from 1–10. Write the last word of the first part of each compound sentence. Next write the proper punctuation mark. Then write the first word of the second part of the compound sentence.

EXAMPLE: We called for Ted but he was not ready.

Ted, but

1. Nancy brought the shovel in and she put it behind the door.

2. The new television season has started but I don't care for any of the new shows.

3. Nobody got the answer the problem was too difficult.

4. Anna shimmied up the rope and Sally watched.

5. I must start now or I will be late.

6. My favorite actress is Cicely Tyson and my favorite singer is Carol King.

7. Tina and Miki went to Mardi Gras but Luanne and I went to Florida.

8. There were over eighty people in line I counted them.

9. Our flight to San Diego was delayed and we missed our connection to Hawaii.

10. We drove through northern Michigan last October the fall colors were beautiful.

Part 3 Compound Sentences and Compound Verbs

A simple sentence with a compound verb looks and sounds very much like a compound sentence. It is important to know how *compound verbs* differ from *compound sentences* for two reasons: (1) They must be punctuated differently; (2) Sometimes you can improve your writing by changing a compound sentence to a simple sentence with a compound verb.

A simple sentence, you remember, has only one subject and one predicate. The subject and any part of the predicate may be compound. Here is an example:

S.   V.   V.
The students rose to their feet and applauded.

In the sentence above, there is one subject: *students.* There are two verbs: *rose* and *applauded.* Both verbs have the same subject: *students rose* and *students applauded.* In this sentence there is only one subject-verb combination. It looks like this:

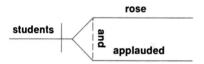

Now let's add a second subject and see what happens.

S.   V.   S.   V.
The students rose to their feet, and *they* applauded.

Now we have two subject-verb combinations. They look like this:

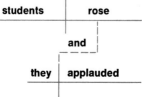

You can see that the simple sentence has become a compound sentence. This has happened because of the addition of the second subject, *they*.

Now let's put the two sentences together to see the difference in the words.

Compound Sentence   The students rose to their feet, and *they* applauded.

Compound Verb   The students rose to their feet and applauded.

By dropping the second subject out of the compound sentence, we make a simple sentence that has a subject-verb combination made up of one subject and two verbs. You can do this whenever both subjects of the compound sentence refer to the same person or thing.

Sam and Andrea arrived, and *they* distributed the uniforms and the equipment.
Sam and Andrea arrived and distributed the uniforms and the equipment.

The shirt was dry, but *it* still looked dirty.
The shirt was dry but still looked dirty.

Do not place a comma between the parts of a compound verb. Study the punctuation of the sentences above.

Exercises Analyze simple and compound sentences.

A. Copy the following sentences, adding commas where necessary. After each sentence write *Compound Verb* or *Compound Sentence* to show which it is.

1. I finished my homework and then I cleaned my room.
2. I like all science fiction movies but I really enjoy the old *Star Trek* programs.
3. The dogs barked wildly and ran after the truck.

4. The dogs snarled at the mail carrier but she paid no attention.

5. The jet made an emergency landing but no one on board was injured.

6. The early bird gets the worm but who wants worms?

7. Has Don arrived or has he been delayed?

8. The lifeguard jumped down and dashed into the water.

9. For an hour we sat by the telephone and just waited.

10. A plane takes off or lands at O'Hare Airport every 45 seconds.

B. Copy these sentences. Underline each subject once and each verb twice. After each sentence write *Simple* or *Compound* to show what kind it is.

1. We saw the King Tut exhibit in New Orleans.

2. The exhibit was a gesture of good will to the people of the United States from the Egyptians.

3. The Wright Brothers flew their plane in Kitty Hawk, North Carolina, on December 17, 1903.

4. A four-cylinder engine and two propellers gave power to their plane, and the aircraft flew a hundred feet for a total of twelve seconds.

5. Queen Elizabeth II became the monarch of Britain and the Commonwealth at the age of twenty-five.

6. Paper currency is printed at the Bureau of Engraving and Printing in Washington, D.C., but some coins are made at the U.S. Mint in Denver.

7. Elfreth's Alley is the oldest continuously occupied residential street in America.

8. It dates back to the 1690's and is one of the historic landmarks of Philadelphia.

9. Jamestown, Virginia, was the first permanent English colony in the New World.

10. The original Fort James was built in 1607, and today's visitors to the fort may see a full-scale reconstruction.

C. Make a simple sentence with a compound verb from each of the following compound sentences. Be sure to use the correct punctuation in your new sentence.

1. In Acadia National Park in Maine, we went backpacking, and we went horseback riding.
2. Our 4-H Club showed black angus cattle, and we displayed home-grown vegetables.
3. In the late 1800's, immigrants flocked to the United States, and they registered with government officials at Ellis Island.
4. On our vacations, we have visited several Amish villages, and we have seen many Indian reservations.
5. A tree fell during the storm, and it landed on our carport.
6. Snow fell all night, and it buried everything in sight.
7. Our hockey team was victorious in the semifinals, and we finished second in the finals.
8. Paint dripped from the brush, and it fell onto the rug.
9. The waves pounded against the small sailboats, and they lashed against the weatherbeaten dock.
10. Vince, Maria, and Kate attended the Chicago concert, and they went out for pizza afterwards.

Part 4 Complex Sentences

Before you can know what a complex sentence is, you need to know about clauses.

A clause is a group of words that contains a verb and its subject.

According to this definition, a simple sentence is a clause since it has both a verb and subject.

s.   v.
Jerry put the boxes behind the garage.

s.   v.
Sue read the announcements.

It will be easier to understand sentences, however, if we think of a clause as *part of a sentence*. We will think of a clause as *a group of words within a sentence*.

How about compound sentences? Do they contain clauses? Do they contain two or more groups of words that have a subject and a verb? Look at these examples:

    s. **v.**   **s.** **v.**
Jane hit the ball, and it flew into the bleachers.

    s. **v.**   **s.** **v.**
We found the box, but it was empty.

The answer is clear. Compound sentences do contain groups of words that have their own subjects and verbs.

Now, let's break up these compound sentences into their main parts and see what happens.

Jane hit the ball. It flew into the bleachers.
We found the box. It was empty.

Each of the clauses in the compound sentences can become a sentence by itself.

Phrases and Clauses

Can you tell the difference between a *phrase* and a *clause*? Look at these examples.

Phrases   of apples
            in the mountains

                   s.   **v.**
Clauses   that you are talking about

                s. **v.**
           who asked for you

A clause has a subject and a verb. A phrase does not.

Main Clauses

A clause that can stand as a sentence by itself is a **main clause.** All the clauses in compound sentences are main clauses. They can all stand as simple sentences by themselves. That is why they are sometimes called **independent clauses.**

Subordinate Clauses

Now we will look at clauses of a different kind:

s.   v.   s.   v.

If the mail has come   When the door opened

Neither group of words above makes a complete thought. Each leaves you wondering, *Then what?*

Now, with your finger, cover the first word in each of these groups of words. What happens? Each group of words becomes a complete sentence. You can see, then, that the words *if* and *when* are important.

We say that these words **subordinate** the groups of words they introduce. They are called **subordinating conjunctions.** They introduce **subordinate clauses.**

Words used frequently as subordinating conjunctions are shown below:

Words Often Used as Subordinating Conjunctions			
after	because	so that	whatever
although	before	than	when
as	if	though	whenever
as if	in order that	till	where
as long as	provided	unless	wherever
as though	since	until	while

Caution: These words are subordinating words only when they introduce a clause. Some of them can be used in other ways.

Exercise Make subordinate clauses.

Using *if, because, when, after,* and *since,* make subordinate clauses out of these sentences.

1. It was very foggy.
2. The window is broken.
3. The car stopped.
4. The dog howled.
5. The power went off.
6. You can go.
7. Our packages are ready.
8. The party ended.
9. The crowd had left.
10. It rained on Saturday.
11. The sun came out.
12. The book was lost.
13. She wore her red sweater.
14. The baby cried.
15. Everything had been said.

Definition of the Complex Sentence

Now that you know about main clauses and subordinate clauses, you are ready to learn what a complex sentence is.

A complex sentence is a sentence that contains one main clause and one or more subordinate clauses.

We left	before you came.
We'll go to the carnival	unless it rains tonight.
We were on the lake	when the storm began.

Exercises **Analyze sentences and clauses.**

A. Find the subordinate clause in each sentence. Copy it. Underline the subject once and the verb twice.

1. Before basketball practice begins, the team always runs 25 laps around the gym.
2. Although the heat was on, the room was still quite cold.
3. Stop and see us when you come back.
4. I put the books in my bag so that I wouldn't forget them.
5. Where were you when I called for you?
6. The water was colder than I thought.
7. Karen never speaks up, although she usually knows the answers.
8. While we were in Philadelphia, we saw Independence Hall and Betsy Ross's home.
9. Although the land around Denver is flat, it is almost a mile high.
10. We can't start the game until the field is drier.

B. Number your paper from 1–10. For each sentence, write *Simple, Compound,* or *Complex* to show what kind it is.

1. Mary and Elyse left in a hurry and forgot their tickets.
2. Close the door when you leave.
3. When the starting quarterback was injured, the substitute showed great talent.
4. Woodworking and weaving are both offered in the fall.
5. Have you finished, or may we help you?
6. Since Chicago is well known for deep dish pizza, we ordered it at a restaurant there.
7. Because of the city's drought, residents had to ration their water carefully.
8. Give us the tools, and we'll finish the job.
9. Jill and I waited in line for over two hours.
10. When we rode the Cog Railway to Pike's Peak, we saw herds of mountain sheep.

Part 5   More About Sentence Fragments

The sentence fragments that you studied in Section 1 were easy to spot. They were fragments because they lacked a verb or the subject of a verb.

Now we meet a new kind of sentence fragment, the subordinate clause. A subordinate clause has both a verb and a subject. It is still a fragment, however, because its meaning is not complete. Look at the groups of words below. Which is a complete sentence? Which is a subordinate clause?

> It is time to leave
> If it is time to leave

A subordinate clause must not be written as a complete sentence. It must always be joined to a main clause.

> Fragment   If it is time to leave
> Sentence   If it is time to leave, we will say good-bye.
>
> Fragment   When you arrive
> Sentence   When you arrive, come in the back door.

You can see that it is important to be able to recognize subordinating conjunctions. Study the list below so that you become familiar with words often used as subordinating conjunctions.

after	if	unless
although	in order that	until
as	provided	whatever
as if	since	when
as long as	so that	whenever
as though	than	where
because	though	wherever
before	till	while

Exercises Recognize sentence fragments.

A. Number your paper from 1–10. Decide whether the groups of words below are sentences or fragments. Write *S* for *Sentence* or *F* for *Fragment*. Add words to make each fragment a complete sentence. Punctuate and capitalize where necessary.

1. after the shower we saw a rainbow
2. after the show had ended
3. where the school always has its football games
4. where is the box of candy
5. since yesterday morning the air has been clear
6. since we have no food left
7. because of the storm, our lights went off
8. because the doctor advised plenty of rest
9. when are you leaving for Europe
10. when the old mine was closed down

B. Follow the directions for Exercise A.

1. down the mountain rolled a boulder
2. since the beginning of school
3. since you agree, we can go ahead with the plans
4. until the manager came out and stopped the noise
5. where the car went off the road
6. when the wind is from the south, we get rain
7. where is the box for this puzzle
8. before the lifeguard could reach the boat
9. while we waited for our ride
10. although the movie was cancelled, we had a good group discussion

C. On page 386 is a list of subordinating conjunctions. Choose six of the conjunctions that have not been used in Exercise A above. Use each conjunction in an original complex sentence. Underline the subordinate clause in each of your sentences.

Part 6   Adverb Clauses

An **adverb** is a word that modifies a verb, an adjective, or another adverb.

Adverb   Pam sat *down.*

An **adverb phrase** is a prepositional phrase used as an adverb. Adverb phrases usually modify verbs.

Adverb phrase   Pam sat *in the rocking chair.*

An adverb clause is a subordinate clause used as an adverb.

Adverb clause   Pam sat *where she would be comfortable.*

Adverbs and adverb phrases or clauses tell *where, when, how,* or *to what extent* about the word they modify.

Remember that a *clause* contains a subject and a verb. A *phrase* has neither a subject nor a verb.

Adverb clauses are always introduced by subordinating conjunctions:

after	because	so that	whatever
although	before	than	when
as	if	though	whenever
as if	in order that	till	where
as long as	provided	unless	wherever
as though	since	until	while

Some of the words above may also be used as prepositions. They are called subordinating conjunctions only when they introduce an adverb clause.

Preposition   *before* the game
Subordinating Conjunction   *before* the game started

Preposition	*after* the party
Subordinating Conjunction	*after* the food was served
Preposition	*since* that day
Subordinating Conjunction	*since* we had already started

Diagraming Adverb Clauses

The adverb clause is placed on its own line below the main clause. A dotted line is drawn from the adverb clause to the word it modifies in the main clause. The subordinating conjunction is placed on the dotted line.

Whenever we arrive on time, we surprise her.

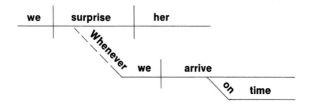

Exercise Recognize adverb clauses.

Copy the adverb clause from each sentence. Underline its subject once and its verb twice. Draw a circle around the subordinating conjunction.

EXAMPLE: Until I was five, I lived in New Mexico.
(Until) I was five

1. When we arrived in Seattle, it was very cold.
2. Before we could visit the small villages, we had to learn Japanese.
3. There was plenty of ribbon because we had saved it from Christmas.
4. Since the mules were slow, several tourists walked beside them.

5. Two partridges rose and whirred away as we approached.

6. As the mist cleared, Pike's Peak came into view.

7. If South American mail planes are late, search planes are alerted.

8. The geyser erupted again before we left.

9. Although he had lived all his life in England, Rick adjusted quickly to his new American lifestyle.

10. If you had been there on Saturday, you would have seen the precision marching.

Part 7   Adjective Clauses

An **adjective** is a word that modifies a noun or pronoun.

apple box

An **adjective phrase** is a phrase that modifies a noun or pronoun:

the box *of apples*

An **adjective clause** is a clause that modifies nouns and pronouns:

I know the cave *that you are talking about.*

Ms. Peters is the one *who asked about you.*

The train, *which had been stopped,* was delayed an hour.

Laura's the one *who telephoned us.*

An adjective clause is a subordinate clause used as an adjective to modify a noun or pronoun.

Usually, the adjective clause comes immediately after the word it modifies. Study the examples above.

Many adjective clauses start with the words *who, whom, whoever, whomever, which,* or *that.* Some adjective clauses start with *where* and *when.*

We passed the place *where you fished.*

It was a time *when everyone was home.*

It was the day *when half of the class was absent.*

Remember: A clause contains both a subject and a verb.

s. v.
where *you fished*

s.   v.
when *everyone was* home

s.   v.
when *half* of the class *was* absent

Diagraming Adjective Clauses

Both the main clause and the adjective clause are written on main lines. A dotted line goes from the word or words that introduce the subordinate clause to the word in the main clause that the adjective clause modifies.

Kelly is the girl who won the race.

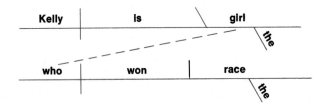

He is the magician of whom we were speaking.

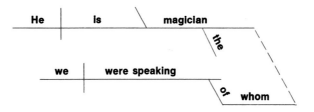

Exercise Recognize adjective clauses.

Copy the adjective clause from each sentence. Underline the subject once and the verb twice. Before the clause, write the word it modifies.

EXAMPLE: This is the book that I borrowed.
   book—that I borrowed

Tom is the one who called you.
   one—who called you

1. The family who owns the snowmobile lives next door.
2. Burt, who was still awake, smelled the smoke.
3. The new bike that I received for my birthday has a generator light.
4. This is the cookbook that has the best recipes.
5. The mayor is a woman who teaches at the college.
6. The team that wins the game gets the silver cup.
7. We couldn't find anyone who had seen the accident.
8. A lady who was carrying many packages sat down beside me.
9. Sam has the horse that jumps the best.
10. Patti owns a collie that has won several prizes.
11. We lost the picture that you gave us.
12. It was one of those days when everything went wrong.
13. Is this the coat that you want?
14. Your camera is in the closet where we keep the skates.
15. This is the book that explains cloud formations.

Part 8 *Who* and *Whom* in Clauses

The words *who, whom,* and *whose* are often used to begin adjective clauses. They tie the clause to the word it modifies in the main clause. When used in this way, *who, whom,* and *whose* are called **relative pronouns.** They relate the clause (called a **relative clause**) to the word it modifies. *That* and *which* may also be relative pronouns.

Relative Pronouns

who   whom   whose   that   which

Relative pronouns have three jobs:

1. They begin an adjective clause.
2. They relate the adjective clause to a word in the main clause.
3. They act as subject, object, or predicate pronoun of the verb in the adjective clause. They may also be the object of a preposition in the clause.

> Kelly is the girl *who won the race.*
> (*Who* is the subject of *won.*)
>
> Is Gayle the girl *whom you met?*
> (*Whom* is the object of *met.*)
>
> He is the magician *of whom we were speaking.*
> (*Whom* is the object of the preposition *of.*)

The subject form is *who.* The object form is *whom.* Which form you use depends upon how the word is used within the clause.

Exercises Analyze relative clauses.

A. Each relative clause is preceded by the word it modifies. Decide whether *who* or *whom* would be used in each clause. Write the pronoun. Then write its use in the clause: subject, object, or object of a preposition.

1. the guide to ____?____ we spoke
2. the doctor ____?____ came to see us
3. the pharmacist from ____?____ we got the prescription
4. the members ____?____ helped us build the float
5. the teacher ____?____ helped us
6. the family with ____?____ I stayed
7. the runner ____?____ always wears a baseball cap
8. the performer ____?____ everyone liked best
9. the miners ____?____ the rescue team found
10. the people ____?____ I counted

B. Follow the directions for Exercise A.

1. the Indians ____?____ once inhabited this area
2. the minister ____?____ performed the ceremony
3. the artist ____?____ painted this mural
4. the construction worker ____?____ handled the jack-hammer
5. the relatives ____?____ they visited
6. the astronauts ____?____ the newscaster discussed
7. the journalist ____?____ wrote this article
8. the goalie ____?____ wears a knit cap
9. the gardener ____?____ grew gardenias last year.
10. the grocer ____?____ sponsors our hockey team

Part 9   Noun Clauses

You will remember that nouns can be used as subjects, as objects of verbs, as predicate words after linking verbs, and as objects of prepositions.

A **noun clause** is a clause used as a noun in a sentence. It can be used in any way that a noun is used. Noun clauses do not modify anything because nouns are not modifiers.

Uses of Noun Clauses

Subject   *What we wanted* was food.
Subject   *What the magician did* astonished us.

Object   We saw *that you were in a hurry.*
Object   We know *whom you mean.*

Object of   Give the clothes to *whoever can use them.*
Preposition   (The clause is the object of the preposition *to.*)

Object of   Jack works hard for *what he gets.* (The
Preposition   clause is the object of the preposition *for.*)

Predicate Noun   The answer was *what we had expected.*
Predicate Noun   The responses were *what we anticipated.*

Words That Introduce Noun Clauses

A great many noun clauses are introduced by *that* and *what.* Some are introduced by *whatever, whoever,* and *whomever.* Other noun clauses are introduced by *who, whose,* and *whom.* Still others are introduced by *where, when,* and *how.*

You cannot tell the kind of clause from the word that introduces it. You can tell the kind of clause only from its use in the sentence. If the clause is used as a noun, it is a noun clause. If the clause is a modifier, it is an adverb or adjective clause.

Wherever he went was a mystery. (noun clause as subject)
No one knew *where we hid.* (noun clause as object)

He left pieces of paper *wherever he went.* (adverb clause)
This is the cave *where we hid.* (adjective clause)

Diagraming Noun Clauses

A noun clause is diagramed on a bridge at the place where the clause is used in a sentence. The word that introduces the clause is placed on a horizontal line above the clause.

1. Noun clause as subject

That she wasn't coming was certain.

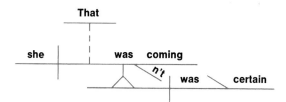

2. Noun clause as object of the verb

Donna could see *who was coming.*

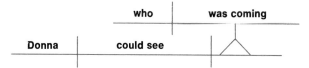

3. Noun clause as object of a preposition

We were surprised by *what happened.*

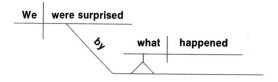

Exercises Analyze noun clauses.

A. Copy the noun clauses in these sentences. Underline the subject once and the verb twice. Tell how the clause is used. Your teacher may ask you to diagram the sentences.

1. I will do whatever you decide.
2. Whoever wins gets this trophy.
3. Do you remember who told you that?

4. I don't know where the Marcuses live.
5. Whoever appeared was put to work.
6. I was just thinking about what you said.
7. Show this card to whoever is at the door.
8. Paula didn't know where Kevin was going.
9. Our class will support whatever candidate is chosen.
10. Where we will go on our class trip hasn't been decided.

B. Follow the directions for Exercise A.

1. Whoever finds Kathy's watch will receive a reward.
2. Why they chose me is hard to understand.
3. Whatever you decide is all right with me.
4. Save these coupons for whoever wants them.
5. Whoever wins the tournament deserves great recognition.
6. We didn't know who was in charge of the ballot box.
7. I was wondering how you did that.
8. Sally doesn't know where the supplies are.
9. Sign the papers for whoever needs them.
10. How you finished so quickly is beyond me.

Exercise Analyze clauses.

Copy the subordinate clauses in these sentences. Tell whether they are adverb, adjective, or noun clauses. Underline the subject once and the verb twice.

1. We arrived when Dr. Jordan was speaking.
2. Is this the coat that you want?
3. Can you study while the TV is on?
4. We did not know who the man was.
5. Jeff ducked before the snowball hit him.
6. The plane that leaves at 7:00 P.M. has a feature movie.
7. I don't believe that the experiment is possible.
8. Someone said that we would have a holiday tomorrow.
9. Dad lived in Colorado when he was growing up.
10. How the dog got out is beyond me.

Additional Exercises — Review

Using Compound and Complex Sentences

A. Analyze simple sentences.

Label four columns *Subject, Verb, Object,* and *Predicate Word.* For each sentence fill in the appropriate columns. Some sentences may have compound parts.

EXAMPLE: Their confidence and determination impressed and surprised the other team.

SUBJECT	VERB	OBJECT	PREDICATE WORD
confidence	impressed	team	
determination	surprised		

1. Their supply of butane gas was low.
2. The sky looks brighter and clearer to the west.
3. The fields and meadows were covered with daisies.
4. The entire week was hot and muggy.
5. The hot sun and the humidity made football practice impossible.
6. Mariners watch the wind and clouds carefully.
7. The shutters and doors flapped and banged.
8. Darnell and I baked cookies for our picnic.
9. The books and the china were all ready for shipment.
10. The librarian ordered some new encyclopedias and a new atlas.

B. Make compound sentences.

Join each pair of sentences by using *and,* *but,* or *or.* Place a comma before *and,* *but,* or *or.* One pair of sentences should not be joined because the ideas are not related. Can you find that pair?

1. Jim groomed four horses. He didn't have time for the fifth.
2. Trudy went at 10 o'clock. The store was still not open.
3. Do you want to make lunch? Do you want to go to Burger King?
4. The short circuit in the toaster blew the fuse. The iron did it.
5. The tide was in. The beach in the cove was covered.
6. We were going to the motocross races. The heavy rain has delayed them until next week.
7. Do you enjoy ice skating? Do you prefer tobogganing?
8. Our class collected aluminum cans. We took them to the recycling center.
9. Marsha counted fourteen hawks. Sara saw eighteen.
10. The bus was full. The driver was nowhere to be seen.

C. Punctuate compound sentences.

Number your paper from 1–10. Write the last word of the *first* part of each compound sentence. Next write the proper punctuation mark. Then write the first word of the second part of the compound sentence.

1. Bill opened the door and two dogs rushed in.
2. I like to read short stories but I really enjoy long, detailed mysteries.
3. The helicopter flew over the park that's its usual route.
4. Mrs. Stuart has about fifty different kinds of plants in her windows you can hardly see out.
5. Our field trip to Knotts Berry Farm was fun but I liked the tour at Universal Studios the best.

6. Should we buy Tim a birthday present or should we make him something?

7. The great auk is a diving bird it is almost 30 inches long.

8. Jeff stood close to the house and Pete got on his shoulders.

9. Sandy pitches best but Lana is the best batter.

10. I'll lend you some money you can pay me tomorrow.

D. Analyze simple and compound sentences.

Copy these sentences. Underline each subject once and each verb twice. After each sentence write *Simple* or *Compound* to show what kind it is.

1. The key was on the table, and I hung it up.

2. He took the receiver off the hook and forgot about it.

3. I threw the trash into the basket, but I didn't notice any magazines.

4. The trees lined the avenue and shaded it.

5. Foreign newspapers come in at noon, and Lee buys one on her way home.

6. A wind started about suppertime and blew hard.

7. I washed the dishes, and Rhonda dried them.

8. José washed the dishes and cleaned the kitchen.

9. Joan and Tom made a hollow around each little tree and watered it.

10. It rained all afternoon, and my sister and I stayed in and played chess.

E. Recognize adverb clauses.

Copy each adverb clause. Underline its subject once and its verb twice. Draw a circle around the subordinating conjunction.

1. If the shelf is too low, move it up.

2. When the alarm sounded, all classes left the building.

3. Wherever he went, he took his Spanish-English dictionary.

4. Since we had lots of time, we stayed for dessert.

5. Juanita hurt her ankle as she was running the hurdles.

6. If you want my opinion, it's available.

7. When you go to Philadelphia, see Independence Hall.

8. Lauren talked as if she would run for vice-president of the French Club.

9. When the trumpet fanfare began, the audience returned to their seats.

10. When the bobsled finally stopped, we could barely crawl out.

F. Recognize adjective clauses.

Copy the adjective clause from each sentence. Underline the subject once and the verb twice. Before the clause, write the word it modifies.

1. This is the store that I had in mind.

2. We enjoyed the postcards that you wrote from South America.

3. Mount Vernon is the home where George and Martha Washington lived.

4. The book that you wanted has been checked out.

5. The speaker whom they want charges $400.

6. Do you remember the time when you fell out of the chestnut tree?

7. This is my friend Tracy, whom I was telling you about.

8. Bob, who had just come back from the dentist, looked rather uncomfortable.

9. It was Ben Franklin who invented bifocals, the electrical generator, and the Franklin stove.

10. This is the album that I want.

G. Analyze relative clauses.

Decide whether *who* or *whom* would be used in each clause. Write the pronoun. Then write its use in the clause: subject, object, or object of preposition.

1. the jockey _____?_____ you picked
2. the pilots _____?_____ United Airlines hires
3. the clerk _____?_____ answered your question
4. the sculptor _____?_____ designed this piece of art
5. the butcher from _____?_____ she usually buys her meat
6. the singer _____?_____ did that TV special
7. the caterers _____?_____ the mayor hired
8. the mail carrier _____?_____ was on duty yesterday
9. the police officer with _____?_____ you were walking
10. the teacher to _____?_____ you talked

H. Recognize noun clauses.

Copy the noun clause in each sentence. Tell how the clause is used.

1. Whoever wins the tennis finals goes to the state meet.
2. The plaque commemorates what she did for the school.
3. How this sewing machine works is what I would like to know.
4. Nancy told me that Maurita wasn't coming.
5. Most of us did not agree with what the speaker said.
6. Coach Larson could see that the defense was tiring.
7. Zebulon Pike was ill prepared for whatever his expedition would face.
8. He did not know that his men would encounter a bitter winter.
9. Carol said that her report was about Renaissance painters.
10. Whoever told you that was wrong.

Section 9

Making Subjects and Verbs Agree

Part 1   Making Subjects and Verbs Agree in Number

When a word refers to one thing, it is **singular.** When it refers to more than one thing, it is **plural.** When we speak of the **number** of a word, we are talking about whether it is singular or plural.

A verb must agree in number with its subject.

If the subject is singular, the verb must be singular. If the subject is plural, the verb must be plural.

SINGULAR	PLURAL
The bird *sings*.	The birds *sing*.
She *listens*.	They *listen*.
It *whistles*.	They *whistle*.

You can see that the third person singular of the verb ends in *s*. The *s* disappears in the plural.

You will have problems in agreement of subject and verb only when you are not sure what the subject is. *Remember:* To find the subject, first find the verb. Then ask *who?* or *what?* before it.

> One of the players *is* my sister.
>
> > *Verb:* is
> > *Who is?* one
> > *Subject:* one

The subject of the verb is never found in a prepositional phrase.

Watch for phrases that lie between the verb and the subject.

> One of the eggs *was* broken.
>
> The *pictures* on the desk *were* torn.

Phrases beginning with the words *with, together with, including, as well as,* and *in addition to* are not part of the subject.

> The *principal,* in addition to the teachers, *is* here.
>
> Mr. *Bard,* together with his children, *has* left.

Exercises Make verbs agree with their subjects.

A. Choose the verb that agrees with the subject.

1. One of my front teeth (are, is) loose.
2. The captain, together with his crew, (look, looks) after the ship.
3. Several pages in the book (is, are) missing.
4. The drawings on display (was, were) done by the art classes.
5. The bus with all the players (arrives, arrive) at three.
6. The schedule for all the sports events (is, are) on the bulletin board.
7. The choice of the judges (was, were) not very popular.
8. All the signs along the road (has, have) been taken down.
9. A popcorn stand in the lobby (was, were) open.
10. The new schedule for the suburbs (has, have) more trains.

B. Follow the directions for Exercise A.

1. The doctor, together with her staff, (are, is) often here.
2. The edges of the playing field (was, were) still wet.
3. My jacket, as well as my ski pants, (is, are) wet.
4. Each of the homerooms (contribute, contributes) to the Toys-for-Tots campaign.
5. Those antique cars in the driveway (belongs, belong) to the Hadleys.
6. A request for money and provisions (was, were) granted.
7. The members of the swim team (report, reports) to the pool every morning.
8. Two of my teachers (coaches, coach) the volleyball team.
9. The girls on the team (like, likes) the coach.
10. The attendants at the airport (requires, require) passengers to check their luggage.

409

Part 2   Compound Subjects

Compound subjects joined by *and* require a plural verb.

The truck and the trailer *were* badly damaged.
The walls and the ceiling *are* soundproofed.

When the parts of a compound subject are joined by *or* or *nor*, the verb agrees with the part nearer to it.

Either Mom or the boys *have* come home.

Neither the boys nor Mom *has* been home yet.

Either the musicians or their leader *has* your music.

Exercises   Make verbs agree with their subjects.

A.   Choose the verb that agrees with the subject.

1. Al and Ken (hasn't, haven't) finished repairing their old car.

2. Either the coach or the co-captains (call, calls) the time-outs.

3. Both winter and summer (is, are) mild here.

4. Either a raccoon or some dogs (has, have) gotten into the garbage.

5. The evening news and the late newspaper (report, reports) the sports results of the day.

6. Neither the tent nor the sleeping bags (arrive, arrives) until tomorrow.

7. Both the tugs and the Loganville ferry (dock, docks) here.

8. Corrine and her family (is, are) arriving tomorrow.

9. Neither my gym shoes nor my uniform (need, needs) to be laundered.

10. The players and the referee (are, is) arguing about the call.

B. Follow the directions for Exercise A.

1. Either Phil or his sister (is, are) bringing us home.
2. Neither the cookies nor the cake (taste, tastes) burnt to me.
3. The water and the beach (look, looks) inviting.
4. Neither complaints nor threats (has, have) any effect on the umpire.
5. Buildings or billboards often (obscures, obscure) the horizon.
6. Neither fishing nor hunting (is, are) permitted.
7. Both the German Club and the Spanish Club (help, helps) decorate the lobby for Christmas.
8. Both the ordinary frogs and the bullfrog (tune, tunes) up at sundown.
9. Either the dog or the cat (stay, stays) home.
10. Either our local newspaper or our local radio stations (publicize, publicizes) our school's sporting events.

Part 3 Indefinite Pronouns

The indefinite pronouns in the list below are singular:

Singular Indefinite Pronouns		
another	either	nobody
anybody	everybody	no one
anyone	everyone	one
anything	everything	somebody
each	neither	someone

Each of the cars *was* given a number.
Everybody *has* a job to do.
Neither of us *has* a good enough report.

The words *some, all,* and *most* are singular if they refer to one part of something. They are plural if they refer to several things.

SINGULAR	PLURAL
all of the paper	all of the people
most of the work	most of the books

The pronoun *you* is always followed by a plural verb.

We know you *have* been working hard.
Is it true that you *were* in Canada last summer?

Exercises Make verbs agree with their subjects.

A. Choose the verb that agrees with the subject.

1. Another of those talk shows (come, comes) on tonight at 10 o'clock.
2. Many of Debbie's friends (were, was) away.
3. Most of the boathouse (need, needs) painting.
4. Either Michelle or Ted (is, are) ushering.
5. Some of the students (earn, earns) extra money as ushers.
6. No one told me that Mike (were, was) moving to South Carolina.
7. Another of her reports (compare, compares) the prices of sporting goods.
8. Everyone in Rock Hill (was, were) here.
9. All of the books (have, has) been shelved in alphabetical order.
10. Each of the ensemble members (play, plays) at least two instruments.

B. Follow the directions for Exercise A.

1. All of the honeydew melons (is, are) ripe.
2. One of my brothers (is, are) in the navy.

3. Neither of the maps (show, shows) Rainbow Springs.

4. These bundles of newspapers (go, goes) to the recycling plant.

5. Neither of us (is, are) ready to give our speech.

6. Most of the hay (dry, dries) in a week.

7. Everyone in the audience (was, were) captivated by the performances.

8. All of the telephones (is, are) busy right now.

9. Most of the players (practices, practice) in the morning and the afternoon.

10. Somebody (is, are) responsible for writing up the club's minutes.

Part 4 Other Problems of Agreement

The pronouns *he, she,* and *it* are used with *doesn't*. All other personal pronouns are used with *don't*.

> He *doesn't* swim well enough.
> She *doesn't* need more money.
> It *doesn't* look like rain now.

> I *don't* dance.
> We *don't* dance.
> You *don't* sing.
> They *don't* know.

In sentences beginning *Here is, There is,* and *Where is,* the subject comes after the verb.

> Here *is* your ticket.
> Where *is* the projector?
> There *are* the keys for the cottage.

Exercises Make verbs agree with their subjects.

A. Choose the verb that agrees with the subject.

1. It (doesn't, don't) look as if the sky will clear before noon.
2. Where (was, were) she taking those packages?
3. Here (is, are) the tube socks and T-shirts the team ordered.
4. There (go, goes) the siren.
5. That idea (doesn't, don't) make any sense.
6. Where (is, are) the box for these ornaments?
7. Here (is, are) all the sheet metal that I could find.
8. Beth (don't, doesn't) want to go apple-picking with us.
9. There (are, is) several deer on the front lawn.
10. There (are, is) the new batteries for the flashlight.

B. Choose the verb that agrees with the subject.

1. There (come, comes) the other team onto the ice.
2. (Don't, Doesn't) Jennie want to ride with us?
3. There (is, are) the float we built for the parade.
4. Erica (doesn't, don't) agree with us.
5. Here (are, is) the magazine you wanted.
6. There (was, were) few skiers on the chairlift.
7. Where (do, does) these cartons go?
8. There (are, is) a fawn and its mother in our yard.
9. Where (is, are) my Disney World T-shirt?
10. Here (is, are) some of the pictures we took last winter.

Additional Exercises — Review

Making Subjects and Verbs Agree

A. Make verbs agree with their subjects.

Choose the verb that agrees with the subject.

1. The sandbars in the Mississippi (cause, causes) many accidents.
2. Some sections of the city (has, have) no bus service.
3. Three students' paintings, including mine, (was, were) chosen to compete in the state art fair.
4. That lady in the gray sweat suit (jog, jogs) five miles a day.
5. The new books in the library (is, are) on a special shelf.
6. The answers to the exercise (is, are) in the back of the textbook.
7. The evidence on these films (looks, look) convincing.
8. The photographers on the yearbook staff (is, are) Raul and Patti.
9. The price of the German binoculars (are, is) too high.
10. Our team, including the coach and the cheerleaders, (take, takes) the bus from here.

B. Choose the right verb.

Choose the verb that agrees with the subject.

1. Neither the fenders nor the license plate (was, were) dented.
2. The principal and the teachers (organize, organizes) a student-faculty softball game every year.

3. Either my alarm clock or the clock in the den (is, are) wrong.

4. If school is canceled, the principal or one of the secretaries (telephone, telephones) the radio station.

5. Both Chico and his brother (was, were) there.

6. Neither porcupine quills nor skunks (stop, stops) our dog Rusty.

7. Either Sean or his grandparents usually (pick, picks) up the mail.

8. Yogurt and frozen yogurt (come, comes) in a variety of flavors.

9. Both the Hershey Company and Sara Lee Kitchens (has, have) tours of their food processing plants.

10. Either a van or a truck (suit, suits) our purpose quite well.

C. Choose the right verb.

Choose the verb that agrees with the subject.

1. Some of these stamps (don't, doesn't) stick.

2. (Wasn't, Weren't) you ready when the whistle blew?

3. Not one of the newscasts (has, have) publicized our candy sale.

4. Most of the time (was, were) wasted.

5. Everything on the two bottom shelves (belong, belongs) to David.

6. All of the fenceposts (has, have) snow on them.

7. Anything made of metal (was, were) immediately magnetized.

8. Neither of the gas pumps (is, are) working.

9. Nobody in the bleachers (cheer, cheers) louder than our Pep Club.

10. Most of our supplies (come, comes) from the school store.

D. Choose the right verb.

Choose the verb that agrees with the subject.

1. Here (is, are) the fire trucks.
2. Here (is, are) what the newspaper says about the eclipse.
3. There (goes, go) the runners.
4. Sam (doesn't, don't) ever take his eyes off the TV.
5. Here (is, are) the photographs that Heather picked out.
6. Where (is, are) the envelopes for these letters?
7. There (isn't, aren't) any time to waste.
8. (Don't, Doesn't) the *Orient Express* run any more?
9. Here (is, are) your tickets for the carnival.
10. She (doesn't, don't) know how to swim the butterfly stroke.

Section 10

Using Verbals

You have learned that there are eight parts of speech. The eight parts of speech are these:

| nouns | verbs | adjectives | conjunctions |
| pronouns | adverbs | prepositions | interjections |

In addition to the eight parts of speech, our language contains three other kinds of words. These are **infinitives, participles,** and **gerunds.** These words are called verbals. A **verbal** is a word that is formed from a verb but acts as another part of speech.

In this chapter you will study the three kinds of verbals, and learn how they are used in the sentence.

Part 1 Infinitives

The **infinitive** is the name of the verbal that usually appears with the word *to* before it. *To* is called the **sign of the infinitive.**

> to go   to see   to run   to walk

The word *to* is often used as a preposition. It is a preposition if it is followed by a noun or pronoun that is its object. *It is the sign of the infinitive if it is followed by a verb.* Notice these examples:

> We went *to the park.* (prepositional phrase)
> We wanted *to swim.* (infinitive)
>
> We stayed *to the end.* (prepositional phrase)
> We tried *to dive.* (infinitive)

Because the infinitive is formed from a verb, it is like a verb in several ways. The infinitive may, for example, have an object. It may also be modified by adverbs.

> Chris learned *to run a lathe.*
>   (*Lathe* is the direct object of the infinitive *to run.*)
>
> We tried *to give the dog a bath.*
>   (*Dog* is the indirect object and *bath* is the direct object of *to give.*)
>
> You will need *to work fast.*
>   (*Fast* is an adverb modifying *to work.*)
>
> Linda wanted *to drive the car to the station.*
>   (*Car* is the object of *to drive; to the station* is an adverb phrase modifying *to drive.*)

The infinitive with its objects and modifiers is an **infinitive phrase.**

Uses of the Infinitive Phrase

Infinitives and infinitive phrases can be used (1) as nouns, (2) as adjectives, or (3) as adverbs.

You remember that nouns are used as subjects and objects of verbs. Infinitives and infinitive phrases can be used as subjects, as objects, and in other ways that nouns are used.

Subject   *To leave early* is sometimes impolite.
       (*To leave early* is the subject of *is.*)

Object   Sue wanted *to leave.*
       (*To leave* is the object of *wanted.*)

Infinitive and infinitive phrases can be used as modifiers. If the infinitive or infinitive phrase modifies a noun or pronoun, it is used as an adjective. If it modifies a verb, adjective, or adverb, it is used as an adverb.

Adverb   Rick went *to see the doctor.*
       (*To see the doctor* modifies the verb *went.*)

Adverb   Tickets for the big game are hard *to get.*
       (*To get* modifies *hard.*)

Adjective   The catcher is the player *to watch.*
       (*To watch* modifies *player.*)

The Split Infinitive

Sometimes a modifier is placed between the word *to* and the verb. A modifier in this position is said to split the infinitive. Usually, a split infinitive sounds awkward and should be avoided.

Awkward   Ann expects to *easily* win.
Better   Ann expects to win *easily.*

Exercises Find the infinitives and infinitive phrases.

A. Find the infinitives and infinitive phrases in these sentences. Write each infinitive or infinitive phrase. Be prepared to tell how it is used in the sentence.

> EXAMPLE: They were ready to drop the whole thing.
>
> Infinitive phrase: *to drop the whole thing*

1. Mary and I plan to watch the Neil Diamond TV special.
2. Mr. Anderson wants to explain the new procedures.
3. To finish this project by Monday is my goal.
4. We tried to remember the address.
5. We plan to visit Washington.
6. Judy and I were told to bring our registration cards to orientation.
7. The vet came to see our horses.
8. This is the best book to use.
9. Bill ran to get a flashlight.
10. Sue still has homework to do.

B. Follow the instructions for Exercise A.

1. This is the path to follow.
2. The best thing to do is to wait.
3. Would you like to eat breakfast at the pancake house?
4. To read the first two chapters of this book is our assignment.
5. Amy has someone to help her to finish the job.
6. Do you want to go shopping tomorrow?
7. He wanted to sail up the coast to Alaska.
8. Did you remember to buy film?
9. Remind me to fill out the application form tonight.
10. Do you want to play tennis after school?

Part 2 Participles

You remember that one of the principal parts of the verb is the **past participle.** The past participle is formed by adding -d or -ed to the present tense: *walk-walked.* The past participles of irregular verbs do not follow this rule and have to be learned separately: *bring-brought, ring-rung.*

There is another kind of participle, called the **present participle.** All present participles are formed by adding -ing to the present tense of the verb: *bring-bringing, ring-ringing, walk-walking.* Participles are always used as adjectives. They can modify nouns or pronouns:

Smiling, Jan accepted the award.
(*Smiling* is a present participle modifying the noun *Jan.*)

Lunging, he hit the fence.
(*Lunging* is a present participle modifying the pronoun *he.*)

Because participles are formed from verbs, they can have objects and be modified by adverbs. The participle with its objects and modifiers forms a **participial phrase.**

Turning the pages, Barb found an old letter.
(*Turning the pages* is a participial phrase modifying Barb; *pages* is the object of the participle *turning.*)

Turning suddenly, Jean bumped into Mrs. Wood.
(*Turning suddenly* is a participial phrase modifying *Jean.* The word *suddenly* is an adverb modifying the participle *turning.*)

Completely exhausted, the swimmer crawled out of the pool.
(*Completely exhausted* is a participial phrase modifying *swimmer. Completely* is an adverb modifying the participle *exhausted.*)

Exercises Find the participles and participial phrases.

A. Write down the participles and participial phrases in these sentences. Show which word the participle modifies.

> EXAMPLE: Flipping the switch suddenly, Ron picked up two possums in the flashlight beam.
>
> Participle   *flipping* modifies the noun *Ron.*
> Participial phrase   flipping the switch suddenly

1. Exhausted, the runners crossed the finish line.
2. Moving effortlessly, the skaters danced across the ice.
3. Jumping clear, Jim opened his parachute.
4. Crossing the old bridge, she passed the old general store.
5. Frozen, the pie tastes even better.
6. Tested in our laboratories, the parts are guaranteed.
7. Spread thin, the glue dries in an hour.
8. Looking through binoculars, Jim could see the skyline quite clearly.
9. Concentrating deeply, the center sank the free throw.
10. Moving quickly, the goalie blocked the kick.

B. Follow the directions for Exercise A.

1. Seeing the rain, Mr. Mill waited.
2. Clutching the receiver tightly, she listened.
3. The ball ricocheted, hitting the taillight.
4. Waiting patiently, the passengers quietly stood in line at the gate.
5. Driving hard, the running back dived over the goal line.
6. Holding her pigeon, Lisa showed us the leg band.
7. Watch for gravel trucks leaving the quarry.
8. Fascinated by the talk, we listened without a sound.
9. He forgot that paperback lying on the table.
10. Breathing hard, Nancy crossed the finish line.

Part 3   Gerunds

A **gerund** is a verb form that is used as a noun. Gerunds can be used in any way that nouns are used:

> *Swimming* is good exercise.
> (*Swimming* is a gerund, the subject of *is*.)

> Karen likes *riding*.
> (*Riding* is a gerund, the object of *likes*.)

> The time for *wrestling* is changed.
> (*Wrestling* is a gerund, the object of the preposition *for*.)

Because gerunds are formed from verbs, they can have objects and can be modified by adverbs. Because they are used as nouns, they can also be modified by adjectives.

> *Riding a horse* scares Kitt.
> (*Riding* is a gerund; *horse* is the object of *riding*.)

> *Running uphill* is difficult.
> (*Running* is a gerund; *uphill* is an adverb modifying *running*.)

> *Careful reading* requires concentration.
> (*Reading* is a gerund; *careful* is an adjective modifying *reading*.)

Gerunds can also be modified by prepositional phrases:

> *Cycling in city traffic* is frustrating.
> (*Cycling* is a gerund; *in city traffic* is a prepositional phrase modifying *cycling*.)

A **gerund phrase** consists of a gerund with its modifiers and objects.

Exercises Find the gerunds and gerund phrases.

A. Find the gerunds and gerund phrases. As your teacher directs, show how the gerund is used.

> EXAMPLE: Planning the sports meet was fun.
>
> *Planning*: gerund, subject of *was*
> *Planning the sports meet*: gerund phrase

1. Skydiving takes nerve.
2. Skiing is an invigorating sport.
3. Cleaning the attic was not my idea of a good time.
4. Washing that wall took all afternoon.
5. Painting the scenery took more time than we thought.
6. Running has become a popular activity.
7. Putting on a play takes teamwork.
8. Chris enjoys baking.
9. Skating on the lake in winter is fun.
10. That dog specializes in digging.

B. Follow the directions for Exercise A.

1. Joe learned fencing last summer.
2. Writing that essay was a difficult assignment.
3. Learning Russian requires homework.
4. Visiting Dallas was interesting.
5. Jack has always liked reading.
6. Wearing sunglasses rests her eyes.
7. They got sick from overeating.
8. Clare likes walking in the rain.
9. Eating outside was cooler.
10. Driving to Alaska was a long, interesting journey.

Distinguishing Between Gerunds and Participles

The gerund, like the present participle, is formed by adding *-ing* to the present tense of the verb. How can you tell whether a word is a gerund or a participle? It depends upon how the word is used. If it is used as a modifier, it is a participle. If it is used as a noun, it is a gerund.

> Walking is good exercise.
> (*Walking* is a gerund, the subject of *is*.)
>
> Walking fast, we overtook the boys.
> (*Walking* is a participle modifying *we*; *fast* is an adverb modifying *walking*.)
>
> Trying is half the battle.
> (*Trying* is a gerund, the subject of *is*.)
>
> Trying, Brenda pushed harder.
> (*Trying* is a participle modifying *Brenda*.)

Exercise Distinguishing between gerunds and participles.

For each sentence, write down the gerund or participle and say which it is. Be prepared to explain why it is a gerund or a participle.

1. Watching television bothers his eyes.
2. Watching television, Terry noticed the colors were wrong again.
3. Fixing steps was Mr. Buswell's specialty.
4. Fixing a sandwich, Gerry listened to the sportscast.
5. Cleaning is done every Saturday.
6. Cleaning the car, Pat found her notebook.
7. Removing the tree was difficult.
8. Panning for gold, the old man waded into the stream.
9. Moving quickly, the paramedics aided the victims.
10. Swimming is good for most people's health.

Additional Exercises — Review

Using Verbals

A. Find the infinitives and infinitive phrases.

Find the infinitives and infinitive phrases in these sentences.

1. We hope to visit Washington this summer.
2. To satisfy his curiosity is impossible.
3. Ask them to come with us.
4. We hope to go to the movie on Sunday.
5. I still have a couple of windows to wash.
6. We were just starting to eat the other half of the pizza.
7. Jill proceeded to explain her proposal.
8. Andy is teaching us to float.
9. To go around by the bridge takes too long.
10. Wendy was planning to go to the beach.

B. Find the participles and participial phrases.

Find the participles and participial phrases in these sentences.

1. Flopping frantically, the trout got off the wharf.
2. Speaking quietly, the librarian explained the reference book to me.
3. Look at the cat carrying its kitten in its mouth.
4. Racing wildly, the horses cross the finish line simultaneously.
5. Elated, Beth told us the news.
6. Cleaning the garage, John found some interesting old newspapers.
7. Bought second-hand, the motor lasted three years.

8. Snorting and kicking, the pinto refused to wear a saddle.
9. Walking slowly, Laura and her dog watched the sunset.
10. Made in Japan, the tape recorder was a money-maker.

C. Find the gerunds and gerund phrases.

Find the gerunds and gerund phrases in these sentences.

1. Tracy likes making pottery.
2. Skydiving requires skill and an adventurous spirit.
3. Talking on the phone tires Mr. King.
4. Walking is good exercise and a healthful habit.
5. Reading is my favorite pastime.
6. Have you forgotten about mowing the lawn?
7. Paneling the den was Dad's idea.
8. You will never get rich by wishing.
9. In basketball, quick thinking is essential.
10. Driving over Highland Pass takes about an hour.

D. Distinguish between gerunds and participles.

Write down the gerund or participle for each sentence, and say which it is. Be prepared to explain why it is a gerund or a participle.

1. Swimming fast is all right for short spurts.
2. Swimming fast, he reached the dock first.
3. Talking a mile a minute, Jan explained her tardiness.
4. Thinking on your feet is not always easy.
5. Talking doesn't take any effort for Pat.
6. Thinking fast, he avoided the collision.
7. Waiting on tables is not hard work.
8. We saw the plow coming up the hill.
9. Finishing the last question on the test, Maria's pen ran out of ink.
10. Playing tennis is Michelle's favorite sport.

Section 11

Capitalization

Capitalization refers to the use of capital letters. To capitalize a word means to begin a word with a capital letter.

Capital letters help a reader to understand what he or she reads. For example, they make the reader notice important words. These might be people's names or the names of specific places. In addition, capitals point out the first word in each sentence. They show the reader where each new thought begins.

This section contains two sets of rules for using capital letters correctly. The first set shows you how to recognize and capitalize proper nouns and adjectives. The second set explains when to capitalize the first word in a group of words.

Just as you treat special people with respect, you use capital letters to show that certain words are special. To write well, you must know which words need to be capitalized. As you write, refer to the rules in this section.

Proper Nouns and Adjectives

Capitalize proper nouns and proper adjectives.

A **common noun** is the name of a whole group of persons, places, or things. A **proper noun** is the name of an individual person, place, or thing. A **proper adjective** is an adjective formed from a proper noun.

COMMON NOUN	PROPER NOUN	PROPER ADJECTIVE
person	Elizabeth	Elizabethan
country	Spain	Spanish
city	Paris	Parisian

Proper nouns occur in great variety. The following rules with their illustrations will help you solve the capitalization problems that proper nouns and proper adjectives present.

Names of Persons

Capitalize the names of persons and also the initials or abbreviations that stand for those names.

J. R. R. Tolkien   **J**ohn **R**onald **R**euel **T**olkein
Ella **T.** Grasso   **E**lla **T**ambussi **G**rasso

Capitalize titles used with names of persons and also the initials or abbreviations that stand for those titles.

Rev. M. R. Eaton   **S**enator Smith   **D**r. Patricia Ryan

Do not capitalize titles used as common nouns:

Have you seen your doctor?   She is the company president.

Capitalize titles of people whose rank is very important, even when these titles are used without proper names.

The **P**resident of the United States

The titles *Mr., Mrs., Ms.,* and *Miss* are always capitalized.

Family Relationships

Capitalize such words as mother, father, aunt, and uncle when these words are used as names.

Note that when the noun is modified by a personal pronoun, it is not capitalized.

Hello, **M**other. Is **D**ad home yet?
My **a**unt is going to visit us next week.

The Pronoun *I*

Capitalize the pronoun *I*.

Is he taller than **I**?

The Deity

Capitalize all words referring to the Deity, to the Holy Family, the Bible, and to religious scriptures.

God	the **L**ord	the **B**ible
Allah	the **V**irgin **M**ary	the **B**ook of **E**xodus

Capitalize personal pronouns referring to the Deity.

God spoke to **H**is prophets.

Exercises Use capital letters correctly.

A. Number your paper from 1–10. Copy the following sentences. Change small letters to capital letters wherever necessary.

1. I told my mother that i had a doctor's appointment.
2. She said, "Please ask dr. hernandez to call me."

3. The new teacher is from paris, france.
4. He is a parisian.
5. Would you tell mom i'll be a little late for dinner?
6. The first book of the bible is the book of genesis.
7. My mother asked aunt rose if tad and maria could stay for lunch.
8. Please take this message to the principal, lynn.
9. She says that ms. holchak is not in her office.
10. Some names for god are jehovah, the lord, and the almighty.

B. Follow the directions for Exercise A.

1. There are seven cities in the united states named springfield.
2. The largest is in massachusetts.
3. Our country is sometimes called a jeffersonian democracy.
4. The new student is toshio kitagawa. His sister is mieko.
5. Both of them were born in japan.
6. Which cairo do you mean?
7. Is it the one in egypt or the one in illinois?
8. Speakers were mr. s. f. paulson, ms. j. p. perez, and ms. p. d. cardelo.
9. All of my aunts and uncles live in california.
10. It was captain sherman who gave sue and ted the booklets on bicycle safety.

Geographical Names

In a geographical name, capitalize the first letter of each word except articles and prepositions.

The article *the* appearing before a geographical name is not part of the geographical name and is therefore not capitalized.

Continents: Europe, Asia, Africa, Australia

Bodies of Water: the Pacific Ocean, Puget Sound, the Columbia River, Hudson Bay, the Straits of Magellan, Lake Superior, the English Channel, the Arabian Gulf

Land Forms: the Mississippi Delta, the Cape of Good Hope, the Mojave Desert, the Atlas Mountains, Pike's Peak, Dismal Swamp

Political Units: Oak Park, Los Angeles, Commonwealth of Puerto Rico, First Congressional District, Utah, Great Britain, the Azores

Public Areas: Badlands National Monument, Grant Park, Shawnee National Forest, the Battery, the Black Hills, Zion National Park

Roads and Highways: Oregon Trail, Lincoln Highway, Broad Street, 34th Avenue, Tri-State Tollway, Riverside Freeway, Drury Lane, Route 23

Directions and Sections

Capitalize names of sections of the country but not of directions of the compass.

Industrial production was high in the North.
We headed south for our vacation.
The pioneers moved west over the Oregon Trail.
The first English settlements were along the East Coast.
The frontier moved westward.
The Southwest is our fastest-growing region.

Capitalize proper adjectives derived from names of sections of the country. Do not capitalize adjectives derived from words indicating direction.

an Eastern school   a north wind
a Western concept   a southerly course

Exercises Using capital letters correctly.

A. Number your paper from 1–10. Find the words in the following sentences that should be capitalized. Write the words after the proper number, using the necessary capital letters.

1. Many wagon trains left from independence, missouri.
2. The trail took them first to fort kearney, nebraska.
3. Then they followed the north platte river to fort laramie.
4. The pioneers crossed the rocky mountains at south pass, wyoming.
5. After they crossed the rockies, the trail split into three parts.
6. The oregon trail went to the pacific northwest.
7. The mormon trail went to salt lake city, utah.
8. A third trail crossed the great basin of nevada and utah.
9. It crossed the sierra nevada mountains at donner pass.
10. Many frontiersmen followed these trails westward.

B. Follow the directions for Exercise A.

1. The trans-canada highway crosses the entire width of canada.
2. Of the seven continents, asia and africa are the two largest.
3. Next week we elect the representative from the eighth congressional district.
4. The track championships will be held in morton township.
5. In the bay of naples there is an island called capri.
6. The blue grotto is a famous tourist attraction on capri.
7. Lake baikal is the world's deepest freshwater lake.
8. The lake is in siberia, in the soviet union.
9. We had our family picnic at the lincoln park zoo.
10. Last summer, we drove along the gulf of mexico to new orleans and then north to memphis.

Names of Organizations and Institutions

Capitalize the names of organizations and institutions, including political parties, governmental bodies or agencies, schools, colleges, churches, hospitals, clubs, businesses, and abbreviations of these names.

General Motors Corporation	Children's Hospital
Oakwood High School	St. Mark's Church
University of Southern California	**U.S.C.**

Do not capitalize such words as *school, college, church,* and *hospital* when they are not used as names:

the basketball team of our school

Names of Events, Documents, and Periods of Time

Capitalize the names of historical events, documents, and periods of time.

Battle of Hastings	Treaty of Paris	Age of Discovery
World War II	Bill of Rights	Middle Ages

Months, Days, and Holidays

Capitalize names of months, days, and holidays, but not the names of seasons.

March	Labor Day	summer
Friday	Fourth of July	Feast of the Passover

Races, Languages, Nationalities, Religions

Capitalize the names of races, languages, nationalities, and religions and adjectives derived from them.

Native American	African	Lutheranism
French	Buddhism	Episcopalian

School Subjects

Do not capitalize the names of school subjects, except course names followed by a number.

Algebra I   History of Civilization II
social studies   physical education

Remember that the names of languages are always capitalized.

English   Spanish   German   Hebrew

Ships, Trains, Airplanes, Automobiles

Capitalize the names of ships, trains, airplanes, and automobiles.

U.S.S. *Constitution*   *Cutlass*
Santa Fe Chief   *Spirit of St. Louis*

B.C., A.D.

Capitalize the abbreviations *B.C.* and *A.D.*

The first Olympic Games were held in 776 **B.C.**
The Norman Conquest took place in **A.D.** 1066.

Exercises Use capital letters correctly.

A. Number your paper from 1–10. Write the words in each sentence that should be capitalized. Use the necessary capital letters.

1. Our car was made by american motors corporation.

2. We saw a honda accord, a chevy monza, and a ford fairmont before buying the buick skylark.

3. My sister is class president at pulaski high school.

4. I registered for ancient history I, algebra II, social studies, english, and music.

5. In 1898 the treaty of paris ended the spanish-american war.

6. The fourth of july is an important date in american history.

7. The declaration of independence was signed on july 4, 1776.

8. My favorite subjects are home economics, english, and physical education.

9. The first woman to fly across the atlantic ocean was amelia earhart.

10. In 44 b.c. julius caesar was assassinated.

B. Follow the directions for Exercise A.

1. In a.d. 1492 columbus landed on an island in the west indies.

2. The prophet muhammad founded the religion of islam.

3. His followers are called moslems or muslims.

4. The u.s.s. *constitution* is also called *"old ironsides."*

5. The *broadway limited* runs between new york and chicago.

6. The new head of brookston hospital is dr. margaret allen.

7. The new social studies teacher is from munich, germany.

8. The head nurse in the emergency room at st. luke's hospital is jeffrey adams.

9. The spanish, russian, french, and german clubs at hersey high school sponsored an international bazaar.

10. My sister is studying russian at u.c.l.a., and my brother is a european history major at u.s.c.

First Words

Sentences and Poetry

Capitalize the first word of every sentence and the first word in most lines of poetry.

My sister likes tennis. She is the captain of her team.

Lines of poetry:

Grow old along with me!
The best is yet to be . . .

Sometimes, especially in modern poetry, the lines of a poem do not begin with a capital letter.

Quotations

Capitalize the first word of a direct quotation.

Ralph Waldo Emerson said, "Hitch your wagon to a star."

Do not capitalize the first word of the second part of a divided quotation unless it starts a new sentence.

"Well," he said, "what you say is quite true."
"I agree," he said. "What you say is quite true."

Letters

Capitalize the first word, words like *Sir* and *Madam,* and the name of the person addressed in the greeting of a letter.

Dear Ms. Gomez   Dear Dr. Perkins   Dear Mr. Castillo

In the complimentary close, capitalize the first word only.

Yours very truly   Sincerely yours

Outlines

Capitalize the first word of each line of an outline.

    I. Improve your handwriting.
       A. Form letters carefully.
          1. Watch *a, e, r, l,* and *t.*

Titles

Capitalize the first word and all important words in the titles of books, poems, short stories, articles, newspapers, magazines, plays, motion pictures, works of art, and musical compositions.

Articles (the words *a, an,* and *the*), conjunctions, and prepositions are not usually considered important words. However, note that an article, a conjunction, or a preposition used as the first word of a title must be capitalized.

Book	*The Good Earth*
Story	"*A Game of Catch*"
Play	*The Miracle Worker*
Magazine	*Sports Illustrated*

Exercises Use capital letters correctly.

A. Number your paper from 1–10. Write the words that should be capitalized. Use the correct capital letters.

    1. eleanor roosevelt said, "no one can make you feel inferior without your consent."

    2. walt whitman wrote a famous poem about lincoln entitled "o captain! my captain!"

    3. the famous humorist will rogers, who was of indian descent, said, "my forefathers didn't come over on the *mayflower,* but they met the boat."

4. I. american history
      A. the war for independence
         1. battle of bunker hill
5. "don't go," he said. "i haven't explained yet."
6. for my birthday I got a subscription to *seventeen*.
7. the morning paper is the *herald tribune*.
8. very sincerely yours,
9. "hurry up!" father said. "if we don't leave soon, we'll be late."
10. we went to see the play *fiddler on the roof*.

B. Follow the directions for Exercise A.

1. dear mrs. weiss:
2. Robert Frost wrote "the death of the hired man."
3. I. business letters
      A. correct business letter form
         1. heading
4. the recent issue of *sports illustrated* has complete coverage of all the hockey teams.
5. he would answer to "Hi!" or to any loud cry
   such as "Fry me!" or "Fritter my wig!"
   to "What-you-may-call-um!" or "What-was-his-name!"
   but especially "Thing-um-a-jig!"
6. the article "images of youth past" appeared last fall in an issue of *life* magazine.
7. Meg finally got to the airport. she asked, "has the plane left?"
8. "i'm afraid so," Janet replied. "we're too late."
9. i have always enjoyed *the wizard of oz*, but I was thoroughly entertained by the stage production of *the wiz*.
10. i think *the call of the wild* is jack london's best book.

Additional Exercises — Review

Capitalization

A. Use capital letters correctly.

Number your paper from 1–10. Find the words in the following sentences that should be capitalized. Write the words beside the proper numbers and capitalize them correctly.

1. Warren e. burger was appointed chief justice of the supreme court by president nixon on may 21, 1969.
2. Is aunt theodosia dad's favorite sister?
3. The reverend doctor martin luther king, Jr. received the Nobel Peace Prize in 1964.
4. Our drama class went to see carol channing in the musical *Hello, Dolly!*
5. Most people think i look like mom, but actually I have my dad's brown eyes and hair.
6. The poet hilda doolittle was known by her initials h.d.
7. Indian civilizations flourished in both peru and mexico before the arrival of the spanish.
8. Allyson would like to become a doctor.
9. Should I send the invitation to ms. anita schilling in care of mr. and mrs. albert romani?
10. Tadeusz kosciuszko, a famous polish army officer, fought on the side of the american colonists.

B. Use capital letters correctly.

Copy the following sentences, changing small letters to capital letters wherever necessary.

1. The gaspé peninsula is part of the province of quebec.

2. My parents were delighted to see the chicago skyline as we drove south along lake shore drive.

3. Which are taller, the rocky mountains or the andes mountains?

4. In one presidential election, the republicans won every state except the commonwealth of massachusetts and the district of columbia.

5. The isthmus of panama in central america was a likely place to build a canal.

6. At that spot, the distance between the caribbean sea on the north side and the gulf of panama on the south is only forty miles.

7. Have you noticed that people from the midwest speak differently than people from the east speak?

8. If you are interested in civil war history, be sure to visit vicksburg national park when you're in the south.

9. By the time we got off of that hot beach, my mouth felt like the gobi desert, the sahara desert, and death valley rolled into one.

10. Lake geneva borders switzerland on the north and france on the south.

C. Use capital letters correctly.

Number your paper from 1–10. After the proper number, copy the words from each sentence that should be capitalized. Use the necessary capital letters.

1. Those three blue fords are still parked in front of rosemont baptist church.

2. So far only six students have signed up for algebra I.

3. The period from a.d. 500 to a.d. 1000 is sometimes called the dark ages.

4. The five countries involved in the six-day war were israel, egypt, syria, jordan, and iraq.

5. Next year rosemont high school will have a winter break during the second week of january.

6. We have to memorize the gettysburg address for our history assignment.

7. A big company like legrow, inc., probably has two or three doctors who work for it.

8. Most of the people in green bay, wisconsin, are catholic.

9. The gregory art museum is closed on memorial day and christmas.

10. The people of switzerland speak either french, german, or italian.

D. Use capital letters correctly.

Number your paper from 1–10. Find the words in the following sentences that should be capitalized. Write the words after the proper numbers, using the necessary capital letters.

1. "there will be a quiz tomorrow," said Mr. Sims, "and it will cover Chapters 1 and 2."

2. have you ever read the poem "song of myself" by walt whitman?

3. my teacher says that *the adventures of huckleberry finn* is a more enjoyable book than either *tom sawyer* or *the prince and the pauper.*

4. I. shakespeare's plays
    A. comedies
        1. *as you like it*
        2. *much ado about nothing*

5. our school library subscribes to *newsweek, time,* and *u.s. news and world report.*

6. death, be not proud, though some have called thee
    mighty and dreadful, for thou are not so . . .

7. because I was raised in the city of chicago, I really enjoy reading the poem "chicago" by carl sandburg.

8. both sculptures, *moses* and *david,* are by michelangelo.

445

Section 12

Punctuation

When you read, you probably do not think much about the punctuation used. But if it were not there, you would be bothered by its absence. You would not know where sentences began or ended. You might not be sure which words were meant to go together.

Punctuation marks are signals. For example, by putting quotation marks in the right places, you can show your reader precisely where a person's exact words begin and end. You can use the apostrophe to show where letters have been left out of contractions. You can show pauses between thoughts, and you can emphasize points that you consider important.

This section will help you use punctuation marks correctly. End marks, commas, semicolons, colons, hyphens, apostrophes, and quotation marks all have uses that can be understood both by the reader and the writer. If you want your reader to get the exact meaning from your writing, give the right signals by using these marks in the right places.

End Marks

The punctuation marks that show where sentences end are called **end marks.** They include *periods, question marks,* and *exclamation points.*

The Period

Use a period at the end of a declarative sentence.

A **declarative sentence** is a sentence that makes a statement. It is the kind of sentence you use when you want to tell something.

My brother delivers newspapers.

A declarative sentence is often shortened to one or two words, especially when answering a question.

Where are you going to put this macramé planter?
Over there. (*I am going to put it over there.*)

Use a period at the end of an imperative sentence.

An **imperative sentence** is a sentence that requests or tells someone to do something.

Please close the door.

If the imperative sentence also expresses excitement or emotion, an exclamation point is used after it.

Look out!

Use a period at the end of an indirect question.

She asked us whether we liked strawberries.

An *indirect question* is the part of a statement that tells what someone asked, but that does not give the exact words of the person who asked the question.

Use a period after an abbreviation or after an initial.

Dr. Marla E. Corona   Trenton, N.J.
Rev. John L. Haeger, Jr.   2:30 P.M.

Periods are omitted in some abbreviations. If you are not sure whether an abbreviation should be written with or without periods, look up the abbreviation in your dictionary.

FM (*frequency modulation*)
UN (*United Nations*)
FBI (*Federal Bureau of Investigation*)

Use a period after each number or letter that shows a division of an outline or that precedes an item in a list.

(An Outline)   (A List)

I. Poets   1. eggs
   A. American   2. milk
      1. Robert Frost   3. butter

Use a period in numerals between dollars and cents and before a decimal.

$18.98   2.853

The Question Mark

Use a question mark at the end of an interrogative sentence.

An **interrogative sentence** is a sentence that asks a question.

Has anyone seen my dog?

The above sentence gives the exact words of the person who asked the question. It is called a *direct question*. A question mark is used only with a direct question.

Do not use a question mark with an indirect question. Instead, use a period.

An *indirect question* is the part of a statement that tells what someone asked, without giving the exact words.

Kelly asked whether anyone had seen her dog.

The Exclamation Point

Use an exclamation point at the end of an exclamatory sentence.

Tim, look out!

Use an exclamation point after an interjection or after any other exclamatory expression.

An **interjection** is a word or group of words used to express strong feeling. It may be a real word or simply a group of letters used to represent a sound. It is one of the eight parts of speech.

Hurrah!   Wow!

Exercises Use end marks correctly.

A. Copy the following sentences, adding the necessary punctuation. Be prepared to tell what punctuation marks you used and why you used them.

1. Where did I put my new sweater
2. Wow that was quite a football game
3. What is Dr Harrigan's phone number
4. Where is Sgt Leslie's office located
5. Help I can't get this door open
6. I was supposed to meet Tom at 10:30 A M.
7. Dr James Coogan, Jr is going to talk about lifesaving
8. Mary, look out
9. Our art supplies will cost more than ten dollars, and I have only $825
10. My appointment with Dr. Wagner is at 11:15 A M on Friday

B. Follow the directions in Exercise A.

1. Dr Elizabeth McMinn is our school principal
2. Please send your requests to Franklin's, Ltd, P O Box 552, New York, NY
3. While in Washington, DC, where did you stay
4. One mile is equal to 16 kilometers
5. Luis asked if he could help me with my homework
6. I have two broadcast bands on my radio: AM and FM
7. UNICEF is the children's organization of the UN
8. My parents were born in Buffalo, NY
9. The Rev James M Butler, Jr will be the guest speaker at the ceremonies
10. Will you mail these coupons to the Clark Company, Inc, 301 E Walton Place, Chicago, Illinois 60611

The Comma

Commas are used to separate words that do not belong together. In speaking, we can keep words apart by pausing. In writing, we must use commas.

Commas in a Series

Use a comma after every item in a series except the last.

The items in a series may be single words, or phrases, or clauses.

Words   The flag is red, white, and blue.

Phrases   The dog ran out the door, down the steps, and across the lawn.

Clauses   How kangaroos run, what jumps they can take, and how they live are explained in this book.

451

Use commas after the adverbs *first, second, third,* and so on, when these adverbs introduce a series of parallel items.

> There are three ways to get good marks: first, pay attention; second, take notes; third, study.

When two or more adjectives precede a noun, use a comma after each adjective except the last one.

> They drove away in a bright, shiny, expensive sports car.

Sometimes two adjectives are used together to express a single idea made up of two closely related thoughts. Adjectives so used are not usually separated by a comma.

> Our house is the little green one.
> Look at the big round moon.

When you say the two sentences above, notice that you do not pause between the adjectives.

Exercises Use commas correctly to separate items.

A. Number your paper from 1–10. Copy the following sentences and add commas where necessary.

1. A strong northerly wind swept the snow against the front door.
2. That little green TR7 belongs to my sister.
3. Red white and blue bunting decorated the speaker's stand.
4. We went to the store and bought Fritos potato chips pretzels and Coke.
5. The race car skidded did a complete turn-around and blew out its right front tire.
6. At the movies, I like fresh salty buttery popcorn.
7. Strong gusty winds blew across the lake.
8. My sister can play the guitar the banjo and the mandolin.

9. In order to finish the scenery, do the following: first nail the supports together; second paint the backdrop; and third put away all unnecessary tools and paint.

10. Sue finished her homework made a telephone call and went to bed.

B. Follow the directions for Exercise A.

1. The committee discussed analyzed and accepted the proposal.

2. A fluffy tiger-striped cat was sitting on our porch swing.

3. A small rabbit scooted across our doorstep through the evergreens and under our back porch.

4. Handball racquetball and squash are similar sports.

5. Bowling tennis and jogging are my favorite activities.

6. A long sleek black limousine pulled up in front of the bank.

7. James Joan and Greg helped design the posters.

8. We need crepe paper balloons and tape to decorate the gym.

9. The speaker stated the hard clear facts.

10. The magician pulled a green scarf out of the air spread it flat on the table and pulled a pigeon out from under it.

Commas After Introductory Words, Phrases, or Clauses

Use a comma to separate an introductory word, phrase, or clause from the rest of the sentence.

Yes, I will go.
After circling twice, the airplane landed.
Although Dick needed help, he said nothing.

The comma may be omitted if there would be little pause in speaking.

At first I didn't know what to do.

Commas with Interrupters

Use commas to set off words or groups of words that interrupt the flow of thought in a sentence.

> Anne, to tell the truth, was quite happy.
> The report, moreover, is altogether inaccurate.

Exercises Use commas to set off words correctly.

A. Copy these sentences. Add commas where necessary.

1. No I don't think the library is open on Sundays.
2. After circling the airport for an hour we finally landed.
3. Although the game was postponed until Friday we had practice every morning.
4. Yes I have finished the dishes.
5. The exam however will be given as scheduled.
6. Mrs. Cassini to tell the truth was quite pleased with our panel discussion.
7. Since the Cubs lost their last ten games they will not be in the play-offs.
8. The results of the student survey however will not be revealed until next week.
9. No the mail has not been delivered.
10. Even though we arrived early we still didn't get good seats for the basketball game.

B. Follow the directions for Exercise A.

1. After we went on the hayride we had a barbecue and played volleyball.
2. Yes the garage has been cleaned out.
3. The game consequently was postponed.
4. The latest weather report however has predicted rain for the weekend.
5. Although the heavy snow tied up the morning traffic most companies and businesses were open as usual.

6. Yes the intramural track meet is tomorrow.

7. Since Mardi Gras is such a celebrated occasion in New Orleans most schools there take a holiday.

8. It is doubtful however that the weather will change our plans.

9. No the garage sale isn't until next week.

10. If you look carefully at these old tintypes you will see how different dress and housing used to be.

Commas with Nouns of Direct Address

Use commas to set off nouns of direct address.

The name of someone directly spoken to is a **noun of direct address.**

If you look, Peggy, you will see the book I mean.
Your firefighters did well, Captain.
Be careful, children, when you cross the street.

Commas with Appositives

Use commas to set off most appositives.

An **appositive** is a word or group of words used directly after another word to explain it.

The speaker, *a famous explorer,* told about Papua, New Guinea.

An appositive may have a prepositional phrase within it.

The leader, *the person on horseback,* moved away.

Nouns used as appositives are called **nouns in apposition.** When the noun in apposition is a short name, it is not usually set off by commas.

This is my friend Rhoda.

Commas with Quotations

Use commas to set off the explanatory words of a direct quotation.

The "explanatory words" used in giving a direct quotation are such brief statements as *Tina said, Christie answered,* or *Bill asked.*

Kate shouted, "Keep your eye on the ball!"

In the sentence above, the explanatory words come *before* the quotation. A comma is then placed after the last explanatory word.

Now look at this quotation:

"I can't find the key," said Patty.

If the explanatory words come *after* the quotation, as in the example above, place a comma within the quotation marks after the last word of the quotation.

Sometimes a quotation is separated into two parts by the explanatory words. This is often done to add variety to the sentence construction. Here is an example:

"The spacecraft," the announcer said, "has just been launched."

The sentence above is an example of a *divided quotation.* A comma is used after the last word of the first part. Another comma is used after the last explanatory word.

Do not confuse direct and indirect quotations. Indirect quotations are *not* set off from the rest of the sentence by commas.

Sylvia said that she had studied for at least an hour.

The Comma in a Compound Sentence

Use a comma before the conjunction that joins the two main clauses in a compound sentence.

Kimberly seemed to agree, and no one else objected.

In a very short compound sentence with the clauses joined by *and*, it is not necessary to use a comma if there is no turn or change in the thought. Always use a comma before *or* or *but*, since these words do change the direction of the thought.

Pete finally arrived *and* we started off.
Pete arrived, *but* it was too late to go anywhere.

Do not use a comma before the *and* that joins a compound subject or a compound predicate.

Sally turned on the radio and sat down to read a magazine.

Exercises Use commas correctly.

A. Copy these sentences. Add commas where needed.

1. "Cheerleading tryouts will be held tonight" began the announcement "and all students are invited to participate."
2. The team captain the player in blue is a good student.
3. I read *Roots* but I preferred the television series.
4. I enjoy reading science fiction novels but I also enjoy reading mysteries.
5. She ran down the stairs and raced down the sidewalk.
6. Ms. Leoni our new science teacher was born in Italy.
7. Sir Georg Solti the famous conductor directs the Chicago Symphony Orchestra.
8. When you are finished Kurt will you help me?
9. Maria finished her tennis practice and then went directly to play rehearsal.
10. John Hancock one of the signers of the Declaration of Independence was from Massachusetts.

1. "Wally" said Barbara "has a good suggestion."
2. Linda showed me her present a cassette tape recorder.
3. I will wash the car but I don't have time to wax it.
4. I asked Ms. Wright our science teacher about lasers.
5. Andrés Segovia the classical guitarist will play at Orchestra Hall in May.
6. Will you come with me or would you rather stay here?
7. Mrs. Watkins our P. E. teacher was a member of the U. S. Olympic swim team.
8. We played soccer for an hour and then we went inside for lunch.
9. "Please take the dog for a walk" said Dad.
10. Pam this is my brother Paul.

Commas in Dates

In dates, use a comma between the day of the month and the year.

July 4, 1776   December 7, 1787

In a sentence, a comma follows the year.

The postmark read September 10, 1981, but we didn't receive the letter until yesterday, October 2.

Commas in Locations and Addresses

Use a comma between the name of a city or town and the name of its state or country.

Miami, Florida
Munich, Germany

In writing an address as part of a sentence, use a comma after each item.

Forward our mail to 651 Sentinel Drive, Wilmette, Illinois 60091, where we will be moving next month.

Note that you do *not* place a comma between the state and the ZIP code.

Commas in Letter Parts

Use a comma after the salutation of a friendly letter and after the complimentary close of a friendly letter or a business letter.

Dear Tim,   Yours sincerely,

Exercises   Use commas correctly.

A. Copy the following sentences. Add commas where necessary.

1. The bombing of Pearl Harbor on December 7 1941 marked the beginning of World War II for the United States.

2. On August 14 1945 Japan surrendered to the Allies.

3. The stock market crash on October 29 1929 marked the beginning of the Great Depression.

4. On August 20 1974 Nelson A. Rockefeller was nominated for the office of Vice President.

5. Send your requests to Mr. R. Joseph Roller 180 North Capitol Avenue Denver Colorado 80202.

6. The first state, Delaware, entered the Union on December 7 1787.

7. The first transcontinental railroad was completed on May 10 1869 in Promontory Utah.

8. In 1874 Joseph Glidden of DeKalb Illinois invented barbed wire.

9. The President of the United States lives at 1600 Pennsylvania Avenue Washington D. C. 20500.

10. George Washington was inaugurated in New York City on April 30 1789 at Federal Hall.

B. Follow the directions for Exercise A.

1. Because my parents work for the government, I have lived in Fairbanks Alaska and Madrid Spain.

2. The Lewis and Clark expedition began on May 14 1804 in St. Louis Missouri and returned there on September 23 1806.

3. John H. Glenn, Jr. became the first American to orbit the earth on February 20 1962 aboard the *Friendship* 7.

4. We ordered our uniforms from the J. C. Wood Company P. O. Box 5835 Richmond Virginia 23220.

5. The 1984 Olympics will be held in Los Angeles California.

6. The charter flight will visit Helsinki Finland and Stockholm Sweden.

7. My sister was born in Tokyo Japan on January 1 1965 and I was born in Frankfurt Germany on January 1 1968.

8. On August 26 1920 the amendment that gave women the right to vote was adopted.

9. The Great Chicago Fire of 1871 supposedly started in the barn at Mrs. O'Leary's 558 DeKoven Street Chicago Illinois.

10. Dear Jill

   Would you please send me the Harrisons' new address? I'd appreciate it.

   Your friend
   Tom

Commas with Nonrestrictive Clauses

Use commas to set off nonrestrictive clauses.

A **nonrestrictive clause** is one that merely adds an idea to the sentence. The sentence would be complete and the meaning would be definite without it.

A **restrictive clause** is one that is essential to the meaning of a sentence. If a restrictive clause is dropped out of the sentence, the meaning changes.

Nonrestrictive:	Cheryl White, whom I have known for years, will go to Purdue in the fall.
	Cheryl White will go to Purdue in the fall.
Restrictive:	Cheryl White is the only person in our school who is going to Purdue.
	Cheryl White is the only person in our school.

Restrictive clauses are often used to identify or point out the person or thing they modify. Without this identification, the meaning of the sentence would not be clear. Nonrestrictive clauses, on the other hand, add no essential meaning to the sentence.

Restrictive:	Janice is the girl *who found the money.* (which girl?)
Restrictive:	This is the book *that has the map.* (What book?)
Nonrestrictive:	Janice, *who is very alert,* found the money. Janice found the money.
Nonrestrictive:	This book, *which has pictures,* is my choice. This book is my choice.

Commas To Prevent Misreading

When no specific rule applies, but there is danger of misreading, use a comma.

Who she is, is a mystery.

Exercises Use commas correctly.

A. Number your paper from 1–10. Decide where commas should be used in the following sentences. Write the word before the comma, add the comma, then write the word after the comma. If no commas are necessary, write *Correct* after the appropriate number.

1. My grandparents who are very active people have just completed a tour of South America.

2. Our dog who recently had puppies is very protective of her litter.

3. This is the bicycle that I repaired and painted.

4. The speed limit which is strictly enforced has reduced traffic accidents.

5. This is the autobiography that I read for class.

6. Mrs. Kruse is the person who owns that flower shop.

7. Those students who are finished with the test may leave.

8. Kyle who is my best friend is moving to Japan next month.

9. The Wades who live next door are well known ocean-ographers.

10. The bus that I told you to take stops at that corner.

B. Follow the directions for Exercise A.

1. This camera which has many features is the best buy.

2. Ms. Larson is the teacher who coaches the volleyball team.

3. The letter you were waiting for has finally arrived.

4. Our neighbor who is an excellent gardener helped us with our rock garden.

5. The coach who anticipated a tough defense shifted her team to a zone offense.

6. This Super Suds detergent which is heavily advertised on television has had increased sales.

7. Mr. Hansen who is our club sponsor will be my English teacher next year.

8. Tomoko Pham is the only student in our school who is from Southeast Asia.

9. That is the book that has all the color photographs in it.

10. Rita Coolidge who is touring with Kris Kristofferson will be in Dallas next week.

The Semicolon

Use a semicolon to join the clauses of a compound sentence when no coordinating conjunction is used.

Dan has finished his homework; Darcy has not begun hers.

When there are many commas in the clauses of a compound sentence, separate the clauses themselves with a semicolon.

McCurdy of Illinois made the most spectacular shot of the game, a toss from mid-court; and Indiana, which had been favored to win, went down to defeat.

When there are commas within items in a series, use semicolons to separate the items.

Hartford, New Haven, and Norwich, Connecticut; Springfield and Worcester, Massachusetts; and Pine Bridge, Mt. Kisco, and Chappaqua, New York, have all tried this experiment.

Use a semicolon before a conjunctive adverb that joins the clauses of a compound sentence.

Conjunctive adverbs commonly used are *therefore, however, hence, so, then, moreover, besides, nevertheless, yet,* and *consequently.*

It was a sunny day; however, it was quite cool.

The Colon

Use a colon after the greeting of a business letter.

Dear Sir or Madam: Ladies and Gentlemen:

Use a colon between numerals indicating hours and minutes.

10:00 P.M.

Use a colon to introduce a list of items.

If you are trying out for the team, bring the following things: a pair of gym shoes, your P.E. uniform, and your consent form.

If there would be no pause in speaking, no colon is used before the list of items.

If you are trying out for the team, bring a pair of gym shoes, your P.E. uniform, and your consent form.

Exercises Use semicolons and colons correctly.

A. Copy the word before and after each missing punctuation mark and add the correct punctuation mark.

1. Jon prepared dinner Paula set the table.
2. Grinning broadly, Lee crossed the finish line 10 feet ahead of the others however, the grin faded when the judges told her she had been disqualified.
3. San Francisco, Los Angeles, and Oakland, California Dallas and Houston, Texas and New York and Buffalo, New York, have professional teams.
4. It was a clear day moreover, it was perfect for swimming.
5. Allen, wash the car Jenny, clean up the yard Joan, take the dog for a walk.
6. New animals in the collection include a cheetah, an okapi, and a harpy eagle from Africa a tiger, two peacocks, and a rhinoceros from India a snow leopard from Tibet and two caribou, a Kodiak bear, and an arctic fox from Alaska.
7. Bring three things to class tomorrow your text, paper, and a blue or black pen.
8. You will need to meet me between 830 and 845 A.M.
9. Dear Madam
   This letter will confirm your reservation.
10. It was a cold autumn day however, it was quite sunny.

B. Follow the directions for Exercise A.

1. Please stop at the store and bring these items home a gallon of milk, a can of tomatoes, and a box of crackers.

2. Tracy was reading a mystery Sandy was hooking a rug.

3. I know that there is not much time nevertheless, the work must be finished by 530.

4. Mother's plane arrives at 655 P.M. Dad's will land at 715 P.M.

5. Jim studied hard for the test yet he thought it was one of the hardest ones he'd ever taken.

6. The Pep Club will handle ticket sales the cheerleaders will help with the ushering.

7. Our bus leaves at 715 A.M. my sister's bus doesn't leave until 830 A.M.

8. The snow was blinding however, the school bus arrived on time at 815 A.M.

9. The running back made a spectacular drive to the goal, a 47-yard run and the defense, which couldn't get organized, was stunned.

10. Bring these items to sewing class on Monday tracing paper, your pattern, thread, and pins.

The Hyphen

Use a hyphen if a syllable of a word must be carried over from one line to the next.

In the library you will find several authorita-
tive books on solar energy.

Only words of two or more syllables can be divided at the end of a line. Never divide words of one syllable, such as *height* or *worse*.

A single letter must not be left at the end of a line. For example, this division would be wrong: *a-waken.* A single letter must not appear at the beginning of a line, either. It would be wrong to divide *sanitary* like this: *sanitar-y.*

Use a hyphen in compound numbers from twenty-one through ninety-nine.

twenty-three cents   forty-two students

Use a hyphen in fractions.

We won a two-thirds majority.

Use a hyphen or hyphens in such compound nouns as *great-aunt* and *commander-in-chief.*

Use a hyphen or hyphens between words that make up a compound adjective used before a noun.

This is an up-to-date edition.
But: This edition is up to date.

Exercise Use hyphens correctly.

Number your paper from 1–15. After the proper numbers, write the words that should be hyphenated. Add the necessary hyphens. Use your dictionary if you need to.

1. We received the store's new, up to date catalog.
2. In ten years I will be twenty three years old.
3. We saw that the lawn was half cut.
4. One sixth of the students voted for Pam.
5. Ninety three students in all voted in the election.
6. Maurita won the election by a three fourths majority.
7. You must write out the amount of the check:
one hundred twenty three dollars and fifty six cents.
8. Our great grandmother celebrated her ninety fifth birthday.
9. The postage for this package is sixty two cents.
10. About sixty eight percent of the residents voted in the special election.

11. When were your great grandparents born?

12. The man had a well to do look about him.

13. Thirty two students were chosen to go to the speech contest.

14. Chester A. Arthur was the twenty first President.

15. The President of the United States is the Commander in Chief of the Armed Forces.

The Apostrophe

One of the most frequent uses of the apostrophe is its use in forming the possessive of nouns. Before you form the possessive of a noun, be sure to notice whether the noun is singular or plural.

To form the possessive of a singular noun, add an apostrophe and an s.

girl + 's = girl's   man + 's = man's
boy + 's = boy's   Ross + 's = Ross's

To form the possessive of a plural noun that does not end in s, add an apostrophe and an s.

men's   women's

To form the possessive of a plural noun that ends in s, add only an apostrophe.

drivers + ' = drivers'   pilots + ' = pilots'

Use an apostrophe and an s to form the possessive of indefinite pronouns.

someone + 's = someone's   anybody + 's = anybody's

Never use an apostrophe in a possessive pronoun.

ours   yours

Use an apostrophe in a contraction.

In a contraction, the apostrophe simply replaces one or more omitted letters.

he's = he is	aren't = are not	I'm = I am
it's = it is	isn't = is not	I've = I have
won't = will not	don't = do not	we've = we have

Use an apostrophe to show the omission of numbers in a date.

the class of '80 (the class of 1980)

Use an apostrophe and *s* to form the plurals of letters, figures, and words used as words.

two *m*'s   four 6's   *and*'s and *but*'s

Exercises Use apostrophes correctly.

A. Copy these sentences, inserting apostrophes where they are needed.

1. Weve heard that there wont be a show today.

2. Beatrix Potters most famous work is *The Tale of Peter Rabbit*.

3. Her writings and illustrations are well known in childrens literature.

4. Billie Holidays life and music were portrayed in the movie *The Lady Sings the Blues*.

5. Diana Rosss performance as the jazz musician earned her an Oscar nomination.

6. Soichiro Hondas company has been producing motorcycles and cars in Japan since the 1940s.

7. Ive always liked the silent movies of Buster Keaton and Charlie Chaplin.

8. All of the teachers meetings are held in the library.

9. Babe Didrikson Zahariass autobiography reveals her intense love for athletics and her zest for life.

10. *The Miracle Worker* is a play about Helen Kellers child-hood and Annie Sullivans efforts to help the blind and deaf Helen.

B. Follow the directions for Exercise A.

1. The *1*s and the *7*s in this ledger are difficult to distin-guish.
2. The graduating classes of 82 and 83 bought a new digital scoreboard.
3. Although she was the first woman to go into space, Valentina Tereshkovas name is not well known.
4. Weve heard Beverly Sillss performance at the opera.
5. Someones moped is parked in the Burtons driveway.
6. Isnt the girls gymnastics meet on Saturday?
7. Clara Bartons dedication in a volunteer nurse corps led to her founding of the American Red Cross.
8. S. E. Hintons novel, *That Was Then, This Is Now,* is one of the best books weve read this year.
9. Jennys sister and Paulas brother are both interns at St. Marys Hospital.
10. Nurses training programs are extensive and demanding.

Quotation Marks

Quotation marks tell your reader that you are quoting directly the exact spoken or written words of another person.

Use quotation marks at the beginning and at the end of a direct quotation.

Donna said, "My cat's eyes shine in the dark."

Quotation marks are *not* used with indirect quotations:

Donna says that her cat's eyes shine in the dark.

Sometimes a direct quotation is broken into two or more parts by explanatory words. In such a case, each part of the quotation is enclosed in quotation marks.

"Do you think," Bill asked, "that you could help me with the dishes?"

The second part of a divided quotation starts with a small letter, as in the example above, unless it begins a new sentence or unless it is a proper noun.

"We got drenched," said Bob. "We had no umbrella."

The first part of a divided quotation is followed by a comma that is placed *inside* the quotation marks.

"Before you leave," said Mrs. Lazar, "I want to talk to you."

Explanatory words in a divided quotation are followed by either a comma or a period *outside* the quotation marks. A comma is used after the explanatory words if the second part of the quotation does not begin a new sentence. A period is used after the explanatory words if the second part of the quotation is a new sentence.

"When you arrive," said Carol, "ring the doorbell."
"I can't go," said Janet. "I have to study."

Explanatory words at the beginning of a sentence are followed by a comma *outside* the quotation marks. The period at the end of the sentence is placed *inside* the quotation marks.

Mother said, "There is someone to see you."

Explanatory words at the end of a sentence are followed by a period. The quoted words at the beginning of the sentence are followed by a comma *inside* the quotation marks.

"There is someone to see you," Mother said.

Place question marks and exclamation points inside quotation marks if they belong to the quotation itself, but outside if they do not belong to the quotation.

Dad asked, "Has Mike closed the garage doors?"
Did Mother say, "Be home by five o'clock"?
"Look out!" Terry shouted.

You may wonder how to use quotation marks when you are quoting *two or more sentences of a single speaker*. Notice how the following quotation is punctuated.

"Is the club going to meet tomorrow?" asked Sue. "I wasn't sure whether we had decided to meet tomorrow or the next day. We have important things to discuss."

Only one set of quotation marks would be needed if the example read as follows:

Sue asked, "Is the club going to meet tomorrow? I wasn't sure whether we had decided to meet tomorrow or the next day. We have important things to discuss."

When a quotation is long, it may consist of two or more paragraphs. In such a case, open each of the paragraphs with a quotation mark, but do not use an end quotation mark until the whole speech is finished.

"There are many ways in which every individual can conserve energy on a daily basis," began the speaker.

"For example, turning off lights, radios, stereos, or televisions when we're really not using them saves a lot of electrical power.

"Being conscientious about our means of travel is beneficial to energy conservation, too. Do we unnecessarily travel by car when we could walk, cycle, or use public transportation? All of these considerations seem minor, but if everyone made an effort to conserve a little energy every day, we'd all benefit enormously."

When you are writing *dialogue* (conversation), begin each speaker's part with a new paragraph, even if the speeches are quite short.

> "It's Saturday again, and here we all are," said Larry.
> "Yes, it's Saturday all day today," Ted joked.
> "It's a wonderful day!" said Anne, happily.

With a quotation *inside another quotation,* single quotation marks are used. Here is an example:

> "It was Patrick Henry," declared Liz, "who said, 'Give me liberty or give me death!'"

Notice that the whole quotation is enclosed in quotation marks. The quotation within the quotation is enclosed in single quotation marks. A comma precedes the single quotation marks at the opening on the inner quotation. Notice how the quotation marks (' ") come together at the end of the sentence.

Exercises Use quotation marks correctly.

A. Copy the following sentences. Add the necessary quotation marks and other punctuation marks. Use capital letters where necessary.

1. Have the committee members come yet asked Molly they are supposed to set up the tables and chairs
2. It was Martin Luther King, Jr. reported Tanya who said Injustice anywhere is a threat to justice everywhere.
3. Would you mind asked Cindy if I borrowed your bicycle
4. Didn't the teacher say we'll meet in the gym at 10:30
5. Andrea Sally said may I borrow your camera this weekend

6. Our history teacher told us John Paul Jones is supposed to have said I have not yet begun to fight

7. Kristen inquired was it Amelia Earhart who said Courage is the price that life exacts for granting peace

8. Bill kept saying It's just one of those things said Nancy.

9. In his inaugural address said Sherry John Kennedy stated: And so, my fellow Americans, ask not what your country can do for you; ask what you can do for your country

10. Will you organize the committee asked Sara and order the decorations

B. Copy the following sentences. Add the necessary quotation marks and any other punctuation marks. Use capital letters where necessary.

1. In her autobiography said Anna Eleanor Roosevelt wrote: Life was meant to be lived, and curiosity must be kept alive. One must never, for whatever reason, turn his back on life

2. Isn't it getting too late Roger asked for us to start making plans for an all-school play

3. In what ways have you, as an individual, conserved energy began our guest speaker

4. There's the doorbell said Uncle Thomas will you answer it, Ramon

5. That's the game yelled the announcer The Yanks have won the Series

6. There's someone to see you my sister said and it looks as if he's bringing back the jacket you lost

7. Is it Burger King or McDonald's whose motto is You deserve a break today asked Debbie

8. Bill said I will drive you to school explained Peg.

9. Joan, have you seen that movie yet asked Dan

10. I never heard of such a thing said my mother quietly are you sure that is what he said

Using Quotation Marks for Titles

Use quotation marks to enclose chapter titles, titles of magazine articles, titles of short stories, essays, or single poems, titles of television and radio programs, and titles of songs or short pieces of music.

Chapter title	Chapter 3, "Americans in London"
Magazine article	"Images of Youth Past"
Short story	"The Headless Horseman"
Essay	"My First Article"
Poem	"The Raven"
Television program	"Sixty Minutes"
Song	"The Star-Spangled Banner"

When you write the titles of whole books or of plays, magazines, newspapers, works of art, long musical compositions, and motion pictures, do not use quotation marks. Instead, underline the titles, like this: <u>Light in the Forest</u>. Such titles should be underlined when you are writing in longhand or when you are typing. Use a single underlining, not a double one. Written or typed words that are underlined are set in a special style of type in printing. This style of type used is called *italics*.

Exercises Use quotation marks and underlining correctly.

A. Number your paper from 1–10. Copy the following sentences, adding quotation marks around titles or underscoring titles where necessary.

1. I liked the story The Monkey's Paw.

2. For my poetry assignment, I read Macavity: The Mystery Cat.

3. Read the first chapter, Discovery in the New World, for tomorrow.

4. The television program The Little House on the Prairie deals with problems and pleasures of pioneer life.

5. Some of James Thurber's stories are The Very Proper Gander, The Shrike and the Chipmunks, and The Owl Who Was God.

6. Our band played the theme from Rocky and the theme from Star Wars.

7. The Charlie Chaplin movie The Gold Rush and Harold Lloyd's film Safety Last are two well known silent comedies.

8. Did you see the movie One on One?

9. Read Chapter 2, How We Came to the River.

10. The Love Bug is a movie about a Volkswagen.

B. Follow the directions for Exercise A.

1. God Save the Queen and America have the same melody.

2. Two of Jack's favorite programs are The Today Show and M*A*S*H.

3. We read the novel The Call of the Wild and the short story Brown Wolf by Jack London.

4. Adjö Means Goodbye by Carrie A. Young is the story of a friendship.

5. My essay entitled Youth Today won an honorable mention in the poetry and prose contest.

6. One Flew Over the Cuckoo's Nest won the Academy Award for the best picture in 1975.

7. Old Man River is a song from the musical Showboat.

8. Last week's editorial was entitled The Mess in City Government—What Are You Doing about It?

9. Barry Manilow, who has recorded such songs as I Write the Songs and Mandy, has also written many popular advertising slogans and jingles.

10. My favorite poem is The Revolt of the Machines by Stephen Vincent Benét.

Additional Exercises — Review

Punctuation

A. Use end marks correctly.

Copy these sentences, adding the necessary punctuation.

1. The order was issued by Capt Thomas E Conklin
2. Jackie Watch out
3. Tomorrow night Dr Linda Marshall and Mr Mark Leopold will lecture on law enforcement
4. Our tour of the FBI Building in Washington, D C, begins at 8:00 A M sharp
5. Did you know that Prof Stevens is teaching in St Louis
6. Wow That relay race was exciting
7. Rev Martin T McDaniel will speak at the lecture hall at 9:00 P M
8. Marcia's report for U S history is on the subject of NATO
9. Be careful There's broken glass in that bag
10. Mr and Mrs Barrett will chaperone the canoe trip

B. Use commas correctly.

Number your paper from 1–10. Copy the following sentences. Add commas where necessary.

1. If I know David, he would beg borrow or even work to go on that camping trip.
2. That long sleek silver Jaguar belongs to Dr. Weston.
3. Leaves and branches were strewn all over the front yard the driveway and the flower bed.

4. While searching the ground for clues, the detectives discovered a thin razor-sharp knife.

5. A feisty mischievous poodle dashed across the newly seeded lawn.

6. Are you sure that only Ginny Pat and Terry need rides?

7. I washed the car waxed it and polished all of the chrome.

8. To get to the ice rink, go two blocks north turn right and park in the junior high school lot.

9. If you want to conserve gasoline, do the following: first start and stop your car gradually; second drive at a steady speed; third don't keep the engine running unnecessarily.

10. While in New Orleans, we visited the French Quarter rode down the Mississippi on a riverboat and heard many jazz bands perform.

C. Use commas correctly.

Number your paper from 1–10. Copy the following sentences and add commas where necessary.

1. Yes I've read several Agatha Christie mysteries.

2. After the photographs have been developed we can choose one for the newspaper.

3. Gary to tell the truth was quite satisfied with the test results.

4. The results of the election however will not be posted until tomorrow morning.

5. No the test will not be given until Monday.

6. Although the game had to be postponed the dance went on as planned.

7. The office fire was consequently a setback for the business.

8. Your decision moreover will affect our plans.

9. After running fifteen laps around the gym the team practiced its defensive plays.

10. Yes the wrestling meet will be held at the high school.

D. Use commas correctly.

Number your paper from 1–10. Copy the following sentences, adding commas where they are needed.

1. Bruce Jenner the Olympic decathlon champion was the guest speaker at our school.
2. If you look closely into the microscope Barb you will see thousands of living organisms.
3. Margaret Hillis the famous conductor directed the symphony at Carnegie Hall.
4. "Weather patterns are changing" explained Mrs. Hammill "and no one is quite sure why."
5. Maria Tallchief and Martha Graham women famous in the world of dance have performed all over the world.
6. Severe drought the worst in twenty years hit the Great Plains last summer.
7. Joyce would you please start a fire in the fireplace?
8. The ballet was in town for a week and every performance was sold out.
9. Curling a sport played on ice with brooms is a rigorous game.
10. Running and swimming are physically demanding activities but they are the top two sports for staying in shape.

E. Use commas correctly.

Copy the following sentences. Add commas where necessary.

1. Please have the package sent to Ms. Kathy Murphy 2439 North Granville Avenue Marion Ohio 43302.
2. All the letters had to be postmarked by January 1 to be considered.

3. Dear Mrs. Brannstrom

Thank you for the birthday gift. It was greatly appreciated.

Yours sincerely
Michael Flynn

4. We visited Bellingrath Gardens in Theodore Alabama and the capitol buildings in Jackson Mississippi while vacationing last summer.

5. The Omni International Hotel in Atlanta Georgia has a huge indoor ice rink six movie theaters and countless shops.

6. My father was born on February 6 1939 in Duluth Minnesota and I was born on February 6 1969 in Evanston Illinois.

7. The Superdome in New Orleans Louisiana and the Astrodome in Houston Texas are phenomenal structures.

8. When you say "Kansas City" do you mean Kansas City Missouri or Kansas City Kansas?

9. On July 4 1876 celebrations for our nation's one hundredth birthday were held in Philadelphia Pennsylvania.

10. Ray Kroc opened his first McDonald's restaurant on April 15 1955 in Des Plaines Illinois.

F. Use commas correctly.

Number your paper from 1–10. Decide where commas should be used in the following sentences. Write the word before the comma, add the comma, and then write the word after the comma. If no comma is necessary, write *Correct.*

1. Whatever you do do well.

2. Janice and Laura are the ones who started the ski club.

3. This magazine which has beautiful color photos is one of my favorites.

4. Laura Eaton who has been my friend for years has moved to Arizona.

5. Franklin Delano Roosevelt was the only American President who was elected to four straight terms in office.

6. Before eating my goldfish darts rapidly around its bowl.

7. After we ate the horses had to be cared for.

8. Paul's camera which has a telephoto lens is ideal for sports pictures.

9. While moving our family stayed at a motel.

10. Mrs. Hogan is the teacher who sponsored the dance.

G. Use semicolons and colons correctly.

Copy the word before and after each missing punctuation mark and add the correct punctuation mark.

1. Jack passed the history test I failed it.

2. The guidebook suggested buying these items leather from Barcelona, Spain, or Florence, Italy wool from London, England, or Edinburgh, Scotland and crystal from Waterford, Ireland, or Stockholm, Sweden.

3. When he finally decided to buy Mrs. Daniels' old car, Ted was happy however, he was miserable when the transmission fell apart three months later.

4. The concert tickets went on sale at 900 A.M. by 945 A.M. they were all sold.

5. Dear Sir
Enclosed you will find your refund check for nine dollars.

6. Keith cleaned out the garage I painted the storm windows.

7. To make the punch, you will need the following ingredients lime sherbet, lemon juice, and ginger ale.

8. At 830 A.M. the following students are to report to the gym Doug Smith, Beth Schleker, and Lynn Kimball.

9. Please bring these items to the testing room two pencils, an eraser, and a spiral notebook.

10. At 730 A.M. Mary jumped out of bed and started getting dressed then she remembered that it was Saturday.

H. Use hyphens correctly.

Copy the following sentences. Add hyphens wherever they are needed.

1. Ninety two is the best golf score Julie has ever shot.
2. Mr. Perez's daughter in law is an up and coming politician.
3. Jake's still life paintings are much better than his por traits.
4. The save the trees resolution passed the City Council with a three fifths vote of approval.
5. Last week Louis saw an accident involving twenty two vehicles.
6. Gina's great great grandfather founded the town of Chenoa.
7. Kelly's Lake, once a quiet, out of the way resort, is now a dirty, evil smelling swamp.
8. Eighty eight children applied to the camp; no more than forty one could be accepted.
9. My great aunt and my great grandmother are both ninety one years old.
10. Eighty five percent of the student population partici pated in the Toys-for-Tots campaign.

I. Use apostrophes correctly.

Number your paper from 1–10. Copy the following sentences. Add apostrophes where they are needed.

1. The head coachs decision to have two extra practices was helpful.
2. The actresss jeweled costume looked as if it weighed at least fifty pounds.
3. I dont think that the art supplies we ordered will be enough.

4. Scott wondered if a member of Congresss salary was as high as a nurses.

5. The *m*s and *n*s in this note look alike.

6. Its supposed to snow this weekend, so well probably be able to go skiing.

7. Dont you think it would have been fun to grow up during the 50s?

8. The girls swimming meet and the boys basketball game are on the same day.

9. Since the municipal parks tennis courts were being used, Sandy and Lisa played on the high school courts.

10. The junior high schools choir and orchestra, and the high schools freshmen chorale, will perform at the new shopping mall.

J. Use quotation marks correctly.

Number your paper from 1–10. Copy the following sentences. Add the necessary quotation marks and other punctuation marks. Use capital letters where necessary.

1. Will the student council sponsor the car wash asked our principal or should another club be responsible

2. If we win tonight said Coach Strand we'll definitely play in the holiday tournament

3. I think it was Ben Franklin replied David who said A penny saved is a penny earned

4. Who said The test is really easy asked Pat

5. I wonder said Wendy if anyone wants to go to the art fair.

6. Trisha asked was it Tolstoi who wrote If you want to be happy, be

7. Juanita inquired What time is play rehearsal tomorrow

8. Yolanda said: It was Mark Twain who wrote Always do right. This will gratify some people, and astonish the rest

9. Did you see the movie with Katharine Hepburn and John Wayne asked Debbie It was on television last night

10. Mr. Pierce said Do the first eight questions said Nancy he didn't say anything about the last two

K. Use quotation marks and underlining correctly.

Number your paper from 1–10. Copy the following sentences, adding quotation marks around titles or underlining titles where necessary.

1. The movie Gone with the Wind appeared on television for the first time in 1976.

2. Many adults enjoy watching Sesame Street as much as their children do.

3. The prize-winning student essay was entitled The Future Belongs to Me.

4. Our class read two of Poe's short stories: The Tell-Tale Heart and Murders in the Rue Morgue.

5. Have you ever read the poem Paul Revere's Ride by Longfellow?

6. Eve Merriam's two poems Thumbprint and Sometimes are two of my favorites.

7. The first chapter of David Copperfield is called I Am Born.

8. The March issue of National Geographic has an interesting article about the Sahara entitled Caravaning Through the Desert.

9. My Fair Lady is based on a play called Pygmalion.

10. The television program The Little House on the Prairie is based on a novel by Laura Ingalls Wilder.

Section 13

Spelling

It is important for you to have good spelling skills. You will use these skills when you write friendly and business letters. You will use them when you write reports on all subjects at school. You will use them when you fill out job applications. If you care about what others think of you and what you have to say, you will want to be able to spell words correctly.

There is no simple way to teach you how to spell. However, there are several methods you can use to attack your spelling problems. These methods are discussed in this section.

How To Become a Better Speller

1. Find out what your personal spelling demons are and conquer them. Go over your old composition papers and make a list of the words you misspelled on them. Keep this list and master the words on it.

2. Pronounce words carefully. It may be that you misspell words because you don't pronounce them carefully. For example, if you write *probly* for *probably*, you are no doubt mispronouncing the word.

3. Get into the habit of seeing the letters in a word. Many people have never really looked at the word *similar*. Otherwise, why do they write it *similiar?*

Take a good look at new words, or difficult words. You'll remember them better. Copy the correct spelling several times.

4. Think up a memory device for difficult words. Here are some devices that have worked for other people. They may help you, either to spell these words or to make up your own memory devices.

> a**cq**uaint (*cq*) To get a**cq**uainted, I will *seek you*.
> princi**pal** (*pal*) The princi**pal** is my *pal*.
> princi**ple** (*ple*) Follow this princi**ple**, *please*.
> business (*i*) I was involved in big bus*i*ness.

5. Proofread everything you write. In order to learn how to spell, you must learn to examine critically everything you write.

To proofread a piece of writing, you must read it slowly, word for word. Otherwise, your eyes may play tricks on you and let you skip over misspelled words.

6. Learn the few important spelling rules given in this section.

How To Master the Spelling of Particular Words

1. Look at the word and say it to yourself. Be sure you pronounce it correctly. If it has more than one syllable, say it again, one syllable at a time. Look at each syllable as you say it.

2. Look at the letters and say each one. If the word has more than one syllable, divide the word into syllables when you say the letters.

3. Write the word without looking at your book or list.

4. Now look at your book or list and see whether you spelled the word correctly. If you did, write it again and compare it with the correct form again. Do this once more.

5. If you made a mistake, note exactly what it was. Then repeat steps 3 and 4 above until you have written the word correctly three times.

Rules for Spelling

The Final Silent e

When a suffix beginning with a vowel is added to a word ending in a silent e, the e is usually dropped.

create + -ion = creation	grieve + -ing = grieving
graze + -ing = grazing	relate + -ive = relative
fame + -ous = famous	continue + -ing = continuing

When a suffix beginning with a consonant is added to a word ending in a silent _e_, the _e_ is usually retained.

spite + -ful = spiteful	taste + -ful = tasteful
state + -ment = statement	move + -ment = movement
voice + -less = voiceless	wide + -ly = widely

The following words are exceptions:

truly   argument   ninth   wholly

Words Ending in _y_

When a suffix is added to a word ending in _y_ preceded by a consonant, the _y_ is usually changed to _i_.

crazy + -ly = crazily	puppy + -s = puppies
seventy + -eth = seventieth	silly + -ness = silliness
hilly + -est = hilliest	marry + -age = marriage

Note the following exception: When -_ing_ is added, the _y_ does not change:

scurry + -ing = scurrying	carry + -ing = carrying
ready + -ing = readying	worry + -ing = worrying

When a suffix is added to a word ending in _y_ preceded by a vowel, the _y_ usually does not change.

employ + -ed = employed	stay + -ing = staying
play + -er = player	relay + -ing = relaying

Exercises Spell words and their suffixes.

A. Find the misspelled words. Spell them correctly.

1. Who is driveing us home today?
2. After writing the letter, I hurryed to mail it.
3. Let's end the arguement before leaving.
4. Ice skateing must be done gracefully.
5. My homework was done sloppyly and hastily.

6. That's the sillyest program I've ever seen.
7. You had me almost believeing your story!
8. Grandpa remembers horse and carryage days.
9. The shiny new car is as noisey as our old rattletrap.
10. Have you truly considered the statment?

B. Add the suffixes as shown and write the new word.

1. write + -ing
2. amaze + -ment
3. care + -ful
4. dirty + -er
5. happy + -ly
6. stay + -ing
7. spray + -er
8. relate + -ion
9. hurry + -ing
10. glory + -ous
11. pray + -er
12. employ + -er
13. lazy + -est
14. shiny + -ness
15. enjoy + -ment
16. skinny + -er
17. mystery + -ous
18. thirty + -eth
19. bounty + -ful
20. sleepy + -er

The Addition of Prefixes

When a prefix is added to a word, the spelling of the word remains the same.

re- + elect = reelect
mis- + spell = misspell
im- + moderate = immoderate
il- + legible = illegible

mis- + direct = misdirect
re- + enter = reenter
dis- + satisfy = dissatisfy
ir- + regular = irregular

The Suffixes *-ness* and *-ly*

When the suffix *-ly* is added to a word ending in *l*, both *l*'s are retained. When *-ness* is added to a word ending in *n*, both *n*'s are retained.

normal + -ly = normally
real + -ly = really

open + -ness = openness
thin + -ness = thinness

Exercise   Spell words with prefixes and suffixes.

Find the misspelled words in these sentences and spell them correctly.

1. The cast imobilized my leg.
2. Our garden is carefuly tended.
3. An ireplaceable vase was broken.
4. The uneveness of the road is annoying.
5. We are learning about iregular verbs in French class.
6. The teacher remphasized the point.
7. I have spent money unecessarily.
8. That was an ilegitimate move.
9. The mispelling was totaly unnecessary.
10. That painting is beautifuly framed.

Words with the "Seed" Sound

Only one English word ends in *sede: supersede.*
Three words end in *ceed: exceed, proceed, succeed.*
All other words ending in the sound of *seed* are spelled *cede:*

concede   precede   recede   secede

Words with *ie* and *ei*

When the sound is long *e* (ē), the word is spelled *ie* except after *c*.

I Before E

relieve   grieve   field   pierce
belief   piece   pier   reprieve

Except After C

conceit   conceive   perceive
ceiling   receive   receipt   deceive

The following words are exceptions:

either	weird	species
neither	seize	leisure

Exercise Spell words with the "seed" sound and words with *ie* and *ei* correctly.

Find the misspelled words in these sentences and spell them correctly.

1. When was Louisiana ceeded to the United States?
2. Hercules' sheild was made of gold.
3. There's one peice of pecan pie left.
4. Nixon preseeded Carter as President.
5. Will aspirin releive this headache?
6. The town was siezed after a fierce battle.
7. The clerk proceded to write a receipt.
8. My leisure hours excede my work hours.
9. The paint on the cieling is chipped.
10. I babysit for my neice every weekend.

Doubling the Final Consonant

Words of one syllable, ending in one consonant preceded by one vowel, double the final consonant before adding a suffix beginning with a vowel.

1. These words double the final consonant if the suffix begins with a vowel.

grab + -ing = grabbing	drug + -ist = druggist
dig + -er = digger	slim + -est = slimmest

The rule does not apply to these one-syllable words because two vowels precede the final consonant.

clear + -est = clearest	loot + -ing = looting
treat + -ing = treating	peel + -ing = peeling

2. The final consonant is doubled in a word of more than one syllable:
> When it ends in one consonant preceded by one vowel.
> When it is accented on the last syllable.

re·gret′   per·mit′   de·ter′

The same syllable is accented in the new word formed by adding the suffix:

> re·gret′ + -ed = re·gret′ted
> per·mit′ + -ing = per·mit′ting
> de·ter′ + -ence = de·ter′rence

If the newly formed word is accented on a different syllable, the final consonant is not doubled.

> re·fer′ + -ence = ref′er·ence
> pre·fer′ + -ence = pref′er·ence
> con·fer′ + -ence = con′fer·ence

Exercise   Double the final consonant.

Add the suffixes as shown and write the new word. Indicate with an accent mark (′) where each word is accented.

1. plug + -ing	11. sleep + -ing
2. prefer + -ing	12. swim + -er
3. control + -er	13. hot + -est
4. prefer + -ence	14. trim + -ed
5. big + -est	15. fat + -est
6. remit + -ance	16. heat + -ing
7. slim + -er	17. scoot + -er
8. tug + -ing	18. motor + -ist
9. permit + -ing	19. slug + -er
10. treat + -ing	20. drag + -ing

Words Often Confused

The following words are often misused. Many of the words are homonyms. **Homonyms** are words that sound alike or are spelled alike but have different meanings. You must be careful not to confuse them.

As you study these homonyms and other words that are often confused, notice how their meanings differ. Try to use the right word at the right time.

accept means to agree to something or to receive something willingly.

except means to exclude or omit. As a preposition, *except* means "but" or "excluding."

> Did the teacher *accept* your explanation?
> Students who behaved well were *excepted* from the penalty.
> Everyone smiled for the photographer *except* Jody.

all ready means completely prepared or ready.
already means previously or before.

> The cast and crew are *all ready* for dress rehearsal.
> Linda has *already* arranged the chess tournament.

capital refers to the large letter used to begin the first word in a sentence, etc. It also refers to the seat of government in a state or country.

capitol refers to the building where a state legislature meets.

the Capitol is the building in Washington, D.C., where the United States Congress meets.

> We use *capital* letters to begin such proper names as New York City and Abraham Lincoln.
> Is Madison the *capital* of Wisconsin?
> Protestors rallied at the state *capitol*.
> A subway connects the Senate and the House in the *Capitol*.

des′ ert is a dry, sandy region with little vegetation.

de sert′ means to leave or abandon.

dessert (note the change in spelling) is a sweet food, such as cake or pie, served at the end of a meal.

> The Sahara in North Africa is the world's largest *desert*.
> The night guard did not *desert* his post.
> Alison's favorite *dessert* is chocolate cake.

heal means to make well, to cure.

heel refers to the back part of a person's foot or of a shoe.

> If the wound is clean, it should *heal* fast.
> When the *heel* of my shoe came off, I walked lopsidedly.

hear means to listen to or to take notice of.

here means in this place.

> When the TV is on, we can't *hear* the doorbell.
> The softball team practices *here* on the south field.

hoarse describes sound that is harsh and grating; especially a voice.

horse is a large strong animal that can pull loads or carry a rider.

> When I get a cold, I am usually *hoarse* for a week.
> Farm *horses* used to pull plows and do other work that tractors do now.

its is a pronoun that shows possession.

it's is a contraction for *it is* or *it has*.

> Sanibel Island is known for *its* beautiful beaches.
> *It's* great weather for a picnic!

loan refers to something given for temporary use and expected to be returned.

lone refers to the condition of being by oneself, alone.

> I gave that shirt to Max as a gift, not a *loan*.
> The *lone* plant in our backyard is really a weed.

lose means to mislay or to suffer the loss of something.
loose means free or not fastened.

> That tire will *lose* air if you don't patch it.
> My little brother has three *loose* teeth.

peace means calm or quiet, freedom from disagreements or quarrels.
piece refers to a portion or part of something.

> If you want *peace* and quiet, go to the library.
> A *piece* of the scenery crashed onto the stage.

principal describes something of chief or central importance. It also refers to the head of an elementary or high school.
principle is the basic truth, standard, or rule of behavior.

> Declining enrollment is the *principal* reason for closing the school.
> We will get our diplomas from the *principal*.
> One of my *principles* is a belief in total honesty.

quiet refers to freedom from noise or disturbance.
quite means truly or almost completely.

> Observers must be *quiet* during the recording session.
> I was *quite* worried when Kevin didn't return.

stationary means fixed or unmoving.
stationery refers to paper used for writing letters.

> The steering wheel moves, but the seat is *stationary*.
> Rex wrote on special *stationery* with his name on it.

their means belonging to them.
there means in that place.
they're is a contraction for *they are*.

> All the campers returned to *their* cabins.
> I keep my coin collection *there* in those folders.
> Lisa and Tammy practice hard, and *they're* becoming very good at soccer.

to means toward, or in the direction of.
too means also, very, or more than enough.
two is the number 2.

> The President flew *to* France for the conference.
> Megan is healthy, and she is happy, *too.*
> *Two* of my friends will be on TV tonight.

weather refers to atmospheric conditions such as temperature or cloudiness.
whether helps to express choice or alternative.

> Computers will soon be able to predict the *weather.*
> Val had to decide *whether* to tell the truth or to save Bob from feeling hurt.

who's is a contraction for *who is* or *who has.*
whose is the possessive form of *who.*

> *Who's* going to the recycling center?
> *Whose* parents will drive us to the movie?

your is the possessive form of *you.*
you're is a contraction for *you are.*

> What was *your* time in the fifty-yard dash?
> *You're* heading the canned food drive, aren't you?

Exercises Use words often confused.

A. Choose the correct word from those given in parentheses.

1. Every country (accept, except) China sent delegates.
2. The nurse's aide had (all ready, already) been trained.
3. The Senator met us on the steps of the (capital, capitol, Capitol) in Washington.
4. Did you and David make apple turnovers for (desert, dessert)?
5. If your (heal, heel) hurts, maybe your shoes aren't the right size.

6. Stand (here, hear) where you can (here, hear) the music better.

7. The bluejay has a (horse, hoarse) call that sounds like a squeaky gate.

8. The magazine prints letters from (its, it's) readers.

9. Toby (accepted, excepted) the gift.

10. Will you (lone, loan) me a pencil?

B. Follow the directions for Exercise A.

1. The pedals on this bike seem (lose, loose).

2. I'd like a (piece, peace) of watermelon, please.

3. When the school (principal, principle) entered the P.T.A. meeting, everyone clapped.

4. Please be (quite, quiet) while we study.

5. The Berkowitzs prefer a houseboat to a (stationary, stationery) house.

6. The networks announced (their, there, they're) fall schedules in the newspaper.

7. Do you think it's (to, too, two) dark to ride our bikes?

8. Even during cold (weather, whether), we walk to school.

9. (Who's, Whose) purse is this on the floor?

10. I admire (your, you're) self-confidence.

Additional Exercises — Review

Spelling

A. Add suffixes to words ending in silent e and y.

Add the suffixes as shown. Write the new word.

1. enjoy + -able
2. ice + -y
3. carry + -ing
4. early + -est
5. waste + -ful
6. believe + -able
7. hurry + -ed
8. continue + -ing
9. employ + -er
10. create + -ing

B. Add prefixes correctly.

Find the misspelled words. Spell them correctly.

1. It's unecessary to change your plans.
2. If you mispell more than two words, you must retake the test.
3. Sharon was dissappointed with the test results.
4. All traffic was imobile after the heavy snowfall.
5. Several cars were parked ilegally in the loading zone.

C. Add suffixes -ness and -ly.

Find the misspelled words. Spell them correctly.

1. Jill's openess made her an easy person to talk to.
2. I realy don't believe Mike actualy said that!
3. The van was illegaly parked by the fire hydrant.
4. The uneveness of this writing is hardly acceptable.
5. Eventualy the rain stopped.

D. Spell words with the "seed" sound and words with *ie* and *ei*.

Find the misspelled words. Write them correctly.

1. Mrs. Barnett succeded Mr. Smyth as corporate treasurer.
2. Lee believed that the cieling needed to be repainted.
3. After we receive all of the reciepts, we will procede with payment.
4. All cars must yeild to the workmen and not excede the limit of 40 M.P.H.
5. Her neice and nephew were here for a breif visit.

E. Double the final consonant.

Add the suffixes as shown and write the new word.

1. drop + -ed   4. slug + -er   7. run + -er
2. run + -ing   5. begin + -ing   8. plant + -ing
3. put + -ing   6. refer + -ing   9. big + -est

F. Use words easily confused correctly.

Choose the correct word from those given.

1. The campers are (all ready, already) for their cookout.
2. I began each sentence with a (capital, capitol) letter.
3. After Seth's broken leg is set, it will begin to (heel, heal).
4. Do you know the (horsepower, hoarsepower) of that engine?
5. (Its, It's) time for Marcia's swimming lesson.
6. Did the Bulldogs (lose, loose) their final game?
7. We printed our (stationary, stationery) in the school workshop.
8. Our class reporter took (to, too, two) stories (to, too, two) the editor of the school paper.
9. (Who's, Whose) the announcer on this radio station?
10. (Your, You're) interested in current events, aren't you?

Section 14

Outlining

When you sit down to write a composition, where do you begin? Once you have gathered all the information you need, how do you organize it?

For both of these questions, an **outline** is a good answer. An outline is a condensed plan for a piece of writing. The ideas that crowd your head when you write can become confused unless you have a plan. An outline will help you put your ideas into a logical order.

Outlining also makes writing easier. Many experienced writers use outlines to prepare for writing. They find that outlining gives them a head start in writing a well-organized composition.

In the chapter "Writing Compositions and Reports," you learned about grouping ideas in logical order. An outline is an accepted form for diagraming that order. The same form can be used for any topic and for any kind of composition. Outlines help you to write explanatory compositions, as well as narrative and descriptive ones. For these reasons, outlining is a valuable skill to learn.

Organizing an Outline

To begin an outline, you should have a clear idea of the purpose of your composition. Then determine the main ideas that you want to develop. These main ideas will be the **main points** in your outline.

Next, consider how you can develop or explain each main point. The supporting ideas for these points will become **subpoints** in the outline. Consequently, related ideas will be grouped together.

Finally, decide which scheme to use for ordering the main points. While time sequence works well for some topics, order of importance is better for others. The best order is the one that makes your topic clearest and easiest to understand.

When you have completed an outline, you will have the skeleton for a composition. By filling in details and building paragraphs around related ideas, you will create a solid composition.

Writing Topic Outlines

A **topic outline** is an informal kind of outline. Topic outlines use words or phrases instead of complete sentences. Topic outlines are effective for organizing compositions.

A topic outline follows. Notice that it does not use complete sentences. Pay attention to the grouping of subpoints under related main ideas.

STREETCARS: YESTERDAY'S BUSES

    I. History of the streetcar
      A. Introduction in 1831
      B. Popularity during the 19th century
      C. Decline during the 1930's
        1. Because of cars
        2. Because of buses
   II. Description of horse-drawn streetcars
      A. Design
      B. Speed
  III. Description of electric streetcars
      A. Power
        1. From overhead wires
        2. From underground wires
      B. Design
      C. Speed
  IV. Effect of streetcars on cities

Using Outline Form

Outlines use a precise form that does not vary. Here are some rules to follow:

1. Write the title of your composition at the top of the outline. Do not consider the introduction or the conclusion as parts of the outline.

2. Arrange numbers and letters of headings in the following order: first Roman numerals for main points, then capital letters for subpoints. Next, Arabic numerals are used. Small letters are used for details under these ideas, then numbers in parentheses for details developing the details, and, finally, small letters in parentheses for subdetails. The arrangement on the next page shows clearly which ideas belong together:

I.
   A.
   B.
      1.
      2.
         a.
         b.
            (1)
            (2)
               (a)
               (b)
II.
   A.
   B.
   (and so on)

3. Indent all headings in the outline. Place letters and numbers of all headings directly underneath the first word of the larger heading above.
4. Do not use a single subheading. There must be at least two. A heading should not be broken down if it cannot be divided into at least two points.
5. Use the same kind of phrase for all headings of the same rank. If, for example, A is a verb, then B should be a verb, too.
6. Begin each item with a capital letter. In a topic outline, do not end headings with periods or other punctuation.

Exercise Make an outline.

Below is a partial outline. Copy it on your paper. Then complete the outline by adding the following headings where they belong.

Necessary toppings	Pepperoni
Baking time	With oregano mixed in
Mushrooms	Prepare the dough
Ingredients	Shape the dough

DIRECTIONS FOR MAKING PIZZA

I. Gather the necessary equipment
  A. Recipe
  B. Pizza pan or pizza stone or baking sheet
  C.

II. Light the oven

III.
  A. Mix ingredients for the dough
  B. Knead the dough
  C.
  D. Place dough in pan

IV. Spread toppings on dough
  A.
      1. Tomato sauce
        a. Made from canned pizza sauce
        b. Made from canned tomato sauce or paste
            (1) With parmesan cheese mixed in
            (2)
            (3) With other spices mixed in
      2. Sliced mozzarella cheese
  B. Optional toppings
      1. Sausage
      2.
      3.
      4. Green peppers
      5. Sliced or chopped onion
      6. Other things you like

V. Bake the pizza
  A. Oven temperature
  B.

Additional Exercise — Review

Outlining

Complete an outline.

Copy the partial outline. Insert the following headings where they belong in the outline.

National   Entertainment
Lead story   Newspaper name
Letters to the editor   Date
Movies   The Congress
                    News section

DISSECTING A NEWSPAPER

I. Front page
   A.
   B.
   C. Weather
   D. Pictures
   E.

II.
   A. International
   B.
      1. Important news from Washington
        a.
        b. The President
      2. Big stories with national interest
   C. Local

III. Editorial page
   A. Editorials
   B.
   C. Opinion columns
   D. Cartoon
   E. Masthead

IV. Other
    A. Features
    B. Business
    C. Sports
    D.
        1. TV and radio
        2.
        3. Plays and concerts

Index

perfect tense of, 292–294
present participle of, 423–424
present perfect tense of, 292–293
present tense of, 291–294
principal parts of, 293–294
progressive forms of, 290–291,
315–316
regular, 294
in sentence patterns, 362–371
separated parts of, 225–226, 288
simple tenses of, 291–294
subject of, 222–225, 227–230,
235–237, 242–244, 363–371,
374–376, 407–417. *See also*
Subject of the verb.
tenses of, 291–293, 316
transitive, 231–234, 243
troublesome, 312–314, 317
Vertical file, 199
Vocabulary, 1–13
See also Words.

we, us, 275–276, 283
who, whom, 272–273, 282, 396–397,
405
Word-finder table for dictionaries,
20
Word order. *See* Sentence patterns.
Word parts
prefixes, 489–490, 498
suffixes, 487–492, 498–499
Words
antonyms, 12–13
often confused, 493–497, 499
connotations of, 169–171
context clues to meaning of, 2–9,
12–13
definitions of, 2–9, 12–13, 25, 82–
83, 99, 103

general, 175–177
"hearing," 94–96
homonyms, 493–497, 499
judgment, 168–172
as different parts of speech, 356–
357
pronunciation of, 22–24
qualifying, 179
sensory, 52, 55, 57, 72–75, 90–96, 103
"sight," 91–96
space, 93
specific, 175–177
spelling, 485–499
syllables in, 21–22, 27
synonyms, 10–13, 26–27
troublesome verbs, 312–314, 317
Writing
compositions, 105–123, 125–139
checklist for, 123
fact or opinion in, 166–169, 181
generalizations in, 178–181
in journals, 51–52
letters, 141–163
paragraphs, 51–103
checklist for, 103
process of, 51–57
guidelines for, 57
using the senses in, 52, 55, 57,
72–75, 90–96, 103
sentences, 29–49
slanted, 171–172
subjects for, 52, 57, 86, 108–109,
130

Yearbooks, 197–199
you as understood subject, 229–
230, 242–243

ZIP code, 162

Acknowledgments

Sources of Quoted Materials

Page 20–21, 30, 31 and 38; William Collins + World Publishing Company, for entries from *Webster's New World Dictionary of the American Language,* Students Edition; copyright © 1976 by William Collins + World Publishing Company, Inc.

Photographs

James L. Ballard: 14, 28, 182, 202, 216, 406.

Magnum: Charles Harbutt, ii, 50, 164; David Hurn, xx; Paul Fusco, 58, 84, 246, 284, 360, 430; Eve Arnold, 70, 318; Martin Dain, 104; Wayne Miller, 124; Burk Uzzle, 140, 372; Constantine Manos, 258, 344, 418; Hiroji Kubota, 446; Mark Godfrey, 484; Costa Manos, 500.

Editorial Credits

Managing Editor: Kathleen Laya
Assistant Editor: Elizabeth M. Garber

Director of Design: Allen Carr
Design Assistants: Ken Izzi, Marcia Vecchione
Cover Design: Sandra Gelak